KEYS TO INDEPENDENCE

KEYS TO INDEPENDENCE

Leaving Home to Study

Rachael Desgouttes, Sheila Partrat, Sophie Paine

PARTRIDGE

To order additional copies of this book, contact
Toll Free 800 101 2657 (Singapore)
Toll Free 1 800 81 7340 (Malaysia)
orders.singapore@partridgepublishing.com

www.partridgepublishing.com/singapore

"There are some things you can't learn at any university, except for one, the University of Life... the only college where everyone is a permanent student." — **E.A. Bucchianeri**, **Brushstrokes of a Gadfly**

"In university, we are taught a lesson then given a test. Whereas in life, we are given a test that teaches us a lesson. — **Habeeb Akande**

Preface

How long does it take to cook rice? Do I keep bananas in the fridge? How often am I supposed to wash my bed sheets? What do I do with my debit card receipts? ... How is it that you always arrive on time and I don't? I'm exhausted and run down. The ATM refused to give me cash – HELP!

Is there a better way to avoid the first years of university communication back home from turning into a "daily life helpdesk" barrage of instant messaging? The focus it took to get into university often meant that academics took all the mental space and time. More practical yet fundamental skills such as money, food, and time management are handled, if at all, on a case-by-case, sometimes crisis-by-crisis basis, over short messages or quick calls.

Money issues create immediate stress, poor nutrition impacts both intellect and vitality, and poor time management shrinks our days. Any of these issues could negatively impact university studies, souring those three or four years, which should be some of the best experiences of our lives.

This book is to provide the tool kit necessary to help keep university, and the years beyond, enriched with positive experiences. It is more than practical advice covering aspects of student life. It also provides a foundation for building sound decision-making skills that will help you in all kinds of situations, wherever you study or live. As much as possible, we have minimised country-specific references, as the lessons put forth on these pages are relevant to university-goers from China to America, and everywhere in between!

There are many ways you can approach this book: read it from cover to cover before going to university, or, using the colour coding, quickly pick up the basic skills you need right now, like how to budget, read a food label and cook a balanced meal, or how to get your day optimally organised. Some information is so important it appears in more than one chapter! This is not because we are becoming old ladies, but because students dip in and read in small chunks. It is THAT important that it needs to appear several times! You can pop back to practical tips as and when you need them. The last pages of the recipe section are even blank, so you can add YOUR favourite family recipes!

We hope this book will help make your university years and beyond as fruitful and enjoyable as they can be. Even if you don't have urgent questions to ask, don't forget to text your parents (they love it!) ... and why not get them to read this book too, to reassure them that everything is under control?

Foreword

By Ariane C. Lellmann

Campus Director for Laureate International Universities Australia

When our children finish secondary school, a major milestone is reached, and a moment of great pride is experienced. They are now ready and eager to spread their wings. Many of them will leave home for tertiary study or other opportunities; possibly in another country. All this is very exciting, but often a step into the unknown for them and their parents.

Leaving the security and comfort of home behind, and taking responsibility for financial decisions and healthy choices, along with juggling time between study, exercise and social events can all be extremely overwhelming. There is a lot to learn, adapting to life away from home. Whether it is our own children, nieces, nephews or young friends and mentees, we dearly want to provide them with a tool kit that not only assists their sound decision making, but that also provides them with guidance to grow to their full potential.

With *Keys to Independence: Leaving Home to Study*, Partrat, Paine and Desgouttes have filled a real gap in the market to help us all cope with this transition period. With its practical approach, this book is a great tool and provides useful tips and well-researched information covering the key topics of money, nutrition & health, home, time management, and safety. It provides practical and sensible advice from experts in each field at the start of this exciting time of transition, as well as being a useful and easily accessible reference as situations arise during this journey.

As an educator at an international higher education institution, I see many young adults arrive at university and struggle with the many aspects of adapting to life away from home and familiarity. Taking responsibility for one's decisions, understanding consequences and juggling the demands of academic expectations, managing a budget and finding part-time work, dealing with homesickness and anxiety is challenging and requires support and practice. The information in this book is extremely helpful, pertinent and well-structured across all the key topics. I am sure it will be of great assistance to both young adults and their parents during this period of exciting, yet uncharted adventure.

Keys to Independence: Leaving Home to Study is an easy-to-read, informative and practical book that provides concrete benefits. This is a guide not just for transitioning to university but also provides practical and relevant advice for the world beyond: the exciting journey of LIFE!

Foreword to High School Graduates

By Alice Burgess

University of Virginia Class of 2017

If you are reading this – *congratulations!* You've made it! All your hard work, late nights, and determination have paid off, and you're onto the next chapter.

While you are probably experiencing a lot of excitement and anticipation regarding the beginning of your professional future, you might also be feeling a tad anxious and hesitant about moving away from home and blazing your own trail. I distinctly remember the countless "firsts" associated with the initial weeks and months of college. My supportive, lovely British parents were shocked at the idea of a liberal arts education and even the prospect of having a roommate, so I had to figure out a lot of the university experience by "trial and error"! I wish I'd had a book like this as a survival guide.

Ultimately, when I graduated, after four of the happiest and most formative years of my life, I had uncovered my passions and made wonderful friends. I had finally learned how to take care of myself, but it took me an embarrassingly long time to learn the wisdom of wellness. Fortunately, you have some keys to efficient and healthy independent living right in your fingertips! My best advice is to attack this book with sticky-notes and highlighters, as it's going to come in very handy over the next few months.

Best of luck in this journey – you'll be brilliant!

About the Authors

This is a collaborative project amongst educators who all share the same motivation to prepare students for life challenges.

Rachael Desgouttes. British born, married to a Frenchman, my children were born and raised in Hong Kong, speaking three languages. After years of giving corporate training in regional management roles, I retrained at HKU. Now a qualified teacher in a Hong Kong international school, I love engaging with teens both in an academic arena and preparing them with life skills. When my daughter moved to the UK for university – we realised what was needed in such a book – and hopefully in good time for my son, who will soon follow!

Sophie Paine. French born, married to an Englishman, mother of two children, I have lived in France, the USA, Hong Kong and China. After a postgraduate degree in Finance, I have worked for more than a decade in accounting and training in the corporate and nonprofit worlds. Thousands of people have attended training workshops through a+b=3, the organisation I founded, empowering them to make better decisions with their money, in order to grow their most precious asset: themselves.

Sheila Partrat. Canadian born, with a degree in Food Science from McGill University and Masters in Economics and Media Studies from University de Paris, throughout her life, she has always retained a deep interest in the pathways between food and health. Following a 2006 move to Hong Kong with her family, not only did they all feel the impact of the pollution and fast life, but a few encountered health issues. She turned to science and found solutions. Since then she has focused on writing and training on the pathways between food and health, as well has co-founded and built an innovative food company, combining health, science and taste, that provides simple yet delicious solutions to help adults and teens alike thrive rather than just survive in a fast-paced world. Last but definitely not least, she is a proud mom of three teens and a dedicated Kundalini yoga teacher and practitioner.

Acknowledgements and Thanks

We started as three writers, but gratefully welcomed contribution from experts who, believing in this project, generously gave their time and knowledge. Combined with the encouragement of our friends and family, we have embodied the proverb "It takes a village to raise a child".

Our thanks are given loud and clear to many professionals; Food chapter co-author Dr. Jean Francois Lesgards, and contributors Denise Fair and Daniel Grimm; Mike Howard and Iain Williamson who educated us all on safety, online and on the streets; Mike Ibbott, who brought from his expertise and experience, valuable insights to the ups and downs students face when alone, Bordeaux wine educator, Wendy Narby who brought cheer and content to the entertaining section; Rachel Jurienz who lent her nursing expertise to the first aid section.

For production we give thanks to Dennis Robinson for his amazing artwork and to talented Maja Howard for her design and layout contribution; to Steven Gibert for his technical wizardry; to Sophie Desgouttes – TCK, student editor, and content advisor; to bi-cultural Alice Burgess who proof-read and commented with diplomacy and student empathy, and to experienced editor Sarah Cunich for her support and tying all the threads together.

Thank you for moral support and valuable advice to Anjali Hazari, Cindy Stevens, Ariane Lellmann and to the many students we interviewed and whom we have quoted.

Finally, we would like to honour our husbands and children who put up with long calls and missed dinners over a few years. Our teens were of course our first target audience and sounding boards. They helped bring our content to life.

Contents

Chapter 1: Money Management

by Sophie Paine

Introduction:

Money management can be summarised in one sentence: *don't spend more than you have*. Simple. If you stick to it, you will be on the safe side and your mind will focus on more important matters, like studying. But be aware that many things around you will make you see money matters as much more complex and make you forget about this simple rule: Shops, money virtuality, friends, your own behaviour. Whether you are already handling your finances or about to, it may be worth spending time reading the basics, and referring to it whenever you need to.

1. MONEY Management – The Essentials

Money Basics

Metal and paper: 4.4%
Virtual: 95.6% (i.e. accounting entries in banks' computers)
Overspending: Debts. Debts have to be paid back, no matter what.
Virtual money is created by commercial banks through loans to customers.
Source: http://www.bankofengland.co.uk/statistics

Consequences of virtual money:

Harder for our brain to manage: We can see cash go down. It takes more mental effort to realise how much virtual money we have left to spend.

Banks create money by lending and make profit by lending. So, there is a strong pressure from banks to lend more.

You don't need a finance degree to manage money. But because it is mostly virtual and the financial environment pushes to borrow, you do need some skills and a frugal mind-set. This is what this chapter is about.

TOP SKILLS to remember:

- Manage the time mismatch.
- Stop and think... before any purchase, (remember, not buying is always an option!)
- Check your finances often and monitor coming expenses.
- No undo button: Beware!
- Learn the finance buzzwords and ask questions.

Skill 1: Managing the time mismatch

Time	Daily	Weekly	Monthly	Quarterly	Yearly	A few times a life
Income			Salary Allowance		Scholarship	
Expenses	Food Transport	Going out	Rent Phone bills electricity	Some bills	Holidays, travel	Moving, furniture
Any time	We decide when: Clothes, going out...					
	We don't decide when: Medical emergencies, repairs...					

Studies show that our human brain focuses on short-term, so the time mismatch between our income and all the various expenses we have to incur requires some thinking: Keeping money for future expenses is not innate.

Think of it like a bottle of water that you can only fill up once a month, or however frequently you receive money. You have to make it last until next refill, for instance until next month, without using it up. In order to plan how much you can use, you must first divide it into types of expenses and set limits.

Skill 2: To spend, or not to spend?

We live in a world of endless choices. Everything comes in multiple shapes, tastes, alternatives, sizes and prices. Everything is packaged to look cool. Instead of getting overwhelmed by the options or feeling the need to spend for the sake of spending, stay cool and don't rush to buy. A second thought may help you really value whether this expense would be life-changing or just another consumer item stuffed into the back of a drawer after a few weeks.

If you do indeed need to make the purchase, narrow the choices. Imagine you are going to a restaurant. The menu has dozens of yummy dishes – all in the same price range – all equally delicious – and you are having a hard time choosing. The waiter comes to take your order and tells you that the restaurant has run out of most of the dishes and only two are left: one you like and one you really abhor. Problem solved! Too much choice makes it really hard on us to choose. It also eats up time and brain energy, and easily puts us off track from what really matters to us.

Choices can be really difficult. What if the restaurant menu looked like this?

When we are purchasing something, our brain focuses only on the choices presented to us right under our noses. Yet we are forgetting about other choices that may have a huge impact on our lives. With a limited income, we cannot forget about our other responsibilities, and thus must make smart and rational choices.

Luckily, there is a solution to prevent you getting paralysed by the prospect of managing your money. List your choices, and then see which ones fit your resources. For instance, if the lunch option that sounds the most delicious is also one that would prevent you from making a timely cell phone bill statement, seek out a more reasonably priced meal. You can't delegate these decisions to anybody else because they may not have the same preferences – especially shops or businesses who have a different agenda.

Skill 3: Don't cross the debt line

With paper money, it is easier to see when you run out, and what a debt means. Virtual money makes spending and earning very abstract; getting into debt becomes much easier. Even though money has a lot to do with our behaviour, preferences, and ethics, its virtual format turns it into a mathematical problem... scaring most of us who don't like maths.

To make virtual money feel more "real", split your income into "munchable" bits: divide what you can spend on food into a daily amount. $10 a day for food gives you a better sense of limit than $300 a month, even though this is the same. (We will discuss a daily spending limit later.) Also, turn virtual amounts into tangible things: this outfit is worth ten cafeteria meals.

Check your bank account often, including your card payments. If you have $200 in your bank account and $100 card spending not debited yet from your account, the real picture is that you only have $100. If you have $200 of rent to pay, you are heading towards trouble. Nobody will warn you until it is too late: you have to monitor your virtual money closely. If you find it difficult to remember to check every day, try to check your account at least once a week.

Something to keep in mind: Life has **no "undo" button**. If you have overspent, it is too late. Money may be virtual, but consequences are real.

Skill 4: Learn the finance words

When communicating with banks and financial advisors, don't be surprised if they speak "finance" and use technical words. Check what they mean, and if you don't understand, never be afraid to ask for a plain and simple explanation.

Skill 5: Budgeting -the ultimate skill

A budget is the solution to money-related issues.

Step by step budget:

List <u>incomes</u> (*) + the <u>expenses</u> you can think of and the <u>amounts</u>.

Incomes:
Parents = 700
Birthday = 400
Odd jobs = 200
Expenses:
Books = 200
Going out = 100
Food = 400
Phone = 100
Presents = 200

(*) Whatever it is = pocket money, scholarship, money from grandparents, summer job, etc....

Time: How <u>often</u> do these incomes /expenses occur?

Parents' allowance → Monthly
Birthday money → Yearly
Odd jobs → 3-4 times a year
Books → Monthly
Going out → Weekly
Food → Daily
Phone → Monthly
Presents → Yearly

Goals: What else would I like to get/achieve later in time?

Holiday: next year
Replace laptop: in 2 years
Down payment for a flat: in 8-10 years

7

Prioritise: That's the jigsaw puzzle ... savings for goals + expenses need to fit in the income. You'll have to make choices!

4

This example shows a month. You can do the same with a week.

	Jan	Feb	Mar
Income			
Parents	700	700	700
Birthday		400	
Odd job			200
TOTAL INCOME	700	1,100	900
Books	50	100	50
Going out	50	50	50
Food	400	400	350 400
Phone	100	100	80 100
Presents			200
Charity/donations	50	50	50
TOTAL EXPENSES	650	700	780 850
Holiday	50	100	50
Laptop		200	70
Down payment		100	
TOTAL SAVINGS	50	400	120 50
Balance?	Yes!	Yes!	Yes!
INCOME – SAVINGS = EXPENSES			

It's never too late to fine-tune the list of incomes/expenses.

GOALS: Save for them bit by bit *Example: holiday cost = 750. You plan to pay for it in 15 months. 750/ 15 months = 50. So, you need to save 50 every month. If you can't save 50 one month, save 100 the following month to make up for it.* **Prioritise your goals**: *better to feel happy to achieve a few than frustrated to achieve none!*

Prioritise! Work out the best solution... on paper... before spending!

Track: Note down all you earn and spend.

5

6

Use what works for you – app, computer, paper... but note down EVERYTHING!

Use your budget: Fine-tune it, include your actual income/expenses, reprioritise expenses to achieve your goals.

	Jan (actual)	Feb (budget)	Mar (budget)
Parents	700	700	700
Birthday		400	
Odd job	100		200
TOTAL INCOME	800	1,100	900
Books	50	90	50
Going out	40	50	40
Food	380	380	350
Phone	100	80	80
Presents			200
Transportation	50	50	50
Charity	50	50	50
TOTAL EXPENSES	670	700	820
Holiday	50	100	50
Laptop	50	200	30
Down payment	30	100	
TOTAL SAVINGS	130	400	80
Balance?	Yes!	Yes!	Yes!
INCOME – SAVINGS = EXPENSES			

2. BEFORE Leaving Home

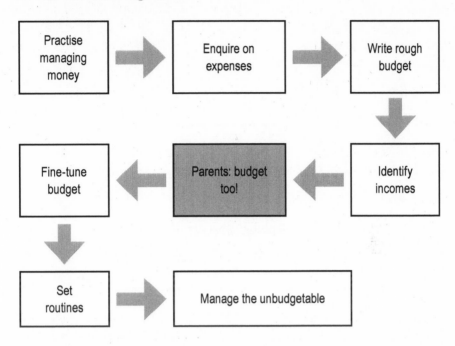

PRACTISE managing money

There is no "being bad with money"... it is just a lack of experience. Did you learn to walk, swim or talk in one day? Managing money is about skills, so practise every day.

Discuss with your parents what expenses you can manage before leaving home.

- Some expenses you can practise managing include: Clothes, phone, transportation, going out, school related expenses (books, lunches), and so on.
- First, agree on a fixed amount. Start with a weekly amount, then move up to a bi-weekly then monthly amount as you get good at it.
- Next, write your budget: List your expenses and plan how much you spend on each type of expenses.
- Set clear rules with your parents: What happens if you spend more than your budget and if you spend less.
- Finally, spend according to your budget.

Budgeting gives us a sense of limits – a track to follow. We set these limits at home – away from spending spots, using our rational brain. So once in the shopping jungle, by sticking to our budget, we know which part of our brain is driving. Like any skill, budgeting is all about practice. Before you know it, budgeting will be second nature, and you'll be an expert in being savvy with your money!

TRADE OFFs

Afraid of losing this exhilarating feeling of spending freely and spontaneously on whatever you want if you write and follow a budget?

Include a workable "mad shopping" amount in your budget.

See how much your shopping amount leaves for other expenses…

Play with the numbers until you reach an acceptable balance.

If you spend more, you have to cut down on other expenses; this is a trade-off.

If you overspend, you have actually spent someone else's money: your parents (if they decide to send you more money) or the bank if you take an overdraft. We will further discuss overdrafts in the bank section.

Find other ways to feel good… far from shopping centres.

Focus your mind not on what you can't do because it doesn't fit in your budget… but what you can do thanks to carefully planning your expenses. Think positive!

You can't escape choices; this is our fate as human beings. We constantly make choices. And our choices gradually shape who we are.

One trade-off you get when you write and follow a budget is peace of mind. You decide carefully with a reason – don't let others decide for you, especially shops, ads and well-meaning friends. If you're true to yourself, following a budget also increases your self-esteem. You can do this!

Pocket-money:

> "*I have managed my pocket money for years. I thought I knew what money management was all about, but what I didn't realise is with my pocket money, I was only choosing between a nice thing I fancied... and another nice thing I fancied. However, when I had all kinds of expenses to manage, I was actually not ready to deal with bills, groceries and paying for my own accommodation.*"

> "*I had never actually managed money before, so it was scary (but exhilarating!) to have a big amount. I wrote a budget with my parents, and I liked how the amount became more real when we split it into rent, groceries, cafeteria, transportation, books, and going out. My father even drew things on the page because he knows I'm very visual. That really helped me know how much I could spend. I tracked how much I spent with an app, and after a month, I wrote the actual expenses with a different coloured pen next to my budget. That helped me fine-tune my budget for the second month ON MY OWN!*"

ENQUIRE: Your first rough budget

For each university you are considering applying to, get information about expenses and list them.

Currency:_____	University 1	University 2	University 3	University 4
Tuition fees				
College fees				
Accommodation (*)				
Kitchen facility charge				
Meals				
Books & equipment				
Extra classes				
Local transportation				
Personal (**): Going out, cell phone, clubs, toiletries, clothes, laundry, miscellaneous				
Health				
Insurance				

Formal clothes (work/ internship...)				
Travel				
Travel home (x times per year)				
TOTAL / year				
Years of study				
TOTAL				
One-offs: Furniture, utensils, vehicle...				
GRAND TOTAL				

(*) Some universities offer accommodation for the first year but not the other years. Your budget may vary from one year to the other. You may also have to spend on storage if you have to change accommodation from one term to another. Check also accommodation possibilities during summer or other term holidays.

(**) At this stage, you can just estimate a total amount. But later on, fine-tune it.

Keep fine-tuning as you gather more information and you decide which university to attend.

QUICK FIX: if you are already at university and haven't done your budget, don't panic... it's never too late. Do it now!

PARENTS: Involve your children in putting together this budget. Planning is a vital skill. Don't do it for them.

THE Incomes

Before freaking out at the huge total of expenses – especially if you multiply it by three or four years' study, stay cool and rational and look at the income part. How much will you potentially earn after graduating, and how do you and your parents plan to finance the total?

Currency:_____	University 1	University 2	University 3	University 4
Potential salary range				
Pay back (years)				

Even if you intend to reap many more benefits from your higher education than just a job and a salary, the expected income matters. Getting an idea of the potential salary range may help you fine-tune your university and major selections, as well as get a better idea of how many years it will take you to pay back your student loan if you have to take one out.

Enquire about the job market for your target career, the preferred study profiles, internship possibilities, university ranking, how quickly you may get hired after graduating, where these jobs are located (and whether your citizenship/visa status matches your target job market), and so forth. Connect with people who have done these majors, attended your short-listed universities, or already work in that field.

The more research you do, the more information you will get, the clearer you will be about what you are heading to and what you want to choose. Tap into all possible information sources: University websites, education websites, college/university counsellor in your school, friends, and acquaintances.

Top Tip: Don't Miss Deadlines!

Plan your research during the year before applying to university. List what you have to do, month by month or week by week. Take it as seriously as any other school subject. List potential costs too – exam fees, travel to visit universities, and so forth.

Do You Qualify for Financial Aid?

Do some research on:

- What are the conditions to obtain financial aid?
- What are the application deadlines?
- In which format are they offered: Scholarships, bursaries, grants, loans?
- What would these amounts cover? Both grants and loans can either cover the tuition fee or the living expenses.

If you are an *international student,* have a look in both your destination country as well as the country you come from, or have been schooled. Most universities make a difference between national and international students, so look carefully at which category you belong to. Being a citizen may not be enough, as some countries require several years of actual residency in order to be able to be treated as a national student.

Understand the Difference Between Grants and Loans!

Grants and scholarships are gifts. You won't have to re-pay them (unless you quit your studies).

Loans have to be paid back with an interest.

Go behind the words used, and always read all conditions in order to be clear whether you will have to pay back or not.

Get a Part-Time Job

Getting a part-time job is a way to explore potential student jobs as part of your university quest. Apart from the income, working while studying has several benefits:

- You get work experience. Even if you work in another field than your major, you will learn a great deal: Complying with strict hours, interacting with people from other backgrounds and age ranges, understanding what your boss wants, interrelation skills (assertiveness, communication, management), work ethic, interacting with potential customers, and more. Take these jobs as a unique opportunity to try out work you may not want to do as a career – to widen your skills.
- Get a better grasp of labour law (make sure your employer follows the law).
- Extend your social network, which may prove useful once you are on the job market.
- Strengthen your CV and make it stand out of the crowd.
- Reap the benefits of less shopping time. When you are busy working, you won't have that much time to spend afternoons shopping – your wallet may thank you!
- Put your studies in perspective. Filling in your schedule with a part-time job means you won't have time to procrastinate the 50-page long essay for another two weeks. This will force you to be more efficient with your time. This can also give you an idea of what skills you need to work on while studying.

> **Your job check-list:**
>
> ✓ Define your goal. Why do you want to work: For the pay, to boost your CV or to meet other people?
> ✓ When are you planning to work? All year long, or only in between terms? How could that conflict with internships?
> ✓ List available part-time jobs and how they fit with your goals. Do you fit their criteria/would they take someone like you? Think of companies/employers in your field who may take interns.
> ✓ Utilise resources from university (career advisor, job board, alumni employment website).
> ✓ Look into the money specifics: What is the pay, what income tax would it qualify for? What are extra costs (like business wardrobe and transportation)? Does a salary impact your financial aid?

MY Income is your expense

Money needs to come from somewhere: Your income is likely to be your parents' expense!

Parents, you too have some homework to do.

1. Adjust your own family budget to include the financial support to your child.
2. Include other additional expenses: You may want to go with your child to help with the big move, or visit universities before applications are due, or visit your child once a year. Adjust your travel expense line.
3. Reduce redundant expenses. You will not pay high school tuition fee or for uniforms any longer, which can contribute to financing university if you wish. You may cancel your child's local mobile phone – but look at the impact if you have a family plan.
4. Go through each line of your budget.

Parents' Quick Fix: Never done a budget? Maybe it's the right time to start! Whether this book reaches you a few years, months, or days before your child leaves home, don't procrastinate: Write your overall financial budget for the next coming years. Start with rough numbers and gradually fine-tune. Write your assumptions so that you can adjust your budget if circumstances change (your child takes a gap year or you move, etc.)

Assumptions:	This year	20__	20___	20___
Job/retirement Residency Children Other	2 spouses work Hong Kong Year 11, 13	2 spouses work Hong Kong Year 12, Uni 1	1 work/1 retired Hong Kong Year 13, Uni 2 consulting work?	1 work/1 retired Hong Kong Uni 1, Uni 3
Income 1				
Income 2				
Financial revenues				
TOTAL INCOME				
Rent/mortgage				
Utilities				
Tax				
Food				
Domestic Help				
School				
Children's activities				
University				
Travel/holidays				
Leisure				
Insurance				
Health				
Family support				
Clothes				
Other				
TOTAL EXPENSES				
INCOME-EXPENSES				

Financial assets				
Properties				
Other assets				
TOTAL ASSETS				
Short term debts				
Mortgage				
Other debts				
TOTAL DEBTS				
ASSETS – DEBTS =				

This budget aims to help you calculate your contribution to your children's university financing and anticipate how to finance a potential deficit in the years where, for example, you have to support several children studying abroad. This may also be the right time to look at your assets and debts by currency. If your child wants to study in your home country with currency A and you get paid in currency B, how will you finance the amount: by transferring part of your income into currency A or by investing in currency A and getting some financial revenues in currency A or selling some currency A investments? Don't forget to include potential tax impacts – in all the places where you have to pay tax – and compare the various options for your family.

Other Financing: Have your grandparents or other family members offered to help – whether with cash or by providing a place to live?– Have they opened a savings account for you decades ago? Time to find out! Depending on your personal circumstances, you may also qualify for some specific support, such as disability, etc.

The Balancing Touch

Currency:_____	University 1	University 2	University 3	University 4
GRAND TOTAL TO PAY				
Potential Financing:				
Scholarships				
Parents				
Part-time job				
Other				
Loan				
Scholarship:				
Application conditions				
Deadlines				

Put all the pieces of financing together and calculate whether you cover your estimated costs or if there is still a gap. Doing a yearly calculation, keep in mind that your studies will last three to four years.

If this does not balance, you have several options: Explore loans possibilities, go through the costs again to see whether they could be realistically reduced and/or look at the income side. Keep working on your budget until you and your parents have found a workable balance. *(Note: More on "Loans" in next sub-chapter.)*

TOP TIP: Common Budgeting Mistakes to Avoid:

- No budget…
- An outdated budget somewhere under a pile or lost in an old laptop
- Too tight and austere
- Unrealistic
- Forgot one big expense…
- Totals don't add up. If you use a spreadsheet, build in "check" formulas to secure your calculations.
- Wrong currency or mix of currencies… your parents send you Hong Kong dollars and you include them as British Pounds.
- Your budget balances at your first attempt… mmm, check it out!
- Your parents did it – and you have no clue what to do with it.
- You lost your budget when your hard-drive crashed… just as you were adding a line for computer maintenance – *Back it up!*
- You left your USB key with your budget along with the file with your credit card pin and other sensitive info – both without passwords - in the library computer. Nobody returned your key.

ENLARGE and fine-tune

As you prepare to leave for university, go over your budget and fine-tune each line. If you plan to visit universities before applying, check out surroundings and shops - look at prices. Try out living on a budget. What could you buy with a set amount of the local currency? Note down the prices of some staples, as that will help you fine-tune your budget.

A closer look at accommodation		
	On campus	Off campus
Costs	Accommodation charge Kitchen facility charge Other charges? Check how many years you can qualify (some universities only offer that possibility for first year students)	Rent Utilities (gas, water, electricity) TV licence (if you want TV) Internet Local tax (check your obligation regarding taxes) Transportation to/from campus
Length	During terms – What about holidays (in between terms/ summer holiday) Extra costs involved (temp accommodation for holidays, place to store your stuff...)	12 months – look at tenure agreement Deposit
Other		Sharing rules between flatmates (What happens if things don't work out? What happens if one flatmate leaves during tenure?) Common life rules (bathroom, cooking area, fridge, living area temperature, cleaning turns and standards, noise and invitation, etc....)

Mobile Phones & Travelling

Be smart... use the free Wi-Fi to stay in touch with your family! There are many apps that are perfect for group communication.

Think over and list what you plan to use your phone for (local calls, international calls, text messages, etc....). Will you use it when you go back to your parents for holiday or if you get an internship back home? Once you know what you want in terms of roaming, text-messages, and so forth, compare the different providers and potential deals – it takes time, and phone plans are usually complex but this is worth doing. Consider how long you may be locked into a plan. If you are not sure what your life style will be, consider getting a simple SIM card to start with to give you time to shop around and compare deals. If you've got family or siblings in the same country, check out potential family plans.

As for travel, book early – that's often the best of deals.

FROM a yearly budget to monthly and weekly budgets

A month before leaving, get more specific and split your budget in months. This is the time to fine-tune this "personal" expense line.

Currency:_____	September	October	November	December	Etc....
Tuition fees					
College fees					
Accommodation (*)					
Kitchen facility charge					
Meals					
Books & equipment					
Extra classes					
Local transportation					
Personal:					
Going out					
Cell phone					
Toiletries					
Clothes					
Laundry					
Clubs					
Miscellaneous					
Health					
Insurance					
Formal clothes (work/ internship)					
Travel					
Travel home (x times / year)					
TOTAL/year					
Years of study					
TOTAL					
One-offs: Furniture, utensils, vehicle...					
GRAND TOTAL					

Potential Financing:					
Scholarships					
Parents					
Part-time job					
Other					
Loan					

Some expenses may be only once a year, but others may be every month. If you rent accommodation outside the campus, you may have a deposit to pay, which is a big lump sum. Be precise. It may also slightly impact the total – play around and see what you can do to adjust it.

Timing is important. For example, you know you will receive a scholarship but it is paid only in October and you have expenses to cover in September. Can your parents bridge the gap?

Establish who pays what: Do your parents pay some expenses directly, for example tuition fees, travel back home, at least the first plane ticket to go to university?

Hey Parents!

Now it's time for all of you – parents and students – to discuss. When will you send the money? If your child has never been financially independent, be careful with sending one lump sum once a year or quarter. Instead, send it once a month, or even twice a month, or weekly. This will help your child learn to manage a fixed income.

Are you worried about bank fees? This may be less than having to send emergency money each time your son or daughter runs out of money, or when there is a need to cover an overdraft. Consider opening (or reactivating) a bank account in the country where your child will study. You can transfer the money once or twice a year to cut down on international transfer fees, and then set a monthly or weekly automatic transfer to your child's bank account. Review your assets by currency.

Keep Enlarging

Split your budget by week. You may have to pay your accommodation on the last day of the month but spend on food every day. A weekly budget will help you manage your monthly income. Compare: (*Note: numbers are using a fictional currency – replace them with your numbers*).

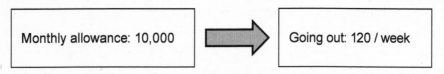

| Monthly allowance: 10,000 | | Going out: 120 / week |

Do you feel the difference?

Split your monthly income:

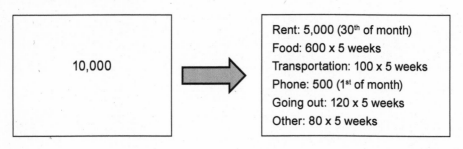

10,000

Rent: 5,000 (30th of month)
Food: 600 x 5 weeks
Transportation: 100 x 5 weeks
Phone: 500 (1st of month)
Going out: 120 x 5 weeks
Other: 80 x 5 weeks

A month has 4.5 weeks, so by taking 5 weeks, you are on the safe side: That will help you keep some extra money.

ALL expenses are not created equal: Focus on key numbers

Don't lose your bearings – your budget is super important, but you can't drive with your eyes glued to the map. So what does "follow your budget" mean? A map is a map; it's static. But you need to know where you are on the map. How can you find out? Use your GPS! Track what you spend. Choose the method that you prefer:

Track everything, then update your budget and readjust it. A budget is a practical tool, not a static piece of art...so change it! If some expenses have changed, for example you underspend on food, or overspend on textbooks, play with the numbers to balance your overall budget.

Key numbers: You can't learn your budget by heart, but you can remember some critical numbers. Of all the expenses you have to manage, some are more important than others: rent, bills, tuition fees (if you are the one paying them). What do these expenses have in common? They are **commitments** you have promised to pay. If you don't pay, these expenses become *debts* (and some may even bear penalties). Is food a commitment? No, you have not promised the grocery shop to spend 600 every week. On the other hand, if you pay a monthly fee to the cafeteria and you have signed up for the year, this is a commitment. Don't mess around with commitments. Here is another way to look at your budget:

Monthly income	10,000
Rent/accommodation fee	5,000
Phone (plan)	500
MONTHLY NET INCOME	4,500
Daily net income	150

+ Income
- commitments
= Net income /30
days= daily limit

◄── **Daily spending limit**

Note: look at your daily spending limit before leaving home: Once you commit, you lose flexibility.

Compare:

Forget about the 10,000 (or even the 5,000 if your parents send you an allowance twice a month), the ONLY number to keep in mind is 150. That is what you have to live on for one day, after setting money aside for your commitments. This is easier to remember than a spreadsheet full of numbers.

You can go further: If you get a fixed monthly allowance, but some expenses are a few times a year – your plane ticket back home for example – include your savings goals in your daily spending limit.

Monthly income	10,000
Rent/accommodation fee	5,000
Phone (plan)	500
MONTHLY NET INCOME	4,500
Plane ticket (7,200 once a year)	-600
MONTHLY NET INCOME	3,900
Daily net income	130

⟵ 7,200/12

(3,900/30)

Food = 110	Transportation = 20

If you need more guidelines and can handle remembering several numbers, split your daily spending limit between food, social/going out, transportation for example. Manage your cash accordingly. Don't walk around with 500 in your wallet if your daily spending limit is 130. Consistency with yourself is the first step towards harmony.

Your Homework:

Monthly income	
Tuition fee/12 months	
Rent/accommodation fee	
Kitchen fee/cafeteria fee	
Phone (plan)	
Utilities	
Other commitments	
MONTHLY NET INCOME	
Text books	
Plane ticket(s)	
Holidays	
Equipment	
Other savings goal	
MONTHLY NET INCOME	
Daily net income	

Managing a big bank account balance

Whether you received one big scholarship or your parents have decided to transfer upfront a big amount once a year, all these zeros look very sweet and awfully deceiving! Be rational and think long term when managing a big lump sum in order to make it last for the whole academic year.

A yearly budget is a must: You have one income and all kinds of expenses to cover for twelve months. Writing a budget will help you see what expenses you can fit until next windfall.

Divide the amount by twelve, and calculate your **daily spending limit** as above.

Open a savings account: Transfer 11/12 of the amount to your savings account then initiate a monthly automatic transfer from your savings account to your current account once a month for a 12th of the initial amount. This will act as a monthly salary. You can fine tune further and only transfer 1/12 of the amount, minus yearly expenses you want to save for (plane ticket back home, holiday). Do whatever works for you so that you see this amount not a luring big pile of money, but a limited amount to make last for twelve months or so.

BUILDING new habits and routines

Include money management when you build your weekly routine schedule. Two minutes here and there, once a day, will make a huge difference. You won't feel it is a heavy workload, and it will give you visibility on your financial situation in order to avoid crises and costly, rushed decisions.

Daily	Weekly	Monthly	Yearly
Note down expenses Note down income if any	Reconcile cash Check bank balance online Withdraw cash for coming week following budget	Check bank statement Check and pay bills Update budget	Tax declaration Next year budget Select charities to give to

If you find the same moment for each task, you are less likely to forget it. Test apps and tools that work for you.

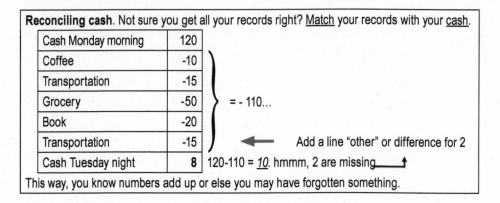

Reconciling cash. Not sure you get all your records right? <u>Match</u> your records with your <u>cash</u>.

Cash Monday morning	120
Coffee	-10
Transportation	-15
Grocery	-50
Book	-20
Transportation	-15
Cash Tuesday night	8

= - 110...

⟵ Add a line "other" or difference for 2

120-110 = <u>10</u>. hmmm, 2 are missing

This way, you know numbers add up or else you may have forgotten something.

Short cut: If you don't want to note down all your expenses, keep the receipts of the biggest ones, and consider the smaller ones as "other". Then, the cash reconciliation is even more useful to know how significant these "small" expenses really are.

Cash Monday morning	<u>120</u>	
Coffee	-10	}
Grocery	-50	} – 80 according to receipts
Book	-20	}
Other	-32	120 - 8 - 80 = 32 -> by deduction, "other" = 32
Cash Tuesday night	<u>8</u>	Count your cash left.

If the "other" looks big and you'd like to get more details to budget your expenses better, you can always track all that you spend with an app or by taking notes.

Shortest cut: If you really don't want to track each expense, then just count your cash at the beginning of the week, and at the end, and see how much you have spent. Don't forget to include any cash you withdrew. At least you know how much cash you use every week! And the amount may make you wonder what on earth you did with such an amount, and encourage you to keep a more detailed record.

Knowing the detail of what you spend helps you control your expenses better and anticipate them. It's a tool, not a goal. If you control your expenses very well without tracking them, that's great! But if your spending pattern drives you crazy – either because you tend to spend too much or your income is so tight – then track. Tracking gives you visibility and self-discipline.

Bank statements: A big part of your expenses may be spent with cards or transfers.

Online banking: (see next section) That's your virtual wallet – so before any big payment, check how much you have left.

The key is to anticipate expenses by looking further than the next bill.

1) Phone bill received	2) Check bank balance	3) Look at budget
120	300	List of future expenses ALERT: Rent 400
4) Launch action plan	**5) Pay bill**	
Transfer from other account or ask parents…		Mission accomplished – Overdraft meteorite avoided

When you check your bank statement once a month, you should:

- ✓ Compare each transaction with your own record (debit/credit card slip, internet payment receipt, cash withdrawal slip) and make sure there are no discrepancies.
- ✓ Look at the fees: Are there any fees that the bank charged you, and you don't understand? Be sure to contest these.
- ✓ Update your budget.
- ✓ Look at the coming week, and anticipate potential issues.
- ✓ Save your bank statements in a specific directory.
- ✓ Read your bills. Most utility bills contain fixed fees (as per contract) and a variable part, such as the units you have consumed (for instance, Kilo Watts, square meters of gas, text messages or phone call minutes…) multiplied by the price of one unit. Spot potential mistakes. Does the fixed fee match your contract? Do the same for the unit fee. Does your consumption look weird? If it does there are three potential situations happening.
  - o Mistake or wrong estimation. For water, electricity or gas bills, utility companies may read the meter only once or twice a year and charge

an estimated consumption based on these readings in between. When you move to a new place and arrange utilities, make sure meters are read at the time of move.

o Leaks: Check whether a tap is leaking, especially a hidden tap behind a washing machine.

o Overconsumption: The third option, which is by far the most common, is that the invoice is right – you did (you alone or with your flatmates) live with all appliances and lights on 24 hours a day, run bubble baths every night, or text your 600-page autobiography to fans at the other side of the world. Let this be a wakeup call! Manage your consumption: Look at what really hurts your bill (Heating/air conditioning? Appliances?) Cut down on what you can. Set limits like timing your shower and setting an alarm clock, make your cup of tea straight after boiling the kettle and don't keep overriding the hot water system. Be frugal with hot water and electricity!

More expense management tips

✓ Managing expenses is easy… but managing oneself is sometimes challenging. Write on calendars / phone when your bills are due and set reminders a week before.

✓ Keep your spending limit as a note in your wallet. If you have budgeted to spend 50 on coffees per week, put 50 in an envelope on Monday morning and only pay for coffees from money from this envelope, and don't cheat yourself. Wait until next week to refill the envelope, don't live on friends' cash, and don't take from your other cash reserves.

✓ Only carry a limited amount of cash.

✓ Write shopping lists using your rational brain, quietly at home, and don't let your emotional brain lengthen the list once in the shops.

✓ Set a virtual limit for online shopping.

✓ Identify what you like spending: Track this even more and set limits. Apps and spreadsheets can alert you if you are reaching these reminders.

✓ Look at best deals with a critical eye: Is this 5-kilo potato crate at -20% really the best deal if you are cooking for one?

✓ Don't buy because there is a discount – but because you need the item and it is on your shopping list.

✓ Find other leisure than window-shopping or browsing merchant websites.

✓ About to be tempted to buy something? What else could you do with the same amount? How will this new item contribute to your well-being in one month's time? In six months' time?

✓ For any big expense (and you have to define what "big" means according to your budget), always look around for the various options and prices or ask for quotes.

✓ Find ways to be social without blowing up your budget: A social night out could be converted to movie night in with home-made food.

✓ Once all these statements and bills are checked, file them. Don't throw them away. You need to find a system which works for you which is:

  o **Convenient:** Enables you to find documents quickly, without excessive pain.

  o **Time-proof:** 12 bills a year … that'll make 36 or 48 by the time you graduate. Keep that in mind and don't start a filing system that works for three months.

  o **Both paper and virtual:** Use real paper folders and virtual directories for virtual documents. Scan your important documents (passport first pages, student ID, insurance card, diplomas and certificates, birth certificates, and driving licence). Copy these virtual documents on a flash drive secured with a password, stored in another place than the original documents.

  o **Safe:** Keep your important papers in a secure place. Tell your parents where they are. If anything happens to you, then they'll know where to find them.

<u>**What to keep**</u>:

- o   Bills
- o   Invoices for items you keep (electronics, appliances, furniture, valuables...)
- o   Contracts (work, rent, insurance...)
- o   Pay slips
- o   Bank statements
- o   Certificates, diplomas
- o   ID

Tip: File your papers by providers: 1) phone, 2) rent, 3) utilities... this will help you spot a missing payment, or an increase. Use the same filing system for your papers and the virtual copies.

RISK Management

We can't plan everything, but that is not an excuse not to plan at all. Anticipating the expense of 60%–70% of future events is better than nothing.

Planning is a skill... and the more you do it, the better you'll become good at it. One big challenge is our propensity to forget about things we should have remembered. There are various ways to tackle this: Either you challenge your brain to become as data-oriented as a computer, or you use computers and reminders and whatever high or low tech solutions that work for you, and enable you to remember bills, trips, and even promises, without overloading your brain. Most financial software and apps, on top of helping you track expenses and budget, have bill schedules with reminders built-in.

Get Organised *(see chapter on time)*

Leave your stuff always in the same secure places! That'll save you literally hours. Have specific spots for your phone, keys, glasses, and credit card.

Don't wait for the last minute to settle payments. Set a reminder a few days before. If you pay by bank transfer online, you can set a future date in most bank websites, or if you pay by cheque, write it with the date the rent is due and put it in an envelope, ready to send.

Why it matters:

Apart from reducing the stress of receiving a phone call because you are late paying, things done on time take less time to do. You will gradually build something that really matters in the money world: trust. You will be regarded as someone who pays on time, who is reliable. What's the benefit of this? Building good relationships with the people you interact with moneywise has obvious and hidden benefits, for example, at the end of the rental year, your landlord will be more willing to rent this place again to you if you have always paid your rent on time; you will have more weight or credibility in negotiating down a rent increase. If ever you have an exceptional cash crisis, your landlord may be more open to grant you a few days relief knowing that you have always been trustworthy. This is a small world... your landlord (or whoever you transact with) may be a relative of your future boss...or sweetheart. Your reputation is what people may hear of you...before they actually meet you. Nurture it, build it – it is fully part of your identity. Your parents may be there to bail you out - but restoring trust and reputation will take your own effort; your parents won't be able to help.

Reduce risks by preventing them. At the end of the day, your health is more important than any money, so look after yourself. Trust others but don't lose your anchor: If others put you in a situation that you are not comfortable with or consider dangerous, get out of it. Your character is also your wealth – so protect it against negative behaviour. Maintain the place you live at a good hygiene standard and make sure it functions. Detect leaks or issues before they get worse... leaks never stop by themselves; so before flooding your downstairs neighbour, get it fixed. Keep your papers safe – especially your IDs. Check your bank account to detect any suspicious amount. Don't share your passwords and make them hard to remember.

I Know Your Password!

123456, password, qwerty... incredibly here are the top three passwords used. And they are very likely to be the same password opening one person's online banking, FB page, Twitter, Amazon or other online shopping websites (with the credit card number stored) and social media, airlines, health, university... the list will get longer and longer.

Not being able to remember all our passwords is a lame excuse: you don't have to remember them. Use an Excel ® file or an app to record your passwords and reduce your mental effort to one password only to remember: the one to your password file.

Make passwords long enough (8 or 9 characters), mix numbers, lower and upper case letters and special characters.

Change passwords often. Include in your file the latest date you updated this password. If you are Excel ® savvy, create a conditional formatting to highlight the passwords you have to change. And if you are not, write the date you last changed it next to your password.

Don't reuse the same password from one website to the other.

When you log on, in a public place, remember to LOG OUT before you leave and ensure cookies haven't stored your password. Being paranoid may save you lots of trouble! Don't click on "remember my password" if you use a public or a friend's computer. If your credit card number is stored in a shopping website, even if it is your own computer or phone, you may prefer to opt out of the "remember me"... in case your phone or laptop gets stolen or used by someone else.

When you shop online, ensure the site has switched to a secure address (https://) when you start any financial transaction. Some banks propose a one-transaction only card (a credit card number is generated only for one online payment), reducing fraud risks. Or use accounts like PayPal that do not divulge your card number to the merchant.

Report any fraud or ID theft ASAP – don't be negligent.

Financial Padding: Keep some savings for emergencies or unexpected events.

Defuse bad surprises: Before committing to anything, understand what you are signing up for. Whether it is a phone or renting a place, read the contracts. Contracts are probably the most boring prose to read. Share the joy of reading (and understanding) your contracts with your parents – it could be a good use of their experience. Read it thoroughly together and then summarise your duties, your rights, what you are expected to pay and what the other party is expected to pay. If you share a flat, make sure your flatmates read it thoroughly too and commit to the obligations.

The unplannable: There will always be unexpected issues popping up. That's life! The sweet thing about planning is that instead of exhausting yourself to deal with tons of unexpected events all day long, you will have fewer to tackle. Keep calm. If the unexpected turns out to be an expense (they often are), list:

- How much it costs?
- Who should pay (that's where reading contracts comes handy)?
- How can you cover this expense (emergency savings? Insurance?)

3. DEALING with Finance Professionals

Banks and financial institutions often present themselves as solutions to address the challenges of managing money. That's their way of seeing things. They can often be part of the challenges too.

BANKS and Financial Services

Most financial institutions are not charities but for-profit businesses. They are even a flourishing industry. There are exceptions – credit unions in the US for example are not-for-profit. Some insurance and banks in Europe are set up as mutual (a kind of cooperative).

Bank accounts are convenient – especially to deal with big amounts (rent to pay, scholarships to receive, transfers from parents, etc.). You just have to learn to use them in your best interest.

Before Opening a Bank Account, Shop Around and Compare:

List the possible banks – your university may have deals or a short-list. That's not enough. Include in your list your parents' bank (see fees), banks recommended by other students, do online research and look at the banks nearby –if you manage your account online, geographical proximity is not critical. Look for banks that may offer specific services (and pricing) for students.

Draft your banking profile: Look at your budget and list what you need from a bank, what services you are more likely to use. This will help you select the bank which offers the best deal for the services you really need. For instance, if your parents transfer money to you every month, focus on zero transfer fees. Look at the app and online services you may use.

Fees: Come in multiple colours, shapes and flavours. Fees are what banks charge you for various services. All banks are different, but there is one thing they all have in common: a wild imagination for fees: monthly fees, ATM fees, overdraft fees, international transfer fees… Gather all the information you can get on fees for your shortlisted banks. Get the fees from the banks leaflets, websites and ask questions. Be careful with opening offers: some banks may waive fees for the first months only. Take a magnifying glass and take the time to read the small print. If this is incomprehensible, ask your parents to help and/or phone the bank and ask them to explain in plain language.

Basic bank language: Banks use different names for similar things. American banks call the most basic account "checking accounts" while British banks call them "current accounts". This book is not country-specific so you may encounter various names for fees and accounts. Learn the words and understand the concepts! Here are a few basic words you may bump into wherever you study:

Banklog (*)	What on earth is that?	Action plan
Overdraft	Is simply a loan or debt. An overdraft is whenever you use (draw) more than the money you have in your bank account. In other words, you use the bank's money to pay for your expenses. Overdrafts are usually very expensive. You may have to pay an overdraft fee plus interest, plus get an angry call from your banker.	Avoid overdrafts. Some banks offer an overdraft limit - check out the conditions. Authorisation in advance to draw more than you have is not a free service. Some banks offer a zero interest overdraft without fee - try to find out why the bank you are cross-checking is offering a free overdraft. (Are the other services more expensive?)

Overdraft limit	Banks (like most finance people) don't like surprises: Many include an overdraft limit (an amount not to trespass): if you go beyond, additional fees and interests are charged. You may receive a call from your bank.	Know the limit and never, ever go beyond. Avoid overdrafts anyway.
Minimum balance	Some banks charge a monthly fee if your bank account balance is less than a set amount.	For students with typical ups and downs in their financial lives, this is probably not a good deal. Fish for banks that offer bank accounts without any monthly fee, let alone fees attached to a monthly balance.
Freebies and rewards	Many banks advertise free services, gifts and various types of reward points.	See through the smoke screen and include the potential rewards in your comparison chart: Will these reward points help you finance an expense you have already budgeted (plane ticket, food, etc....) or will they just be additional stuff on your shelves that you will have to get rid of when you move out? Look at the conditions to get them: would you qualify with your budgeted level of expense, or will you be pushed to spend more in order to qualify?
Direct debit	Is an authorisation you give to your bank to pay a specific supplier or third party.	This saves time and stress to pay for utilities or rent. You don't have to spend time transferring money or writing and posting cheques. But make you sure you have enough in your bank account so that direct debits can be processed.
Direct deposit	This is a convenient way to receive any amount like a salary or a scholarship.	Check the fees before. It's annoying to get one's income cut down by a fee.

Online banking	Bank branch on internet: you can check your bank balance, download your statement, transfer money, pay bills from your computer or phone.	This is very convenient. Look at what your short-listed banks offer online or on apps. Double-check the security features.
ATM	Automated teller machine, you insert your card, type your pin, and you can withdraw cash, deposit cheques, check your account balance, etc....	In many countries, fees are charged when you withdraw money from an ATM belonging to another bank network. If you don't travel and your bank has an ATM conveniently located, this is not a problem. If you plan to travel or if the bank you have chosen is a local bank only, this may cause extra expense: check out your bank network coverage to avoid paying fees.
Mobile payments	You can initiate payments or receive money using your mobile phone.	Look at the bank app and what it requires. Check your bank conditions in case of fraud.
Contactless cards	Some countries have cards that you charge beforehand and let you pay small amounts.	Enquire on conditions and fees if any.

(*) the bank language!

Manage your bank account actively!

Anticipate: Use your budget to forecast your bank balance; if you use Excel®, use colour-coded alerts (conditional formulas are great) to monitor your balance and avoid costly overdrafts. If your budget is tight, update it on a daily or at least a weekly basis to get visibility on potential shortfalls. If you forecast a deficit, think hard how you can finance it, parents, delay some expenses, or free overdraft if your account offers that possibility, etc. Warn your bank before it happens. Use a personal finance app or software to track your ins and outs, schedule your bills and calculate your bank balance in advance. React before you have hit the bottom. If you pay your bills with a cheque, make sure you have enough in your bank account in the coming two to five days before a cheque gets debited. Bounced cheques (cheques that your bank will refuse to pay on your behalf because you don't have enough on your account) are very costly.

Check your bank statements: Either online, whenever you feel like it, or at least once a month. Learn to read your bank statements: credits are amounts added up to your account; debits are amounts taken out of your account. Most personal finance software will help you "reconcile" your bank statement – which is the technical word for ticking each transaction (ins and outs). Are you spotting a transaction you don't agree with? Double-check with another record (bill, card receipt, online payment receipt) and if you don't agree, contact your bank ASAP to solve the issue. Keep payment receipts until your account has been debited, to support any claim. Errors can happen.

Set reminders: The nice thing with a personal finance app or software is that you can set reminders. With your busy life, use that feature to avoid paying bills late or checking your bank statements.

Track the fees: Do you understand why your bank charges you these fees? Do they comply with your bank account conditions or contract? If not, phone your bank to find out why you were charged these fees and possibly get a credit back. Manage your fees: If you are charged fees for transactions that you can do differently, it is worth changing your habits. If you get an ATM fee for instance, because it is easier for you to use the campus ATM but you could get cash for free by walking a few hundred meters more, plan your walking expedition according to your cash needs.

Safety:

- Memorise your pins and keep them in a safe and locked place. Never ever share them – not even with the bank. The bank won't ask for your pin. If someone claiming to be your bank asks for your pin, this is a fraud.
- Keep your passwords in a protected file.
- Avoid using the library computer for online banking. If you can, use your own computer or phone. Ensure you are on a secure webpage (https page). Don't forget to log off (even though most bank online platforms will automatically log you off after some idle minutes). Learn how to use the various features of online banking.
- If your bank has provided you with a security device (little gizmo that generates a one-time pin for example), store it in a locked place and remember where you stored it!
- Keep the emergency bank contact numbers in a convenient place in case you need to call your bank for an urgent issue like a stolen card.
- Hide the screen when you enter your pin to withdraw money or make a payment.

- Second bank account: if you get a big lump sum, it may be easier to transfer it to a second bank account (current or savings) and transfer it back to your main account once a month as you pay for your bills. Why? Mostly to avoid living under the impression you have tons of money to spend.

LOANS

Banks provide loans – beside fees, that's actually how they earn money: by lending money with interest. For further reflection on interest, read "The ethics of interest" below.

INTERESTING FACTS

Key feature of the current financial system
Extra amount charged by the lender to the borrower.
%: extra charge for 100 borrowed. 5% = you borrow 100, you pay back 105. You borrow 200, you pay back 210, etc....
Always be clear on the time reference (% per month? year?)
Interests grow: ("compound"): Unpaid interest becomes a debt that will bear interest too (see below the maths behind interest)

ACTION PLAN:
Pay your credit card, in full, every month to avoid interest growing out of control.
Always pay any debt in time.

The maths behind interest: Let's take an example: I borrow 1,000 at 10% monthly interest. After one month, I have to pay back 1000 + 10%:

(10 for each 100 borrowed = 10/100x1000=100) = 1,100.

If I don't pay back, the due interest from month 1 becomes a debt. So at the end of the second month, I owe:

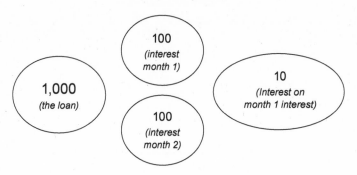

If maths is not your cup of tea, just remember that interest keeps growing, like weeds; if you don't clean up your garden, weeds spread. If you don't attend to your debts, interest multiplies.

Loan vocabulary:

Fixed interest: Is set. For example, you borrow at 5% a month. It stays 5% a month, until your last repayment. Read the small prints: make sure no clause may transform this fixed rate into a variable one.

Variable interest: Interest goes up and down. Therefore so does the monthly loan payment. Variable loans are usually "tied" to a reference or index. They look like: "LIBOR + 0.5%", "Prime index + 0.425%".

What's the point of taking a risk (or bet) on the interest rate? Variable interest loans are often offered with a variable interest which is slightly lower than the current fixed interest loan, making it more appealing. Some loans come with a "cap", or maximum rate. But things can change quickly. So on top of the uncertainty of your first job, you add the uncertainty of how much you will pay back, an uncertainty that depends on world economic trends and financial situation – so not much you can do about.

LIBOR is the London Interbank Offered Rate – that's THE interest reference. Many loans are indexed (tied) to it.

Fees: Yes, loans come with fees too! Words vary – application, origination... but the idea is the same. There's an extra charge to pay when you sign for a loan.

APR: Is the attempt to have all banks speak the same language. Loans costs are so multifarious: one-off fees, yearly fees, monthly interest, etc. The APR or Annual Percentage Rate gathers all these fees and interest for one loan and turns them into one rate only. This way, you can more easily compare various loans. Let's take a simple example. You are hesitating between two loans: One has a lower fee but higher interest (and the other, the other way round). What's the best deal?

	Option 1	Option 2
Loan amount (principal)	1,000	1,000
Loan fee	10	5
Interest rate	5.00%	5.40%
Interest (1000 x interest rate)	50	54
Interest + fee	60	59
APR = (interest + fee)/loan amount=	6.00%	5.90%

The second option turns out to be cheaper.

Principal: This is the amount you have originally borrowed. It's the basis for the interest calculation. If you borrow 3,000, the interest payment is calculated on the 3,000 (interest rate multiplied by the principal).

Monthly payment: This is the amount to pay back every month. Part of it is the amount you borrowed, and the rest is interest. Fixed interest loans often include a fixed monthly payment – usually easier to plan and manage, especially if your income and most other big expenses like accommodation are fixed. The bank will show you an amortisation table with many numbers. Let's take a short example: You borrow $1,000 at 5% monthly interest for two months.

	Principal still to pay	Interest amount	Principal paid back	Monthly payment
	The amount borrowed minus whatever you have already paid back	(5% x principal still to pay)	Monthly payment minus interest	Big maths formula[1]
Month 1	$1,000.00	$50.00	$487.80	$537.80
Month 2	$512.20	$25.61	$512.20	$537.80
Total		$75.61	$1,000.00	

The monthly amount stays the same, which is easier to manage. over time, it bears less interest, so you pay more and more the principal back.

At first, your monthly payment is mostly interest (x% of a lot is a lot).

But as you pay back the principal over time, it bears less interest, so you pay more and more of the principal back.

Length or duration: This is how long it will take you to pay back fully. If you borrow for a longer term, your monthly payment is lower as the payback is spread out over a longer period. BUT, the longer the duration the more expensive it is as interest adds up for longer.

---

[1] For those who want the formula: . You can also use the PMT formula in Excel ®.

Loan principal	$10,000.00	$10,000.00
Yearly interest rate	12.00%	12.00%
Loan duration (months)	12	36
Monthly payment	$888.49	$332.14
Total payment:	$10,661.85	$11,957.15
Total interest	$661.85	$1,957.15

Monthly payment times the duration
Total payment minus the principal

Terms and Conditions: Read them... because that's where all the details on fees, potential charges etc. are lurking. Be especially careful about offers that depend on your status (hence the word "conditions".) For instance, you may qualify for a benefit or a reward but only if you are an undergraduate for example. Use your critical mind! Pay attention to the repayment options, especially whether you can repay sooner and what potential penalty or fee applies.

The (false) magic of interest: Most financial books or literature marvel at the magic of interest when it works your way: for your savings. Stay cool headed and compare the interest on a savings account to the interest on a loan or a credit card. Interest paid on savings accounts is minimal, especially after you deduct the inflation rate. You are likely to end up with a negative real interest. So don't get excited. You won't get rich by getting interest on your savings account – getting an income by studying and graduating, and spending less than you earn are better avenues to wealth. Interest is statistically much more likely to hit you as a borrower.

The doubtful ethics of interest: Interest is not a law of nature, it is a man-made phenomenon. It even goes against the law of nature: unlike natural resources, plants, animals or people, money does not decay or rot, it keeps growing with interest.[2] That causes a first ethical issue: how do we re-pay more, how do we create the money to pay the interest, when any production of wealth on Earth is directly or indirectly linked to the natural resources on our Planet? This pressure

---

[2] Read the beautiful analysis of Mankind's relation to money written by C. Eisenstein in the 'Ascent of Humanity."

won't be sustainable for ever. The second ethical issue is social: those who lend money are those who have money – so interest is the reward of having money in the first place. It redistributes money to those who have some already. It is also an asymmetrical relationship (based on power – not on fairness) as the pressure to pay back with interest is much higher than the lender's risk of not being repaid. This is why many religions and philosophers reject interest. Practically, if you prefer to avoid interest, there are emerging financial institutions that offer non-interest-bearing accounts or financing modes that do not involve loans and interest, and a more balanced share of risks.

TOP TIP: Before taking a loan

Always, always, always plan how to pay back your loan BEFORE taking one. Don't be over optimistic in planning your incomes or extra minimalist in forecasting your expenses. Don't forget to include interest payments in your budget. A loan is a bet on the future and your ability to pay back plus the interest. So it's risky, especially as you are actually lacking big pieces of the jigsaw, such as how long it will take you to get a job, how much you will earn, where you may live, etc.

A loan is a burden: Don't take too many loans.

Don't take a loan to pay back another loan (unless you "refinance" the first one, meaning you borrow money at a lower or zero interest rate to pay back another loan at higher interest rate.) You will just add an extra burden. It is like starting a second fire to put out a first fire.

Compare various ways to finance your project or purchase. Write several budgets with each assumption: savings, loans, in-kind/cash donations, reducing your project/purchase amount, or a mix of all the above. Financing your holiday or plane ticket home may be cheaper, if you save for it and book well in advance when fares and deals are still open, compared to buying a last-minute ticket on your credit card and hence paying for your holiday for months and months.

Shop around: If your assumption is that it is best to take a loan, don't rush to the first bank: enquire about the terms or conditions (APR, fees, interest, monthly payment, repayment options, etc.) and find out what suits your finances best.

Once in Debt. Managing Your Loans:

Your credit history: This is your financial CV or resume. It aims to tell lenders how reliable a borrower you are: your credit history tells what types of loan you had/ have, when you borrowed, how much you borrowed (and your credit limit for credit cards for instance), how much you still owe, whether you paid back on time. Your credit history is summarised in a score, a number.	**Refinancing:** Is borrowing at a lower rate to pay back an older loan at a higher rate. Before rushing to a bank when interests go down, do your maths. Read your original loan terms and conditions and look at the repayment options. If there is a penalty fee to pay it all back in advance, include the penalty cost in your APR calculation before comparing with new loans.
Credit reporting agencies (note that that varies from country to country) issue this number by compiling and grinding lots of data on you – your credit history, any payment defaults, how long and how often you use credit, etc. Does the score matter? Credit is so prevalent in our world that it is hard to shun it completely. Lots of people will look at your credit score as an indicator of your reliability.	
Consolidation: Is taking one loan to pay off several other loans. Do the maths first: Is the amount you will pay back lower than before, including the potential longer term you obtain when consolidating your debts? Is the rate lower? Is it a way for you to postpone the inevitable: get a plan to get out of debt?	**Caution!** Be careful with pieces of advice you can get on refinancing, credit, consolidation, etc. especially from people who work for lending institutions. Lending is a thriving business and their objectives are not the same as yours.

Credit Score:

As a system designed by lenders, credit scoring does not only try to assess how risky you are as a borrower, it also assesses how potentially profitable a customer you may be: So, if you don't have debts, or only a very limited number, what potential lenders see is that you are not likely to borrow – so not a very interesting target. The scoring system values how people manage debts and don't value those who are outside it. You may want to stay outside the credit scoring system and try to pay fully and immediately what you buy – but at some point, you will cross the path of the credit scoring. Credit scoring is used whenever you ask for a loan: It sets the rate you will be able to borrow to buy a house for instance (the lower your credit score, the higher the rate) and even one percent on a sum with lots of zeros ends up being a hard to swallow pill. Even sooner than that, if you want to get a phone plan, the phone company is likely to check your credit score. The system is used extensively in some countries (namely the US) where credit score is also looked at by potential employers – so even if you don't like the system, play smart with it.

Have one (or two) credit cards and pay them in full every month (before any interest): That shows you can manage your debt sensibly. Have your monthly card balance paid by direct debit, meaning you authorise the credit card company to pay your monthly purchases with the money on your bank account – this way you don't let credit card debts grow and grow. That requires you to be disciplined and manage your credit card usage to avoid an overdraft.

Don't multiply credit cards or store cards that you either don't use or with old balances. One or two max.

Pay bills on time – all of them, and always on time. Careful when these bills are shared with flatmates (or boy/girlfriend): don't let others impact your score.

React quickly – if you have taken too big a debt to swallow, write a plan to pay it off in a few months.

Don't take a new debt to pay back another one (see below).

Student Loans: Are loans. You borrow money and will have to pay it back with interest. What makes student loans special is that they offer a grace or deferment period. Unlike most loans where you have to start paying back the month after you get the loan, student loan pay backs are deferred until you leave, whether you graduate or drop out, and start working.

But grace doesn't mean free. As you diligently study and use your loan money, the interest compounds. Note that some loans require students to make monthly payments during their studies.

In the UK, student loans are deducted from your salary when you start earning above a certain threshold. If you become unemployed, or earn less than that threshold, repayments stop and will start again once you get above. Student loans can also have progressive repayments: The more you earn, the more you pay back. So the decision to finance your studies with or without a loan is based on a big question mark. How much are you likely to earn for the 10 or 20 years following your graduation?

As for any loan, think and plan ahead. Write a multiple year budget to see how you will juggle with your other expenses while paying back your loan. If you are getting good at spreadsheets, write various budgets with various assumptions: Lower income, higher income. Keep it simple. If you don't like numbers, estimate your potential income once graduated (let's say for the first years), and your debt pay back.

	Low	High
Income >	2.000	4,000
Monthly debt instalment >	400	400
What's left to live on =	1,600	3,600

Go a little further and subtract a typical rent and food. See what's left for all the other expenses and some savings for your longer-term projects. Keep exploring how to finance your studies until you find a workable solution.

TOP TIP: Check List:

- ✓ List your study costs (tuition + accommodation + living expenses + travel...) as previously explained.
- ✓ List the incomes.
- ✓ Do you need a loan to bridge the gap?
- ✓ How much do you need to bridge the gap? Play around with the numbers to get a workable budget.
- ✓ Look at how much you will pay back and how much is left for living expenses such as rent, etc.
- ✓ Once you have an idea of the amount, look around at the various loan options and compare APR rates, conditions, grace period, etc.
- ✓ Decide – gather paper work.
- ✓ Manage your loan – start saving or paying back (or at least the interest) while studying if you take a job for example.
- ✓ Study and graduate and get a job. This is the surest way to pay back your student's loan.

CREDIT cards and debit cards

The cool thing about being independent is the magic plastic card! 47 square centimetres od plastic, unlocking a world of possibilities. Cards are really convenient – and most of the time safer than cash. But they are not just about entering a pin or signing a receipt. It is worth learning how to use them. If they do open up possibilities, these are not endless – they are only at the height of the money you have.

There are roughly two big types of cards: the debit and the credit cards.

They look the same: Same size, same plastic; many have chips and a black band on the back side; most of them are issued by banks and carry the bank's logo.

DEBIT	CREDIT
"DEBIT" is often written on it. **Immediate payment:** The expense is taken out of your bank account within one or two days at most. **Declined payments:** Because the debit card is linked to your bank account, if you try to buy something for 100 while you only have 60 in your account, your card will be declined, i.e. you will have to either use another payment type (cash, credit card...) or leave the shop without buying for 100. If you have negotiated an overdraft limit with your bank, your card may be accepted but you'll have to pay the overdraft fee and interest on that purchase (which will make the cost of your daily grocery look like gourmet food). **Fraud protection:** Your pin protects you - but if someone steals your card (or just its number to make a new card), they may reach your bank account in one day and empty it. The bank will investigate and restore your fund but that may take several days or a couple of weeks. Depending on how quickly you phone and declare the fraud or theft, you may not be fully paid back the stolen amount.	It carries the name of the bank issuing it (acting as the credit card company) and the credit card network (Visa, MasterCard, American Express, Discover, etc.) Note that American Express, Discover are both networks and card issuers. **Deferred payment:** The expenses are paid by the credit card company (the one who issued the card) to the shop. At the end of the month (or the beginning of next - the "cut-off" date depends on each card), the credit card company sends you a statement with all the expenses you owe them. **Paying your purchases:** At that point, you have two choices: pay your balance fully – and that's it, or drag the amount for another month or so. That's where the credit card company starts charging interest - usually at a high rate. **Credit limit:** The card company sets a limit to your card. If you go over, they are likely to call you and you may pay an over limit penalty.

Cash withdrawal: You can use it to withdraw cash. **Fee:** It depends – some debit cards come without fees.	**Fraud protection**: Is often higher on a credit card. The credit card company may call you to ask you about a fishy transaction with your card. (If that was a genuine one from you, let them know.) The credit card company won't charge you for the fraudulent purchase. **Rewards:** Many cards come with points and rewards (purchase points, air miles etc.) Whenever you use them for a purchase, you get points that you can redeem later. **Credit score:** Showing that you can use a credit card sensibly boosts your credit score. **Cash withdrawal:** Check it out - in some countries, using your credit card at the ATM comes with a fee. **Fee:** Most credit cards are not free: You have to pay an annual fee.

Some Statistics[3]

US$8,220: average debt per credit card in the US, taking into account only the cards that usually carry a balance.

US$885 billion of revolving debt in the US (mostly credit cards debts) (January 2015)

$499: average balance among college students in 2013.

£58.5bn: outstanding credit card balances in the UK (Q3 2014) out of which 42% were non-interest bearing.

40% of UK consumers paid off outstanding balances in full each month vs. 70% in the US.

---

[3] http://www.nasdaq.com/article/credit-card-debt-statistics-cm393820
http://www.creditcards.com/credit-card-news/average-credit_card_debt-1276.php?aid=32392dee
http://www.creditcards.com/credit-card-news/credit-card-industry-facts-personal-debt-statistics-1276.php
http://uk.creditcards.com/credit-card-news/uk-britain-credit-debit-card-statistics-international.php#sup2

Behind the Card

Credit Card Network

Authorise and process transactions between credit card users, merchants and credit card issuers.

Define where cards can be used.

Set conditions and terms such as merchant fee (for each payment paid by card, the shop receives the amount less a fee), fraud liability rules.

Get paid by a fee on each transaction.

Credit Card Companies:

Issue the card after assessing the applicant's risk profile (they check the financial credit history for instance, or/ and the disposable income).

Most of them are banks. Note that American Express and Discover are both credit card networks and companies.

A profitable business: the credit companies get fees (annual fee on each card), interest charges and a fee on each transaction.

Now the big question is… which one is best? If you have a piece of bread, or a carrot to cut in slices, which one is easier to use?

The credit card offers more advantages but like a sharper knife, there is more risk of cutting yourself. You have two approaches: learn to use a credit card, or if you don't trust yourself, stick to debit card.

Be a transactor not a revolver: Use your credit card like a debit card, i.e. as a payment tool, not as a loan.

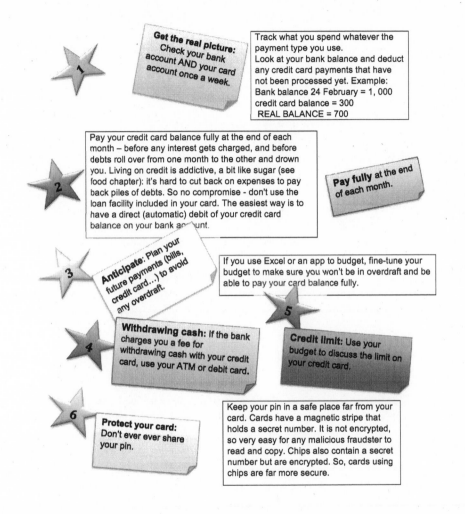

1 Get the real picture: Check your bank account AND your card account once a week.

Track what you spend whatever the payment type you use.
Look at your bank balance and deduct any credit card payments that have not been processed yet. Example:
Bank balance 24 February = 1, 000
credit card balance = 300
REAL BALANCE = 700

2 Pay your credit card balance fully at the end of each month – before any interest gets charged, and before debts roll over from one month to the other and drown you. Living on credit is addictive, a bit like sugar (see food chapter): it's hard to cut back on expenses to pay back piles of debts. So no compromise - don't use the loan facility included in your card. The easiest way is to have a direct (automatic) debit of your credit card balance on your bank account.

Pay fully at the end of each month.

3 Anticipate: Plan your future payments (bills, credit card...) to avoid any overdraft.

If you use Excel or an app to budget, fine-tune your budget to make sure you won't be in overdraft and be able to pay your card balance fully.

4 Withdrawing cash: If the bank charges you a fee for withdrawing cash with your credit card, use your ATM or debit card.

5 Credit limit: Use your budget to discuss the limit on your credit card.

6 Protect your card: Don't ever ever share your pin.

Keep your pin in a safe place far from your card. Cards have a magnetic stripe that holds a secret number. It is not encrypted, so very easy for any malicious fraudster to read and copy. Chips also contain a secret number but are encrypted. So, cards using chips are far more secure.

You may ask: What's the point of using a credit card like a debit card?

1) Credit cards are more secure and carry some rewards (see below).
2) All your big transactions (bills, rent, credit card balance payment) are all at the end of the month. You may not fully benefit from the 29 to one day credit but as soon as you get a monthly salary, paid at the end of the month, having all your big expenses paid when you get your salary makes them easier to manage.

The laptop case:

You have bought a laptop for $5,000. Good deal, you can get a nice $500 rebate on top! You paid it with your credit card. The minimum monthly payment is the bigger of these two numbers: 3% of the balance or a flat rate of 50. Every month, you only pay the minimum. The credit card charges 20% interest a year. Any idea how long it will take you to pay your laptop fully?

Two years? Three? Five maybe? No, a whopping six years – by that time, you'll probably have replaced your laptop once or twice already, so you will still be paying for an item you have dumped and no longer use. Total cost? $7,329. Interest keeps flourishing on the balance which decreases so slowly every month that you end up paying nearly half the purchase price in interest. Good deal? Not to mention that you didn't get the rebate - you had to mail the proof of purchase with a voucher to a company and you just waited too long and found it too much of a hassle to do.

Moral? Pay off your credit card fully each month – don't let it get out of control.

Online Shopping: To Click or Not to Click... Too Late, I've Clicked!

The Major Issue: Convenience, effortlessness, lots of choice, online shopping has tons of advantages. And you are already online anyway. All it takes is to shift to a merchant screen, a few clicks and before you realise it, your virtual cart is full of super cool stuff. When you open your wallet and pay cash, you get a strong sense of limit. **Online, the delay between pressing the BUY button and the financial aftermath can take so long that money looks limitless, your virtual cart is bottomless, buying feels without consequences until your statement arrives or you get a call from the card company.**

Is all online shopping bad? No, you can actually save time and travel money, get things online for a cheaper price, or things you wouldn't be able to find otherwise. But stick to the item you are searching for and do not look around in the real shop and buy other stuff too. You need to become a Zen master in full self-control mode.

Know yourself: Identify your sweet spots – the online shops you like hanging around. For these ones, stick a big post-it (actual or virtual) on your screen with your monthly limit. Look at your budget to find out how much you can spend. If you buy something, deduct it from your monthly virtual envelope. Be firm with yourself.

Delay: Instead of clicking on BUY NOW, put the item in your wish list - on the site, or if the site hasn't got any, save the link and copy it to one file with all your wished items. Wait for a week or two. Go back and look at your file – do you still crave the items that have been on the list the longest? How much do they all add up to? Looking at your budget, how much can you afford?

Think before clicking: What will this thing change in my life? If I don't buy it, how will not having this stuff impact my life? Next time I move (which happens often when you study), how many boxes will I have to carry along? Get a sense of the volume of stuff you arrive with - and keep it the same.

Cap: Keep a low credit limit on your credit card. Turn down your banker's offer to increase it.

Wean yourself: Stuff and screens are addictive.

TOP TIP Safety:

- HTTPS: always, always check that the merchant site is secure before entering your credit card number. The site address should switch to a secure address (with an s in it): https:/;
- Don't store your card number and other information on the website – it will take time to retype, but if you use a library computer or any device which may be used by someone else, you don't want to share your data, let alone have it hacked. Besides, retyping your card will take you time - time for you to think twice whether this purchase is or is not a good idea. That will make your purchase a bit more thoughtful and less automatic. Manage your cookies to avoid too much personal information getting public, erase them regularly.
- Avoid using public Wi-Fi to buy online or check your bank statement; if you can do it from home, with a proper firewall and antivirus, you'll be on the safer side.

- Don't ever give your pin or other numbers other than the card number (16 or so digits on the front of the card), your name (as on the card), expiry date and security code (three or four digits on the back or the front of your card).
- Other ways to pay online: You may also consider using a PayPal account to add another "screen" between your card and the outer world. Some banks issue one-time or "disposable" credit cards: they issue one credit card number for each of your online purchases at your request. Check the fees and conditions. The drawback of the one-time number is that it no longer exists after you have made the purchase – so it may not be great using that type of card to buy a plane ticket for instance, if the airline agent asks for the credit card you used to book the flight, as you are checking it. It may make returns trickier too.
- Avoid using debit cards online, as you are hardly protected against fraud.

Online Gambling: A No-No

Online addictions: Screens and virtual worlds are addictive - set your limits and find alternatives before you get dragged into costlier online addictions, like online gambling. Casinos, on or off-line, are for-profit businesses – not some kind of benevolent wealth redistribution scheme, so odds are against you, even if you win a few times. Stop and get more fruitful ways to get fun and pass your time. If you still think you can "win" money, just track your ins and outs – I don't need to bet to know that your net will be negative. If gambling has become part of your life, get help to quit[4]. How do you know you have a gambling problem? Like other addictions, gambling invades your life – your number one motivation to get out of bed is to play; playing stresses you but you can't stop; you would do anything to get money to go on playing; your daily schedule is built around playing; friends, studies, family – all of them seem boring and pointless.

---

[4] this website has interesting resources: http://www.youthgambling.com/

Other Cards and Loans:

Store cards: Are credit cards that you can use for a specific store network or brand. Why on earth would stores offer them if they hit their profit? Store cards are usually hard-sold with fabulous rebates on a first purchase, marvellous enough to make you forget to read through the conditions that include an interest rate that will knock you down on the second month if you haven't fully paid your balance (and will wipe clean the initial rebate). Credit stores also make you feel nurtured and special – you will receive constant care and attention from the store or brand, messaged to you as special offers, exclusive to you. These reminders will make it hard to resist buying anything, especially as thanks to surveys or just your spending pattern with the card, the store knows you very well. In other words, unless you have an iron will and get a good rebate on one expensive item that you pay fully and return the card after a few months, don't sign up for a store card.

Prepaid cards: Are cards that you load with money then use to pay wherever cards are accepted. Many come with theft or loss protections (like credit cards). Many people in the US use them instead of a bank account, but that comes at a high cost: fees are displayed in all types of format: set-up fees, monthly maintenance fee, fees when you load them, when you withdraw cash from an ATM, etc. Think twice and open a bank account and manage one credit card linked to your bank account.

Payday loans or cash advances: Are loans often obtained when showing a proof of income. They are also used by unbanked people (people who don't have a bank account) to cash cheques for example. They charge very high fees and interest.

INSURANCE and Risk Management

One thing to keep in mind is that insurance is a business – not a social business, not a non-profit but a profitable business. How do insurance companies make profit?

The insured persons pay a sum:

Customers (individuals, businesses) take out an insurance contract. This contract specifies what risks are covered, for how long, under which circumstances, lists the exceptions if any, and how much will be paid to the customer if the risk happens. All customers pay a premium.

They may get a payment back if something bad happens to them.

Insurance uses the premium to pay for the doctors, hospitals, medicine manufacturers, car repair, and menders of all kinds that will fix the problem if/ when it happens. They may not pay fully though - often insurance companies won't bother covering small amounts (these amounts may seem low to them but big to your student budget): that's the "deductible".

The insurance companies earn money with the difference between premiums received and risks paid + investing the premiums.

They also use part of the premiums to pay their employees and manage all these claims, sell their contracts, find new customers, advertise, etc. and keep some for their shareholders (profit). The difference between the premiums received and the claims paid is the "underwriting profit". As often with money, timing plays a lead role. Risks are likely to be spread out. They won't happen all on January 1st when premiums are paid. So the insurance companies get a lot of cash that they are not going to use straight away. What do they do? They invest it. They buy and sell financial products on the market and try to make additional profit from these investments. What happens to the profit made by an insurance company? It either stays in the company or is distributed to its shareholders who own the company.

How does the insurance company calculate premiums? By compiling lots of statistics, running probabilities and taking a bet on the future. If 10% of customers get involved in an accident, 15% need new glasses, 30% have teeth decay to be fixed, 5% get robbed and 2% have a fire in their kitchen on average per year, this would cost a certain amount to pay per year. They divide that amount to pay by the number of people taking out an insurance. In reality it is a bit trickier than that, as insurance companies calculate different premiums according to different types of risks and risk profiles. This is why young drivers have to pay higher premium. (This kind of kills the idea of pooling risks among a large group if you start splitting people in groups with similar risks profile.

Deductibles: Let's say my neighbour's dog chewed on my heavy brand-new astronomy text book and it costs 90 to buy a new book – my neighbour will pay for my book but is most likely unable to claim the money back from the insurance company.

There is another type of insurance company: The **mutual insurance company** – worth mentioning as in several countries, insurance for students follows this scheme. In a mutual insurance company, people signing up for an insurance contract are also the company owners (often referred to as members), so they have their say in how the company is managed and have a share in the profit. They are closer to a risk pooling association based on solidarity. Being far from the quarterly profit announcement pressure, they are usually more long-term focused. If the premiums exceed the claims and operational expenses, the members can decide to share the profit or reduce next year's premiums, but they may also have to pay more the following year in case the mutual underestimated the premiums. There is also less conflict of interest between what's good for shareholders and what's good for policyholders (insured people) as they are the very same people. Definitely an option to explore even after finishing university.

As with everything, enquire before signing up. The first risk you will have to deal with is the information overflow, written in very technical language. Don't be taken aback. Turn that into a strength: ask questions (drill your parents first) and obtain reliable and understandable pieces of information. If you can't understand and explain it yourself, maybe that insurance contract is not for you - provided you have put in a minimum effort to try to understand it! Insurers have imagination (yes!) and have come up with tons of different insurance products over the years. Stick to the basics. You can't eliminate risk and get coverage for everything. Life is risky from day one, but manage your risk.

Find out first what is compulsory and what is optional. There is a minimum you can't do without (medical, liability, if you rent a place, own a vehicle...). This differs from country to country, so enquire.

Compare: Shop around – check whether your university offers one or more mutual insurances.

Read the contracts: Read the small print. What's covered, what's not? What are the exceptions and conditions, premiums, deductibles, etc.? Your parents may help you with a guided reading.

Trade-offs: Look at what is relevant to you: There may be some options you don't need. Look at the coverage offered on general health, dentist, optician, sports for instance. The other trade-off is between keeping the cost for you to pay, (the deductible amount + some uncovered risks) and having it paid by the insurance company. The trick is to find the balance which may suit you best. Unsurprisingly, the more coverage you get, the more premium you pay. So sometimes you may be better off taking a larger deductible amount on you but paying a lower premium.

Here and there: Make sure you still have some medical coverage when you get back home too and when you travel. Your local university contract may not include an overseas medical coverage for example. Discuss with your parents who is going to pay.

Careful with over-insurance: Beware of the hidden and duplicating insurances. Credit cards often include insurance. List what your cards and insurance cover; what risks, under which conditions, in a spreadsheet to spot duplicates or potential gaps; the sports you do, or countries you travel to. Your parents too should double-check their contracts and avoid paying for you, on their insurance policy, while you have your own.

How to claim: Once you have signed up and paid, enquire what to do in case of accident, hospitalisation or theft, etc. Keep the contact phone number and your insurance policy number handy but secure. This will save you stress, time and possibly money the day of a mishap.

Update: Your life may change, you may start working, driving, change address etc. Review and update your insurance contracts.

Self-insurance: Prevention is Better than a Cure

Risks are part of life – whatever insurance you take or don't take, prevention is better than cure.

Manage your level of risk: Your body is your first wealth: manage your health, nurture a positive mind and respect your body. If you haven't done so already, read the chapters on food, sleep, friends, hygiene. A focused brain in a well-fed body that has had enough sleep, and is surrounded by supportive people, is likely to be your best insurance!

Managing deductibles: Even if you are over-insured (which you should be careful to avoid if you have read this chapter), you are likely to pay some medical or repair expenses out of your pocket. Budget for them!

Emergency savings: Don't eat up all your scholarship or loan straight away. Keep an emergency fund in your bank account. Even if the cost is paid by the insurance, you may still have the deductible to pay, or have to pay first befor being reimbursed, depending on your contract and the mishap, so don't get cash-strapped.

Alert: Be wary – keep your papers, especially IDs, safe. Check your bank account and credit card often to detect potential fraud. Lock up your belongings, be wary of scams - too good to be true offers are just what they are: not true. Get help if you fall victim to frauds or crime.

DEALING with Currencies

If you study abroad, another ingredient to spice up your financial life, will be exchange rates. Your parents' residence country and your university country will use two different currencies. A bit like two objects floating on an ocean, they are likely to move up and down independently - or conversely. Let's look on the bright side: this is excellent to practice your mental maths and an efficient preventive remedy for neuro-degenerative diseases J. It is another uncertainty to deal with so let's see how to minimise it.

Exchange rate and fees: What you need to know

- **The ratio between two currencies is called the exchange rate:** – several scenarios there: The rate can move up and down every minute as traders buy and sell these two currencies. The rate can be fixed too (the currency may either not be traded on a market or they may, but the central banks buy and sell big loads of them to keep the same rate). If you study in Qatar for example, or in Denmark, their respective currencies are "pegged" (meaning fixed) to the USD (for the Qatari riyal) or the Euro (for the Danish krone). Third case, the rate may move within a "band": that's the case of the Hong Kong dollar, pegged to the US dollar between 7.75 and 7.85.

- **Get your rate right**: Whenever you have to convert don't get mixed up. The exchange rate is the price between two currencies so it depends on your reference point. For example, Peter is sitting to the left of Bob also means that Bob is sitting to the right of Peter. So if 1 Euro equals 1.13 US Dollar, that also means that 1 US dollar is equal to 1/1.13=0.88 euros. Remember which one shows bigger numbers to remain accurate in your calculation.
- **Buy and sell rates:** That's for the official rate or market rate. But when you convert (change) currency, you will see two rates on the bank screen or at the bureau de change. The bank or bureau de change takes a profit (they call it "spread") so they buy at a cheaper price to sell at a higher price. This profit also aims to cover their risk: if a currency keeps going up and down (it is "volatile"), they want to avoid buying at a price higher than the rate they will have to sell tomorrow or in a few days. Note that sometimes, on top, the bank may take a fee.
- **Currency codes:** Very often banks will use the currency three letter nickname: the first two letters are the country code, and the last letter stands for the currency (usually the initial letter of the currency). Exception: EUR for Euro.
- **Prices:** Exchange rates don't explain all the price differences between countries. For example, your favourite Happy Cow strawberry yoghurt costs HKD 20 in Hong Kong, but GBP 1.40 in the UK. If you do the maths with an exchange rate of 12 HKD for 1 GBP, your Hong Kong yoghurt should cost GBP 1.67.

Practical tips:

Count local: Become bilingual in your new currency from day one. Stop converting all the prices when you go shopping. Get to know your key numbers, especially your daily spending limit, in your new local currency. The very first days you arrive, go around and window shop – make a list of prices of staple products (rice, bread, milk, bus trip, laundry, etc.) This will help you fine-tune your budget which has to be in the currency you will use.

Adapt your diet and lifestyle to your new home: You may find some food relatively cheaper or more expensive in your new country. Eat local!

Changing cash: The "spread" (the difference between the buy and the sell rates) can be high, especially in hotels. Banks may offer you better rates. However, withdrawing cash from an ATM is usually the best deal (if your card has been authorised to be used abroad.)

Using a foreign credit card: Until you open a bank account in your new home country (top of your to do list), you may consider paying with your home credit card. Ensure it is activated to work abroad before leaving home. You can generally do this by phoning the bank. Check the conditions (especially the applicable fees), what to do if stolen. As soon as you have a local card, switch and use the local one. Likewise, when you go back home, don't use your foreign card but a home country card. Check your card statements to check the foreign currency movements (make sure these are movements you have initiated and check the rates and fees applied). In the same way, over the summer, if you come back home, keep paying any bills due back at your studying place through online banking.

Minimise currency transfers: You get hit by exchange (either negatively or positively) when you move currencies around. So if you work in the summer in your new country for one month, keep your income in your local bank account. Negotiate with your parents an amount in your home currency if you spend the rest of summer back home, so that you don't transfer money.

The real challenge is to manage an income in one currency (parents' transfers) and expenses in another: The agreed upon 1,000 (in your new local currency) may gradually become 900 or 1,100 over the year because of exchange rates. On the other hand, your parents may not be happy either to start sending you 1,000 and have to increase the amount gradually so that you get the same amount.

PARENTS:

Consider sending one big yearly transfer to set the exchange rate once and for all.
Check the fees: On top of taking a lower exchange rate, both the sending and receiving banks may charge an overseas transfer fee. Include it in your budget. If the transfer fee is a fixed amount, it is definitely worth sending bigger amounts once or twice a year rather than smaller amounts monthly.
(See "Before Leaving Home" above for longer term strategy.)

---

4. MONEY is Social

What is money really? Money is a social convention. The round-shape pieces of metal or the rectangular colourful flimsy papers in your wallet only have value because you and all the other people in your circle, neighbourhood and country accept and trust them as valuable. As a socially invented tool, money obviously impacts and is impacted by our relationships with others.

TAX

Are you excited to leave your parents' nest and trace your own path? Along with the excitement, these are your first steps as a citizen. You are acquiring your own social identity – own address, own social security number or ID card, depending where you live and reside. Part of the package is the fiscal identity. As a student, without an income, you may still be dependent, i.e. on your parents' tax declarations. But you need to check your status, obligations and rights with a tax specialist. Your university may be able to provide some basic pieces of information, or you can go to a local tax office. Taxes are country specific so you must enquire what status you will have. Don't play with tax, computers remember you.

Income tax: If you earn an income, you will have to declare it, and you may have to file in your own income tax declaration, especially if you work abroad.

Age: Several countries put a limit to the dependency status: after a certain age, your parents may not be able to file you in their tax declaration and you will have to do your own.

Double taxation agreements: Double taxation is paying a tax twice on the same income: If you earn an income in one country but you reside in another, you may have to pay an income tax in your residency country and in the country where you earned the money. Many countries have agreements to avoid double taxation. That adds a bit of extra research homework for international students.

Local tax: If you rent a place, depending on the country law and whether you are a full time or part-time student, you may have to pay local taxes. Even if you have checked that you are not liable, also check whether you need to get a formal exemption paper. Be aware, that if you share a place with several people, local tax status may depend on your flatmates too.

Other taxes: TV licence, social contributions (based on a salary if you work) which fund national compulsory health and retirement public insurances.

Coming and going: Check what to do when you leave the country permanently or you start working there full time, or any change of immigration or residency status. This is likely to impact your tax status too.

> **TOP TIP** Don't forget to register and vote. Be a full citizen! Even if you are not a citizen of the country where you study, contact your nearest consulate to register and be able to vote from abroad. Keep in mind that EU citizens can vote in their EU country of residence for local and European elections.

MONEY and friends: Sharing space and bills

Many students choose to move to a place with friends after their first year of university.

Choose your Flatmates: Different daily routines, different standards in cleanliness, noise level and sleep pattern, can quickly turn best friends into the meanest enemies. Think ahead: if you are planning to move out of the campus and share an accommodation, your first year in the hall is the year to get to know your friends and assess (in)compatibilities. Know yourself too and draw an ideal flatmate portrait. – What you are not ready to compromise with, and what can you be flexible about?

MUST		PLUS
Doesn't smoke	WANTED — FLATMATE	Can invite friends but not every night,
Tidy		Can cook whatever food, provided she cleans up the kitchen,
No loud noise after 11pm		
Spends less than 20 minutes in bathroom in the morning		Positive minded
No durian		Doesn't snore

Flat Rules: Don't be afraid to sound silly or rigid by asking to discuss rules before moving in. It may be the best way to keep friends, your sanity or at least your peace of mind, plus your sleep which could impact your studies. This is also good screening test for choosing your flatmates. Bear in mind that you don't have to be best pals to move in together – focus on the lifestyle compatibility. You can always meet your best friends elsewhere. Discuss the rules by topic.

1. Smoking and alcohol: No/yes?
2. Kitchen: Food allergies, smell dislikes, fridge and cupboard sharing, food sharing, cooking space sharing, cleaning turns, garbage turns
3. Bathroom: Morning and evening timeshare, maximum duration of shower/ bath, cleaning turns
4. Noise: Silent hours agreement, weekday/weekend rules
5. Friends: Number of parties (per week/ month), maximum of friends and time
6. Boy/girl-friends: Are couples allowed or not?
7. Pets: Yes/no – if yes, what kind? Where? (pet owner's bedroom only or all rooms or common areas only?)
8. Heating: Temperature agreement
9. Phone and internet: Usage requirement; individual or collective bills
10. TV: Yes or no? Shared bill or for one person only?
11. Bills: Sharing rules, which ones are individual and which are collective. Which name? Payment process (see below). Damage payment rules (in case).
12. Other shared expenses: Cleaning products, garbage bags, electric bulbs, cooking utensils, additional furniture if needs be, etc.
13. Parents: Who will be the guarantor?

Choosing a place: The first test will be to agree on a place to move to. Once again, before rushing to the first place, hold a first discussion with your potential flatmates to agree on a short list of requirements and questions to ask regarding your future den:

1. Location: Which area? Access to public transport, time to university. House or flat?
2. Numbers of bedrooms (and their size!)
3. Kitchen and bathroom: What appliances? Size, number of bathrooms/toilets.
4. Internet, phone...
5. Other: Floor, South-North orientation, neighbourhood safety and appearance, points of interest nearby (parks, cinema), insulation, type of heating, bike lot if needed.

6. Rent, how much? What utilities are included and what are not. How are utilities calculated? Average cost of utilities that are not included. Deposit (how much, when). Summer term payment?
7. Furnished?
8. Other facilities: Bike storage place?
9. Guarantor? Very often, landlords will ask your parents to be guarantors; they will sign a document where they commit to pay the rent if you don't and even pay for damages you.

Insurance

Budget: Calculate together your target and maximum budget adding the rent and other expenses (utilities if not included, internet, fuel for heating), transportation to and from university, one-offs if any (additional furniture for example), cleaning products and stuff (sponges, broom). Make sure your share of these costs fits in your budget. Most of these expenses are commitments (see first part), so don't overcommit.

Check what the law says about rent increases: know your rights and obligations as a tenant. Remember that as co-tenants, you have a joint responsibility: if one damages something in the accommodation, the landlord will have to be compensated by one or all of you. This goes for the rent too: if one of you cannot pay her/his share of the rent, the others will have to pay.

Check where to get accommodation listing: your university (students' union for example) may have some. If you go through an agent, understand first what commission the agent will charge.

Check each other's availability for house-hunting. You can share the fun, but preferably, visit in pairs or small groups to compare your feelings and findings. Take notes while you visit and debrief your flatmates. Decide together.

Paperwork

Read all the tenancy agreement. Many pairs of eyes will hopefully help spot strange clauses, if any. Scan a copy to the guarantor for thorough review.

Negotiate if you don't agree on some clauses or if you want some repairs or improvements done before.

Get help before signing if things don't look crystal clear especially on charges, duration etc. (Consumer protection associations and your university accommodation office for instance may have model agreements and be able to give you some advice).

Get a receipt for all payments and keep a copy of all documents. Check whether other paper documents are needed.

Written agreement: Even if you stick to the "each one pays her/his share now" rule, write and sign who pays what. The first payment may be the deposit which can be one or more months' rent, so not a small amount. At best, you will never look again at these payment papers signed between you and you will discard them a few years after having moved out. But if things get sour with your friends, and disputes arise, these documents will settle the points.

Moving in	Moving out
Be clear on the handover process (date, keys – including numbers of keys, gas/water/ electricity meter reading), who tells utility agencies about the change of tenant.	☺ Can be smooth - you have a nice last dinner together, a few selfies, you all move your stuff out, clean up together, get the meters read, pocket your share of deposit back and hand the keys to the landlord. Don't forget to stop the utilities and notify your change of address where necessary.

Take pictures of the place on the day you move in. You may want to clean BEFORE you put your stuff in. Post the rules agreement on a strategic place like the fridge door, the bathroom door or the living room: this may be a friendship-saver.	☺ Can be rougher - the landlord is fussy about some alleged damages (the photos taken on day 1 will prove useful) or drags his feet to pay back the deposit. Or, your flatmates have a different end of year and packed a few weeks before. You get the joy of cancelling the utilities, cleaning up the place and dealing with the landlord while you still have to submit your 400-page thesis on osteoporosis among female mammoths and its impact on climate change. ☹ Even rougher scenarios can always happen when you can't stand your flatmates any longer and you leave in the middle of the year, or you get kicked out, or the upstairs neighbour played a sequel of the Titanic and you have to leave the flat for several weeks. Keep calm and polite. Many situations build up over time so keep your sensors alert and anticipate potential issues. Do your best to sort out the financial side and in any case, pay your debts.

Living in: Apply the rules! But if you all feel some need adjusting, discuss and improve.

Be safe: Lock the doors; don't let strangers come in; don't advertise you have just bought a flashy TV or computer by leaving the empty box outside your front door; be low profile. Burglaries do happen. Check for potential gas leaks.

Rent: Gather the amount a few days before it is actually due to be paid. Agree on the payment process beforehand: do you each pay your share separately (note that the landlord may not be happy with multiple cheques or transfers), or does one of you collect the payment from others and do one payment to the landlord? If you opt for one payment, who pays the landlord: the same person or do you take turns? To avoid defaults, you may want to discuss how each flatmate will ensure timely payment: if some of you have received a big lump sum at the beginning of the year (scholarship for example), multiply the rent + utilities by the number of months you have to pay until your next scholarship payment - this is the amount you have to keep in your bank account or open a second bank account and leave it there. If you receive a monthly payment, then if the rent is due monthly, set aside the rent amount as soon as you receive the money. Calculate your daily spending limit. If you get a biweekly or weekly allowance, save half, or a quarter, of the amount of the rent + utilities from it as soon as you receive the money.

Maintain your flat in best condition: Clean it. If you detect an issue (leaks, clogged pipes), tell the landlord asap.

Be considerate and respectful with your flatmates, but also with your neighbours. Build good relationships and be helpful. You may be thankful if you are the one who needs a hand.

Be considerate with Mother Earth: Don't waste water, electricity, gas, food.

Reap the $$$ benefits of living in a group: Discuss what items (food, soap, washing powder) you can buy in bigger and cheaper packaging. Set a common pool or kitty to pay for them. Encourage each other to spend sensibly.

Be clear: Unresolved issues keep growing (especially over money) until they become hard to deal with. Discuss with calmly with tact how to sort out or prevent an issue. Tackle an issue positively: you are likely to learn lots of life skills like negotiation and listening that will be useful in future professional and family settings. If accounts don't seem right, get your signed papers out of the drawer and redo the maths on what was paid by whom and whether all expenses were shared equally or according to your initial agreement.

Be the flatmate you would like to live with. Apply the rules to yourself first; manage your money and budget and anticipate all the bills and rent.

Crisis and debts: It may happen that one of you has a financial crisis.

Minimise crises: Go through the payment tips above together. If one of you is more money-savvy, and one of you is having serious headaches with budgeting, go ahead and help her or him. Don't try to prove your point and triumphantly observe: "I knew you couldn't save that much until the end of the month!" If you feel a problem coming, be tactful, not nosy. Give a helping hand – not money, but practical advice on how to anticipate rent and bills and control other expenses accordingly.

Advance payment: If your flatmate is broke, discuss the various options to solve problems:

- Emergency help from parents,
- Tap into other savings they may have somewhere,
- Advance payment from the other flatmates: be clear on how the defaulting flatmate plans to pay back - work on a realistic plan together. Don't leave the discussion until you have agreed on a workable plan and signed a document recognising the debt to pay. Harsh? No. Good accounts make good friends. It doesn't mean you can't be generous with friends who need help. But make sure mismanagement doesn't strain your friendship because one of you keeps defaulting. The plan must work for you too – if you can't pay your share plus some of your friend's, don't propose this solution.
- Once you have agreed on a plan, implement it and make sure your friend pays back as promised.

FRIENDS and money: pressure, pride and jealousy

You don't have to live with flatmates to experience money hitches with friends. Money is linked to so many of our human activities – from taking a coffee to exploring the universe and all the variations in between – that there is no way you can finish your three or four-year studies without a financial blunder.

Financial styles and habits

The truth is you start university with 17, 18 or 19 years' experience of managing money. Since your very first days you have been immerged into an ocean of financial choices - the place you were born, the clothes you wore, the food you ate. You have lived a life style that depended on what your parents could afford and wanted to afford; you have watched your parents shop, choose their holidays and cars, buy appliances and groceries, (don't) talk about money, give to charities... Even if you didn't observe them carefully, you will have taken lots of habits from them, willingly or not, consciously or not. Leaving the nest will give you the time to reflect on all that you have taken for granted and make your own choices.

Very soon you will meet people with different backgrounds and this may cause friction or some misunderstandings. Be open-minded and sensitive. Re-construct your financial style: some habits are good to keep (budget, shopping lists, spending carefully, donating regularly, saving for specific projects, de-cluttering wardrobes and cupboards) and others may be good to reconsider (having ten or more credit cards, never talk about money, rush to the ultimate gimmick as soon as it is out, never check one's statement, don't have a long-term plan, buy something each time we go out or travel, throw the most lavish birthday possible, etc.) Fortunes go up and down so don't feel you are entitled to something just because you can afford it. Be sensitive: Some of your less well-off friends may resent some of your purchases or your life-style. Be aware: You may pressure your friends without realising it.

Food for thought

Unless you are already forced to do it, pick a day a week or a week a month where you live on a tight budget: Experience and build your empathy towards your billions of Earth-fellows.

Break the social barriers: Trying to get friends from all walks of life, sharing your experience and viewpoints will be enriching. If you don't do it as a student, it will be even harder later on.

Money conveys all kinds of values and feelings: Jealousy, generosity, stinginess, carelessness, honesty, pride, greed. Build your relationship with money around the values you feel strongly about. How?

- Select and write these values; Not sure what values you feel strongly about? Think of people you admire and find out what you admire in them.
- Observe yourself – when you deal with money in various situations, what is your state of mind or what value does your action convey? Note them throughout the days.
- Compare the observed values and your target ones: How far are you from your "ideal you"?

Work on a practical plan to go from how you feel about money now (from your observed values) to your target. For example, if you tend to be stingy and generosity is one of your target values, give to some charity once a week; if you tend to be careless, note down what you spend, and force yourself to think before buying. What's the reward? Huge - be in line with who you would like to be and cultivate peace of mind. Contradicting oneself is stressful.

On the other hand, don't resent your more well-off friends for buying stuff you can't afford. Keep a clear mind on why you came to study. Write your personal goals and see how this stuff fits in the bigger picture of your life. Buy with a purpose, not because others have it. Be cool and don't take offense easily. Put yourself in other's shoes – and go beyond your own view point. Sprinkle your day with compassion and you'll experience how wealth gaps impact people's behaviour with a calmer heart.

Practical tips for a bunch of friends with different budgets:

Going out:

Before going out, be considerate and gently enquire if everybody is comfortable with the idea and choice of place. Decide how the bill will be split (if some of you choose less expensive food for instance, they may resent "sponsoring" the others). Factor in tax and service if not included.

Include cheaper (and healthier) options in your routine social time: pot luck, home cooking, a bike ride (if all of you have one), a walk in the park.

Concerts, cinema and theatre: look for the students' cheapest prices. You may want to get a cheaper (not so centrally situated) seat, just to stay with your friends. Look at what matters to you – great view or a great moment with friends. Buying well in advance may help you get a deal.

Clothes:

Don't be brand-obsessed and spread your brand enthusiasm to your friends. Have a thorough reflection on what role your clothes play in your life – go beyond the mirror and the advertisements.

If you really like changing and exploring styles, swap with friends. Recycle older clothes with different accessories or combine tops and bottoms differently to create new styles. Or just be you.

Train your ears to be selective: don't listen to either praise or derogatory remarks on how you look today. You will look different tomorrow, won't you? Try to remember a few childhood friends you haven't seen for a while: what do you remember most about them? Chances are you don't remember what they wore, but how silly, kind, bubbly, fidgety they were. What will friends remember of you in one, five, ten years' time? That's more an area to work on and improve than your wardrobe. Likewise, train your eyes and tongue and look at the more lasting qualities of your friends rather than the brands they sponsor.

Books: Having friends with various financial constraints is an opportunity to help (or be helped.) Turn other expenses into social ones too: for example, books that can weigh heavy in a student budget: share them, give them a social life, donate them.

Sports (membership, equipment): Sports can be seriously financially discriminating. Marketers know that and put an extra spending-pressure on accessories and clothes.

Enquire what you would like to do as a group, or what you like to do on your own. You don't have to hang around with the exact same bunch of buddies all the time.

Look at the prices and options and budget. Be cautious: Your enthusiasm may not last a yearly membership. Set a time in the week that works for everyone. It's better to realise you can't agree on a time and day before paying a yearly membership and buying the gear.

Holidays (weekends, longer travel): Spending a weekend or a week away with friends is great for making real friends (or losing them!)

Plan ahead – discuss openly what budget each can afford and explore the various options (destination, transportation, accommodation, food, outings and visits) within this budget. Make sure everyone is comfortable. If you know or feel you are the most well-off person of your group, have another friend take the lead of the budget discussion. Planning ahead can help you get better deals and optimise your visiting time.

Explore your area – there are surely tons of scenic spots, historical buildings and museums to enjoy. Take advantage of any free days museums may offer. Some local associations may organise guided tours for free or at a very low price. Volunteer with organisations that organise what you like – they may need volunteer ushers, waiters, cleaners, guides and you could get cheaper access to exhibitions, plays or concerts this way, plus meet interesting people - and get out of your student circle.

Credit cards may help you get deals or accumulate points you can redeem on things you like. These point schemes are one thing to consider when you choose your credit card. If you are likely to take the plane once or twice a year for example, a card earning points with a relevant airline could save you some bucks. Don't get carried away. Don't spend to get points but get points when you spend.

TOP TIP Lending to others

Keep a log of the dates of what you lent to whom, and what you borrowed from whom.

Put reminders so that you give things back when you said you would.

Write your name on books you want back.

Be clear. When you borrow, ask when the lender wants it back. Say when you want your things back.

Take care of the things you borrow.

Be cautious: If the same person never gives you back things, just don't lend to them any longer.

Don't lend things that do not belong to you, unless the owner knows and agrees.

TALKING about money

Money is about numbers and facts - straight forward, dry and precise. So how come in a discussion, money very often becomes fuzzy, impressionistic and emotional… provided these discussions ever take place, or go beyond a comment on the latest shopping spree?

Do talk about money. Most money talk evolves around "that's cheap" or "that's expensive". Going further is like walking on a landmine. In many cultures, talking about money goes from embarrassing to downright rude. So you may not have experienced many constructive family financial discussions. Money is the shadow actor of so much of our daily life that you can't pretend it is not there and not talk about it.

Talking with your parents: There is probably still a money flow between your parents and you. You have to talk about how much they will give you – whether it is an allowance or a loan, for how long, how often, what they pay and what you pay, what support they can give you if there is an emergency (medical, emotional, financial). Be clear before going and during your studies. Budgeting is a great way to work together on facts (even if some facts are still assumptions before you go, at least they are not judgements or impressions). Try to stick to a dispassionate discussion. If things slide to judgements, such as "You spend too much on clothes anyway!" or shift focus; "At your age, I was up at 6am distributing newspapers while reviewing my Spanish lessons." gently bring back the talk to the numbers and how to balance them in a satisfactory way for both parties.

FOR STUDENTS ONLY	FOR PARENTS ONLY
Ask for your parents' advice in a way that flatters them (don't forget that as you leave they feel they are losing you, so be compassionate – you are the centre of their universe) say something like: "You have so much experience, how would you make ends meet if you were in my situation?"	Don't talk to your children like babies. Maybe they've never done a budget or have no experience in managing money (which is only partly true, see "financial styles and habits" above), but if you want them to act responsibly, talk to them as you would talk to a responsible adult.

The dialogue should not stop after you have left home. Track your ins and outs and update your budget. If in your plan, you come up short - re-do your plan. Think through solutions and talk to your sponsors giving them facts to back up your discussion. Don't wait until the last minute – that will narrow down the possible solutions and end up being costlier in money and in trust at your parents' mental bank. Be fully transparent as long as they are funding you. Once you are fully financially independent, it is up to you to manage what you want to tell them about your financial situation.

☹ If a big useless expense has dipped you into negative territory, avoid sugar-coating the blunder and speaking in half-truths. Your numbers won't add up, the more suspicious your parents will become, and the tougher the talk will be. Check your facts, think of possible solutions and explain clearly the situation as soon as possible. If you feel the discussion will be tense, prepare even more, write what you want to say, and breathe. Reformulate the discussion on facts and solutions to get a clear outcome.	☺ If you are managing your money well and things are smooth - just tell them. A "thank you" to acknowledge receipt of a transfer (even if it was planned and agreed on), will make up for failing to wish your mother a happy birthday on time. If your parents see that you are in control, maybe they will ask you to help them with their budget next time you come home.

Talking with your friends: Trust is the big bond between friends (not just pats on the back and parties). Friends are people you care for? So be careful, focused and clear.

Careful: With what you tell them about your own finances, including what you show them about your finances through your spending pattern, (see "financial styles and habits") and even more careful in what you tell about them to others. Rule of thumb: speak of others as if they were with you, including money matters. If your flatmate has a financial crisis, it does not have to make the front page of the college bulletin. With some perseverance, your name won't appear in the financial hall of defame for the three or four years of university.

Focused: Keep the money talk focused to the necessary, i.e. where others' money interacts with yours. If you plan to go on a weekend together, calculate how much you can spend and include that in the discussion. Your friends don't have to challenge why you don't want (or can't) devote more to it – the only exception is about shared commitments like rent. If you can't pay, they can drill you further to find the money (see "sharing space and bills"). On the other hand, you don't have to hide that you are taking money management seriously. What's the big deal if they see you ask for a receipt, note down an expense or work on your budget? If you have gained some practice in money management and it's getting known, some fellow students may approach you. If you are confident enough to go through how to write a budget with them, great. But otherwise, don't feel obliged to be the financial helpdesk.

Clear: Your interaction will not just be with words – it will probably involve real money as well - friends asking to pay for a coffee or buying a book or concert ticket for you, expecting to be paid back of course. University is an information-saturated environment – so chances are your brain will archive or skip the information and you will forget or remember the wrong amount or ask twice - especially if nights have been nibbled up by coming exams or an essay deadline. Before you know it, you will resent your friend for not paying you back this quadruple latte or your best friend will hardly mumble "morning" and will stare at you with a murderous look. Debts are like weeds, they can smother good plants very quickly – and seriously damage relationships.

TOP TIP Good accounts make good friends	
What you owe:	What others owe you:
Note your debts immediately – on whatever you look at daily - your phone, diary, your morning mug.	Small amounts: track, find a balance, and share the cost.
Pay it back ASAP.	Big amounts: formalise them on a written agreement; manage the financial and friendship relation.
Thank your friend.	

Small amounts: Like paying a coffee here and there. Do what you can. If you feel like treating your friends, once a year, from time to time, or regularly, that's up to you. Track it and update your budget accordingly and see if it fits.	Big amounts:
	Formal agreement: for substantial amounts (substantial is relative to your situation), write a paper with the amount + date + the agreed payback plan + both signatures. The paper is there in case your friend forgets her/his commitment to pay back, or you disagree on the amount.
Be clear with yourself: Don't let your talk contradict your hand. If you want to be the generous guy, don't say it – do it. But if your friendship is bugged by you paying the weekly pizza more than your turn, find a strategy to fix the problem for future dinners: Stick a pizza turn list on the fridge for all to see.	Tact: If things get really sour and your friend can't or doesn't want to pay back, it is up to you to see how far you can go - including how much you value your friendship and you can both overcome the unsettled debt drama. If you decide to be lenient, be clear – say it: find a quiet moment, far from others' ears, and just say, you know, the xxx you still owe me, let's forget it – that's fine. Bring the paper to formalise the write-off. Your friend may be relieved or disagree. Self-esteem has a price and you can't deny him that. So discuss further with tact.
Be clear with others: Talk and decide on clear rules like, Bob pays the 1st week of the month, you do the 2nd week, Charlie the 3rd and Preston the 4th. You go Dutch if there is a 5th. Sharing the cost equally as a rule is a way to avoid open and unsaid squabbles.	Do your plan first. You can give a helping hand only if you are in a stable position yourself. Mentally consider the amount you lend as a loss or a gift. When you get it back, be thankful (this friend gives you the opportunity to help, that's something to feel grateful about). Be aware that the "when" may become "if" at any time. So don't take a substantial loan lightly.

Negotiating with Third Parties: Adults will expect you to be like everybody else, fuzzy, impressionistic and emotional when talking about money – and even more because you are "young". STAND OUT: BE PRO!

Don't Wait: As a rule, the more you wait, the more financial issues rot and stink... so be on top of your finances and if you smell something fishy, dig it out immediately and settle it with whoever you have to settle it.

Check your facts before any financial discussion – you'll catch the other party by surprise and won't let them tell you stories. It is worth spending 30 minutes preparing your case rather than discovering it in front of the other party. Note that if you have tracked your ins and outs regularly, this will take even less time. Improvisation doesn't work so well with money because the strongest party will gain the upper hand, even if (s)he's wrong. By re-checking your facts, you may find the problem and solve the issue quickly over the phone.

KEY POINT: Check Your Facts:

If you are being interviewed for an internship or a job, check the average compensation or salary beforehand and labour laws.

If you are moving out from your flat, re-calculate how much you owe the landlord or he owes you using all the information you have gradually compiled in your computer, back it up with the invoices and receipts you have kept and neatly filed, and re-read the contract and your rights and duties as tenant.

If you have to talk to your banker, check your bank statements, update your budget, prepare your questions.

Prepare: Write what you want to obtain from the discussion, what is not negotiable and where you are ready to give some leeway.

Being a pro builds trust. You hear over and over about credit scoring but there is one thing which is much more important to build: trustworthiness. When it has gone, it takes a hell of a time to rebuild.

Helpdesks: If things get bad and you hit the wall, you may need serious help – many consumer protection associations, student unions and non-profit organisations can give you some professional advice on how to get out of debt or solve difficult situations. You will discuss through your issues and your anonymity will be ensured. Don't procrastinate: research these associations, double-check they are reliable and registered, then push the door and get some free help. If they ask you to pay, get out.

RESPONSIBLE Spending

The "what" perspective	The "why and who" perspective
When we buy, we tend to be (very) short-sighted: we just focus on the wonderful thing in front of our eyes and forget about all the rest (the bills to come, what we wanted to save for, the other things we bought not long ago, and where does this thing come from and who made it).	Buying is an exchange: not an exchange of money vs. a good or service, but an exchange of money between people and people matter. Mass market retail and complex supply chain make it hard to know how our purchases impact others but give it a thought whenever you buy something.
THINGS	**PEOPLE**

Food for thought:

Fair trade: Are organisations that strive to make the products you buy a bit more transparent so that you can "see through" who made them and under which conditions. They set standards helping producers in developing countries get a fairer price, encourage better treatments of their workers (wages based on the work done and according to local labour laws, health and safety standards) and that products are made in a sustainable way (see below). They audit (inspect) these producers to grant (or not) a fair trade label and help them reach these standards.

Slavery: Still exists. Numbers are hard to find… as obviously traffickers don't fill in government surveys, but the ILO (International Labour Organisation) has estimated at around 21 million people trafficked, exploited or forced to work for nothing, of which 14 million work in agriculture, construction, domestic work or manufacturing. The ILO estimates the profits from forced labour at US$150 billion. (http://www.ilo.org/global/topics/forced-labour/lang--en/index.htm).

Sustainability: Is one of these trendy words you may have come across. Put simply, it means to keep the resources for those after us – to avoid depleting the Earth for our children or ourselves in a few years or decades' time. It sounds like a natural and obvious thing to do. But it often takes more effort and money to use less energy, recycle or minimise waste, reduce water consumption and cut down on pollution or preserve wildlife. This is a trade-off that many businesses – small or big – and governments still struggle to do as pollution for example is not necessarily priced. Consumers definitely have a big role to play. Keep informed, recycle, use energy sensibly and don't buy things only because they are cheap.

Sustainability: Is one of these trendy words you may have come across. Put simply, it means to keep the resources for those after us – to avoid depleting the Earth for our children or ourselves in a few years or decades' time. It sounds like a natural and obvious thing to do. But it often takes more effort and money to use less energy, recycle or minimise waste, reduce water consumption and cut down on pollution or preserve wildlife. This is a trade-off that many businesses – small or big – and governments still struggle to do as pollution for example is not necessarily priced. Consumers definitely have a big role to play. Keep informed, recycle, use energy sensibly and don't buy things only because they are cheap.

Carbon Footprint: Is the carbon dioxide (and other gases creating the greenhouse effect) produced by human beings whenever they take the bus, drive their car, buy products that have been manufactured and transported, heat their homes, dump rubbish, etc...

Locavore: Is not a worm or medicine name; it just means to buy stuff produced locally and it is usually used for food. The rationale is to reduce carbon footprint and support the economic network of the place where you live. It will impact your plate – if you decide to study in Northern England and focus on local food, oranges and tropical fruit will disappear from your plate. It is fun (and humbling) to tie your plate to the season. You will eat whatever has been harvested this month. It may end up more expensive – fruits produced far away with lower wages and better yield may be cheaper than local ones despite the transportation costs. That's a matter of choice- just like when you vote.

Recycling: Monitor your rubbish production! This also includes cutting down on bags and using recyclable containers. Second-hand and swapping (clothes, books, etc.) with friends can help make use of the same resources while limiting the impact on the planet. Use things until they wear out (vs. until a new fashion is out). Learn to fix those that can live another more year or so.

SHARING

You may wonder why give... while your student budget looks so tight already.

Get out of your bubble: You are not alone! Researching causes and giving to them will open your eyes to real-life problems others face. Isn't it part of education? It may also help you build some inner strength if one day you too face hardships and feel grateful for your health and situation. Your contribution will also help improve and restore lives... and as all humans are interconnected one way or another, helping has a positive ripple effect.

Life-long habit: Give regularly. These university years are great to experiment and build good habits. Life will go even faster when you start working so the sooner you get good foundational habits, the readier you will be in life's race! Consider giving regularly to one or a few stable charities. You may want to set up a monthly direct debit for example, and definitely include them in your budget.

Generosity is healthy: Giving builds empathy. Various researchers show strong links between generosity, gratitude, happiness and longevity. They find causations between generosity and better sleep, less anxiety and depression, better social life, even lower blood pressure.

Giving is not just about money: You can donate time, things or just be helpful with people around you. BUT, give - don't dump things you want to get rid of, or lower your work standards when you volunteer.

Brain and heart: Careful research (see choosing a charity below) is a great way to practise reading financial reports, cross-check information, compare various providers, etc. Why not use similar skills with your other expenses? When you absolutely want that Super Brand, why don't you download their financial report first and see how they will use the money you give them!

How much to give?

The answer lies within yourself.

Religious benchmarks: Most religions encourage giving and sharing; they also often give guidelines on the etiquette of giving, and some set percentages:

- ✓ The tithe: 10% of your income (Bible)
- ✓ The zakat: 2.5% of your financial assets[5]

Do like the others: align to national statistics, or to your parents or friends.

Plan: See how much you can give in your budget, how much time you can give. Develop a sharing attitude that you feel comfortable with.

Plan your time as well to calculate what volunteer commitment would fit your schedule.

Too poor to give?

Did you know that people with lower incomes tend to give a larger percentage of their income than wealthier people[6]? Have a double look at your budget and see what leeway you have. It is a matter of choice (again): What matters most to you, as a human being living with other human beings: A second pair of the Brand sports shoes or contributing to a medical research, or helping a student like you on the other side of the world go to university, or feed a family for a holiday?

Once you have identified a cause (or more) you really feel strong about supporting (medical, hospitals, overseas development, disabled, children, homeless, environment, religion, education, animals), search the various charities (or non-profit or non-governmental organisations) working in that field.

---

[5] Check religious sources for detailed rules

[6] Reports from the Chronicle of Philanthropy and the National Center for Charitable Statistics in the USA showing a U curve: middle income people give less proportionally; a 2014 UK study from Charities Aid Foundation shows a declining curve: the percentage of income given in charity goes from 4.5% in average for the lowest income to a bit above 1% for the people earning an income of GBP 100,000 and above.

Choosing a Charity

Cause: Is it clear? Look at their mission statement and vision.

Registration: Are they a registered charity? If so, in which country?

Structure: Board, staff, countries of operations, number of staff.

People: Who founded them? What is their story? Are the founders still on the Board?

Accounts: Download their financial report and read it. How old is the latest report available? Are the accounts audited? Are they rated by any transparency agency ("watchdogs") like GuideStar, the BBB Wise Giving Alliance, and Charity Navigator?

What are you looking for?

Administrative costs: FALSE - charities tend to show nice pie charts about their expenses, regrouping them in three main categories: programme, administrative and fundraising. There is a wrong perception that the lower the administrative costs are, the more efficiently run the organisation is and the more likely your donation will go to the field.

Like all donors, you don't really want the money you give to go into expensive offices and fat salaries but charities with very low administrative costs may either split some overhead costs between programme, fundraising and administration, or they may underpay their staff, underinvest in efficient systems or audit or use volunteers at administrative tasks that would require professionals.

Impact: Is more important, even though it is harder to measure. Does their website publish impact indicators? Charities love using cases and stories, especially to fundraise, so use your critical mind: cases are great to help donors visualise what the money is used for and how it changes recipients' lives... but cases are not statistics and a heart-breaking case may be isolated and hide a statistical desert. Read studies or books written by economists or ethnologists. Compare various charities operating for the same cause.

Sustainability: You don't want your money to go to a charity that will close its operations in a few months. How long has this organisation been operating in that particular area? Do they partner with local organisations and other agencies (local governments…)? Look at the amount in their bank accounts, cash and financial investments (from their financial statements) and divide it by the amount of total expenses and overhead expenses: this will give you how long they can go on operating in the event they lose all funding sources. Who funds them (individuals, aid agencies, private charitable funds) and is the funding structure stable over time?

Transparency: Are their accounts audited? Rated? Give a donation and see how long it takes them to process it, including sending a tax receipt. Have you got a choice of which programme to give to? Is their website up to date and does the donation page have a secured https:// page?

Leadership: Listen to their CEO or other managers (online or face to face during events): are the people directing the organisation inspirational? Do they express a clear vision you agree with?

Trust: Meet people working in that charity: attend their events, offer to volunteer. That will give you a good feeling whether you want to support them.

Crowdfunding: Besides charities, you may also be solicited to give for a "crowdfunded" project: people or organisations put together a project and publicise it on a crowdfunding platform. The platform helps them with the narrative and nice videos, and spreads the word. Donors give money for that project through the crowdfunding platform. Crowdfunding is not necessarily for charitable causes - it can be for anything! Enquire as you would for a charity: who are you funding? Transparency? Impact?

MONEY and dating

Love has struck!

Read the section on "Friends and Money" to get a first idea of do's and don'ts. Here are a few more specific ones:

Do	Don't
Budget presents, going out and see what fits.	Pay for everything.
	Let the other pay for everything.
Talk about money: be clear on what expenses you are sharing especially if you pay a rent, or go on a holiday together.	Feel obliged to pay for the most expensive things each time.
	Let financial frustration build up.
Save for presents (consider homemade ones too).	Rely on the other to pay for more than her/his share.
Alternate cheap and simple days with some more special days (budget permit).	Show off and spend over the top.
	Mention the price of what you give.
Know yourself.	Make money the centre of your relationship.
Understand and communicate: you may have different spending patterns: talk about it and how much difference you can each tolerate.	Finance your dating with credit.
	Confuse dating with financial support.
Stay alert: Don't let love blind you and make you overlook some worrying behaviour from your dating partner.	Cheat, pretend or lie.

What you want to be sure of, is that the person you are dating and trying to build a relationship with is trustworthy as (hopefully) he or she also has the same aspirations. Trust is built over time and tests.

Frustration and squabble prevention lab:

1. Talk about it, but without judgement, sarcasm or shouting.
2. Frustration notepad: Write about it in a share notebook. This is less aggressive and gives more time to think.
3. Acknowledge your different attitude to money and spending pattern.

4. Be clear and factual: I can go out twice a month – otherwise I can't save for my trip back home, for example. You can show the maths: plane ticket = $$, going out x 2 x 30 weeks without showing your whole budget as long as you are sure your date is solid and may be long term. Your finance is yours only.

5. Use money as a test: If you clash on money, what does it tell you? Are there other values you disagree about? What does the way your partner handles money unveil about her/his personality? What does the way you handle money unveil of your personality? If your dating gradually evolves into a life-time partnership, you'd better find out sooner than later how to manage money together. [Reminder: the first reason for divorces in the US is about money].

5. AFTER Graduating

PREPARING for after studies

Graduation is getting nearer from the first day you start university. So get a head start. Gather contacts and information. You will need them when you step out and have a few days to accept or refuse your first job offer.

Get ready list:

Job	Place
Network.	Explore your new living area (landmarks, neighbourhood, nature, etc....).
Meet professionals.	
Keep contacts in an orderly system.	Is it a place you may consider living after graduating?
Do internships	If not, where else?
Fatten your CV: Work on projects, papers, volunteer.	What's the job situation like?
Manage your studies actively: how does what you learn integrate in your life plan?	Enquire about the different neighbourhoods, prices, housing style, safety, transportation, proximity to employment areas, to shops etc.
Plan your two or three coming years.	

The salary is not what first matters in a job. Most people quit their jobs for other reasons than the payroll. Among the top reasons found by recent surveys[7]:

Bad boss: Your boss doesn't seem to care or appreciate what you do, or make you grow in your job.

Bad fit: The job didn't turn out to be the one you were expecting; or you don't like the employer's culture.

Bad commute: Daily commute takes a real toll on people's well-being so think twice. Consider moving nearer (once your job is secure enough), or negotiate working from home part-time, or just find a job closer.

Get ready:

Internships: Give you a good idea of what a job is, people you appreciate working with, what a "company" culture entails and how you fit. Vary experiences: try small and big structures to get a feeling of the working style you best thrive in.

Summer jobs: They may be out of your field – but they still are great ways to understand what working implies.

Document and reflect: During and right after an internship or job, take an hour and write what you liked/disliked, things you want to improve, and whether you would re-contact them for another work opportunity (don't forget to keep contact names and details and any important documents like payslips). Send a thank you letter.

---

[7]   Gallup   poll   on   7200   adults   in   the   US: http://www.gallup.com/business journal/182321/employees-lot-managers.aspx for instance

Be your boss: Do you want to start your own business?

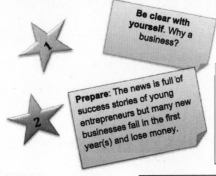

Be clear with yourself. Why a business?

What is your number one motivation to start a business? If it is to get money you may be better off looking for a job with a real monthly salary.

Prepare: The news is full of success stories of young entrepreneurs but many new businesses fail in the first year(s) and lose money.

Have a solid business idea and plan. Get experience. Don't push aside getting employed first - you will learn a lot both from the positive and negative. Remember to take notes and reflect on what you are taking away from this job.
Save a big chunk of your salary for your future business.

Work on the financials

Calculate your personal budget and your business budget: How will you live until your business makes enough to pay you every month?
Minimise fixed costs: Consider starting small from your home. Calculate your breakeven point - how much you need to sell to pay for your costs: That will give you a sales target.
Find out how to finance it – polish your plan and business pitch to investors.
Know when to stop - it's hard for an entrepreneur to keep the emotional link with her/his "baby". So before you even start, while your head is still cool, decide the maximum debt you can take (if any) or loss you can reasonably bear.

Get organised

Account for all ins and outs; take bookkeeping lessons.
Track your time and focus on priorities – working "freely" without guidelines is challenging, especially if you work with friends from home. It is easy to get distracted.

Friends' venture:
You'll have more motivation and skills to start with a team.
Keep the financial deal clear and written from day one; write a partnership contract with rules on sharing losses and profits and everyone's respective contribution (both in money, assets and work).
Track everything professionally (in other words, bookkeeping), and review the accounts together once a month.
Decide on how to exit (either all of you or one of you) before starting.

How to choose?

These years are heavy in big decisions: What to major in, what job, where to live...

Think of possible consequences of my decision (in the short, medium and long term):

- ✓ How could it benefit me?
- ✓ How could it harm me?
- ✓ Consequences on others, family, friends?
- ✓ Consequences on environment?
- ✓ Consequences on my financial situation?
- ✓ Balance of benefits / downsides: Are there more benefits?
- ✓ Does this decision fit my values or does it go against them?
- ✓ What happens if I decide not to do it?
- ✓ Imagine you are ten years older and look back: will you still be okay with this decision?
- ✓ Others' opinions: What will my family and friends say?
- ✓ A good night sleep to see things with a fresh mind.

Job	Place
Do I have a clear idea of the job?	Monthly rent compared to my income
How does that fit in my life plan and goals?	Amount of deposit
Will I like the boss?	Other costs (electricity, tax, etc.)
Will I fit in the culture?	Where it is (far from work?)
Is there room to grow, learn more and evolve in another job in the same company?	Number of rooms
	Size?
What will the job bring me in terms of experience?	Bathrooms and facilities
	Neighbourhood (safety, shops, transport)
What's the salary?	Notice period
What are the other compensations in the package?	
Do I like the environment? Is it easy to commute to?	

Don't get excited by your salary - focus on managing it.

Being independent implies:

Feeding oneself.
Living somewhere.
Doing the laundry.
Cleaning up and sorting out where to live.
Ensuring own safety.
Taking decisions.
Respecting others.
Respecting others' property.
Earning money.
Paying tax and contribute to society.
Managing expenses.
Managing papers.

Food for thought: Is adulthood about independence or interdependence? Adults are interconnected. Others rely on our skills as we rely on others – in a fashion.

Additional tips – once you start working and getting paid.

The paperwork: Don't wait for the pile to turn into Everest before you DO SOMETHING.

File in a way that makes sense to you. Test your system: How long it takes you to find 1) your diploma, 2) your birth certificate, 3) your payslip from three months ago?

Think long term: Is your filing system time-proof: is it easy to use even when you will have accumulated 48 payslips?

Mirror your e-filing with your paper files. Files by topic and/or third party are usually easier to navigate and help you spot issues more quickly: one monthly invoice missing or a change in pricing.

Ask your parents for the missing bits they may still keep (birth certificate, high school diploma, etc.,) after kindly requesting them to scan them first.

Back-up: Scan your important papers and copy them either to a secure internet site that you can easily retrieve and give access to one or two other trusted people in case something happens to you, or to a flash drive, which you store in a place other than next to your computer.

Payslip: Learn to read your payslips. Payslips vary from country to country – but there are some common pieces of information.

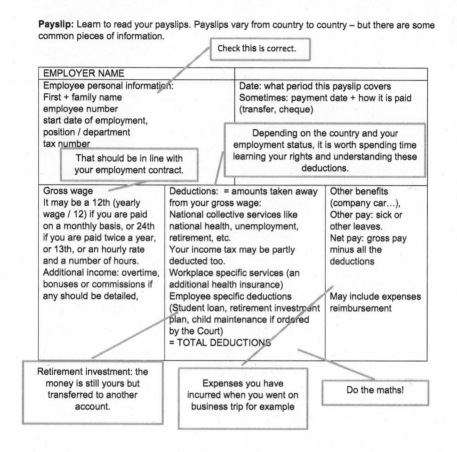

Check this is correct.

EMPLOYER NAME	
Employee personal information: First + family name employee number start date of employment, position / department tax number	Date: what period this payslip covers Sometimes: payment date + how it is paid (transfer, cheque)

That should be in line with your employment contract.

Depending on the country and your employment status, it is worth spending time learning your rights and understanding these deductions.

Gross wage It may be a 12th (yearly wage / 12) if you are paid on a monthly basis, or 24th if you are paid twice a year, or 13th, or an hourly rate and a number of hours. Additional income: overtime, bonuses or commissions if any should be detailed,	Deductions: = amounts taken away from your gross wage: National collective services like national health, unemployment, retirement, etc. Your income tax may be partly deducted too. Workplace specific services (an additional health insurance) Employee specific deductions (Student loan, retirement investment plan, child maintenance if ordered by the Court) = TOTAL DEDUCTIONS	Other benefits (company car…), Other pay: sick or other leaves. Net pay: gross pay minus all the deductions
		May include expenses reimbursement

Retirement investment: the money is still yours but transferred to another account.

Expenses you have incurred when you went on business trip for example

Do the maths!

Get information and know your rights

Tax:

Gather information on your obligations as soon as possible. Don't wait for your first income. After all, you can vote. Tax and representation go together.

Register as soon as you have graduated and are clear on your new residence.

You may already pay local taxes linked to where you live, so these ones will be familiar.

The income tax should be new to you. Many countries have a tax withholding amount taken from the salary. You may have a choice of the amount deducted when this is set up:

Too low	About right	Too high
You feel confident you can save every month for your tax... do what you have signed up for then and transfer the savings for your tax to a savings account for example to make sure you can pay on time.	Tax payment should be relatively painless and eventless. No extra amounts to pay or tax credit jackpot to feast upon.	You use the government as your savings account. When your actual tax payment is calculated, a tax credit is paid back to you. If you have trouble saving, this is a way to force you to save, unless you use the tax credit for a shopping spree. This lacks flexibility and doesn't earn any additional revenue.

Learn how to fill in your tax declaration before it is due. Get it straight from the horse's mouth: tax agencies usually give information for free. Write the date with a reminder well in advance.

Follow up on any mistakes! Don't let them get worse.

BUDGET!!!

Update your budget (the one you did as a student) with your new income and new expenses, including your student loan to pay back if any.

	Month 1	Month 2	Month 3	Month 4
Income				
Other revenues				
TOTAL INCOME				
Rent				
Utilities				
Tax				
Food				
Domestic Help				
Student loan				
Travel/holidays				
Leisure				
Insurance				
Health				
Family support				
Charity, donations				
Clothes				
Etc…				
TOTAL EXPENSES				
INCOME - EXPENSES				

Financial assets				
Properties				
Other assets				
TOTAL ASSETS				
Student loan				
Short term debts				
Mortgage				
Other debts				
TOTAL DEBTS				
ASSETS – DEBTS =				

Know where you are going: Calculate your daily spending limit and have it clearly in mind:

Monthly income	20,000
Rent + utilities	6,000
Student loan	3,500
Phone (plan)	400
Insurance (yearly 1200)	100
Income tax (yearly 1200)	100
MONTHLY NET INCOME	**9,900**
Daily net income	**330**

Daily spending limit

Don't overcommit: The more you commit (rent, clubs, etc.), the less flexibility you have for other expenses and potential downs.

Refine your budget and limit to add your savings goals.

What	When	How much	Monthly savings
Summer holiday	6 months	1,200	200
Bike	3 months	600	200
Emergency		100	100
Down payment for home	3 years	90,000	2,500
Master degree	2 years	28,800	1,200
TOTAL			4,200

Monthly income	20,000
Bills...	10,100
Monthly net income	9,900
Monthly savings	4,200
Monthly limit	5,700
	/30
Daily spending limit:	190

Can you live within this limit (food, transportation, health/hygiene, leisure, etc.)? If not, prioritise goals and expenses until you get the balance between present and future that works best for you.

Plan long term: Keep learning, include a personal development line in your budget, start saving for big events (down payment to buy a house, wedding, etc.).

Keep tracking your actual expenses and updating and adjusting your budget.

Consider paying your recurring bills (utilities) by direct debit to cut down on administrative time, as well as some donations you regularly make.

Check your bank and credit card statements.

Start learning about the various investment possibilities.

DOMESTIC Finances

Continued from… Money and Dating. Things are looking stable and you have decided to move in together and maybe even get married. Do's and don'ts stay the same.

Money meeting: You need to have a serious, unpassionate, fact-based discussion and agree on how your partnership is going to operate. Unromantic? Yes, but you want your love venture to travel on smooth water not on a storm created by distrust and squabbles. Here are some recipes for calm waters:

Rent: Who pays how much? Is the lease contract in both your names?

Utilities: who pays which one? Which name? Don't have all of them under the same name as some countries national agencies may sometimes ask for them as a proof of residence.

Grocery: Who pays what?

Furniture and equipment: Who brings what, who pays for what?

Repairs/home improvement: Who pays for what? While you are at it, define rules for house chores too and a tidiness standard (couples also split over dirty socks left on the floor for too long).

Write your family budget: Discuss what works best for you two:

- A unique budget: Where you merge all your incomes and expenses in one big budget, add a column to say who pays for what.
- A common budget: Budget what you share rent, utilities, etc. and your own personal budget for the rest. You can start with a common budget then move to a unique one.

Set goals: From furniture purchase to holiday, and longer term goals too.

Monthly meeting: To review if the water is still smooth and update your budget, check how you are doing with your goals.

Learn the law: Legally in most countries, as long as you are not married, all items bought will belong to one of you only.

Married? Add a few more items for your meeting:

- Set an amount above which purchases should be discussed together.
- Bank: Stay put or open a joint account?
- Family support: Discuss how to deal if one has to support her/his family.
- Notify insurances, utilities, tax, etc. about your new situation.
- Set up a money management software and split the work.
- Optimise your filing system so that it is orderly and clear for both of you.

Write a will.

DEALING with unemployment

Mind wise	Money wise
Consider your job search as a job: get up early as if going to work, get a daily routine. Go out once a day.	Budget: List your expenses (accommodation, food, transportation) including those related to your job search (transportation, internet, phone, business clothes).
Organise your search in a professional way: list potential employers, contact, if you know them, search their websites, etc. Network. Exercise.	How can you pay? Do you need to move back to your parents or a relative? If you do, how far are you from your targeted employers? Can you work part-time: How much can that cover your expenses?
Stay active: Consider a part-time job (to get out and get money). Eat regular meals (stay away from the fridge in between).	If you co-share a flat, be clear with your flatmates on your commitment to pay (or not) the rent. If you live on your savings for a while, calculate your spending limit using part of your savings as income.

Savings for safety:

Many websites give a three to six-month rule of savings to keep in case we lose our revenue. The truth for many people, is that this is not realistic because they cannot save that much - full stop.

Build your minimum safety net before graduating: Don't spend all your income – whatever it comes from (summer internships, jobs, loan, scholarship, etc.). Target one month expenses to start with, go through your budget and flag (you may want to create a "survival" column in your spreadsheet) expenses you cannot do without (really – we're talking about an emergency plan): Rent, minimum food for one month, transportation; how much does that add up to? That's your first savings target.

Work on plans B, C: If you are out of work for two to three months for example, how can you survive? Work out different emergency scenarios before the storm is on you. They will come in handy when you have to take quick decisions and your brain is too stressed by it all.

Money Management in a Nutshell:

Don't spend more than you have.

Some expenses are more important others: Prioritisation is key!

Plan ahead: Write a budget.

Note down all that you spend and receive: It will be easier to prioritise and plan.

Think long term: write down your goals and save for them.

Never borrow without a plan for paying it back.

Have an emergency fund.

Compare: Calculate the pros and cons of any choice (big purchase, telephone plan, etc....).

Donate.

BUDGET SAMPLE:

Currency:_____	September	October	November	December	January
Tuition fees					
College fees					
Accommodation (*)					
Kitchen facility charge					
Meals					
Books & equipment					
Extra classes					
Local transportation					
Personal:					
Going out					
Mobile phone Toiletries					
Clothes					
Laundry					
Clubs					
Miscellaneous					
Health					
Insurance					
Formal clothes (work/internship)					
Travel					
Travel home (x times / year)					
TOTAL/year					
Years of study					
TOTAL					
One-offs: Furniture, utensils, vehicle					
GRAND TOTAL					
Potential Financing:					
Scholarships					
Parents					
Part-time job					
Other					
Loan					

Money Management

February	March	April	May	June	July/August

Monthly income	
Tuition fee/12 months	
Rent/accommodation fee	
Kitchen fee/cafeteria fee	
Phone (plan)	
Utilities	
Other commitments	
MONTHLY NET INCOME	
Savings goal: _____	
Savings goal: _____	
Savings goal: _____	
Savings goal: _____	
Savings goal: _____	
MONTHLY NET INCOME	
Daily net income	

Chapter 2: Keeping Organised with Efficient Time Management

by Rachael Desgouttes

1. INTRODUCTION

Unfortunately, TIME is a finite commodity. That is the problem!

Have you ever felt you have more to do than the time available to do it in?

Are there things at the bottom of your list that just never get done and keep nagging at you?

Have you ever woken up feeling stressed because there are more things on your "To Do" list than you can possibly fit in the day?

Do you regularly study all night because there is a deadline tomorrow?

Do you grab a chocolate bar and bag of crisps because you haven't got time to go to the supermarket, never mind cook something tasty?

Does a spontaneous late night out mean you donate the following morning to sleep and your study plan is ruined?

You are not alone! I often seem to have more to do than time allows. Whilst these scenarios are always going to be a part of life, and not just as a student, they should be the exception rather than the rule. The better we can plan and manage our time, the better we can reduce stress and accommodate our fun time without impacting the rest of our commitments.

2. GENERAL Overview - Real Time! Rocks, Pebbles, Sand

I am sure you know the story of the professor who demonstrated to his class how to fill a large jar. He filled it with tennis ball sized rocks. He asked his students if the jar was full. They all agreed it was. He then tipped handfuls of small pebbles into the jar and they filled up the gaps between the rocks. He asked again if the jar was full. The answer was again, yes. So yet again, the teacher poured sand into the jar, which filled the small gaps between the rocks and pebbles. Was the jar full? he asked. Yes.

Finally, the teacher opened two cans of lager and poured them both into the jar. The liquid filled the empty space between the sand, pebbles and rocks.

The teacher finally explained that the jar represents life. The rocks represent the most important things; pebbles are the other things in life that matter to us, and the sand is everything else.

If you put the sand in first, there may be room for some or all the pebbles but certainly not all the rocks will fit. If you spend all your time and energy on the small stuff, you will never have room for the most important things.

The key is to identify what the "rocks" are in your life. These will have changed from when you were at school, and will shift again as you journey through life. But fill up your hours and days with rocks - the things that really matter. Minimise the sand that you allow in!

One of the students sheepishly asked the teacher what the beer in the experiment had represented? The teacher smiled and replied; "I'm glad you asked. Beer shows that no matter how full your life may be, there's always room for a beer!"

Task: Fill up the container! Small stuff first = too little space Big stuff first – fit in priorities

3. TIME And Culture

Punctuality can be identified as having cultural variances! Generally, British people tend to be amazingly punctual, French are regularly 10-15 min late, and there are many stories of complete time misunderstandings when working with Latin Americans or Middle Eastern cultures.

> *"My Indian friends invited me for a dinner. I arrived as instructed at 8.30. No other guests arrived till after 10, and food wasn't served till almost midnight! I was starving!"*
>
> --Joseph M. Oxford Brookes

4. PUNCTUALITY - Time Is A Frame Of Mind

We all know people who are regularly late. Have you ever told a friend to meet you half an hour before the real time, as you know they will be late, or arranged a rendezvous time, and planned to be late yourself because you can rely on your friend being so too? Or maybe this late person is YOU! Whilst we can all fall behind occasionally from an interruption or external delay, if either you or your friend is regularly late, it is not a coincidence. We can all find excuses: bus was late, alarm didn't go off, heavy traffic, bad weather caused problems etc. Often we make a gesture to avoid timing problems: set the alarm earlier and add an additional alarm clock for good measure, skip breakfast, shower but not wash hair and a host of other initiatives and quick fixes. The truth of the matter is that these small problems are not isolated, but part of a much larger issue which includes:

INTRINSIC versus extrinsic motivation

Intrinsic means coming from within. By the time we are at university, we should be studying because we want to, rather than in school days when it was an obligation. The pressure to get work done, however, is often driven by deadlines, and hence the motivation is extrinsic – the external threat of being kicked out of class is enough to make us stay up all night!

How can we turn around the pressure? We want to continue enjoying the subjects we selected, yet we mustn't allow an inefficient and or ineffective study process, lack of sleep, or an imbalanced life make it an exhausting chore.

5. SELF-MANAGEMENT - How Am I Doing So Far?

Have you ever wondered why it is that we can get to the movies on time?

Do you ever not-have-time to "like" and comment on the latest party photos on social media?

If it is cold and raining, is it justifiable to stay in bed and not go on the run that was planned for 7am before class?

If a seminar runs over time by 15 minutes – what adjustments need to be made for the rest of the day?

Have you ever exhausted yourself the day before you go on holiday by shoving two or more days' worth of "to dos" into one day?

Have you lived with a guilty feeling because you never got round to doing something you intended to? Examples may include writing a thank you letter to Great Aunt Bessie, returning a faulty item to a shop, doing the pre-reading assigned for a seminar.

Managing ourselves in order to complete ordinary tasks is something that we often overlook; it seems too obvious to consider. When we set our tasks, we need to consider elements other than just how long it might take. What are the entry and exit criteria – the environmental factors that allow us to go ahead, or alternatively cancel or postpone?

6. PRIORITISING

Human nature means we do the things we want to do first. Do you remember as a child being told to eat the vegetables first to get them over and done with? Have a look at the TED talk called "Inside the mind of a master procrastinator" by Tim Urban, published April 6th, 2016. The question is, how can we find the inner discipline to balance ourselves to execute the "must do" and "urgent" list, yet reward ourselves by interspersing the "want to do" or less urgent tasks?

ESTABLISHING priorities

> *"I feel very proud when I see my students graduate and leave for college or university all over the world. Within the first six to twelve months, I often receive an email. The most common struggle they have is finding the right life-balance between domestic, social and study time."*
>
> -- M. Caulfield International Secondary School Teacher, Hong Kong

> *"The party scene was so vibrant that for the first two months I barely made it to class. Even after that calmed down, my studies were not my first priority. I grew up in a small farming town, so being in a big, bright city was thrilling. However, I never really caught up, and by the end of the first year, I failed my exams and finally decided to leave the course."*
>
> -- Tom S., opted out of an Engineering degree

Whilst living at home, priorities fall into place like magic. Behind the scenes, family and teachers often assist, setting out your priorities for you. Laundry, shopping, cooking, cleaning and transportation are mostly taken care of by adults around you. School, study and socialising become the focus of your world. As we mature, we earn more social freedom and have to make decisions about balance.

Time management and our schedule are an automatic result of the environment: other people, events, regular school hours, even the school bus timetable. These elements dictate what has to happen, and when.

If your mother nagged, "Have an early night because you have a big exam tomorrow!" it might have seemed exaggerated. Students gaining their independence at university soon realise that this was one of many essential "hidden" time planning tools for optimum performance that was done for you!

If ever you missed your school bus, your routine was thrown out of order. You would have had to arrange an alternative way to get to school. This may have been an inconvenience, and there might have been a cost – in either time, money or both. Perhaps being late to school would have generated a punishment, causing further disruption and inconvenience to your schedule, and possibly that of others too.

WHAT is a priority? The Eisenhower Matrix

It seems too obvious to have to ask, but what is a priority? Simplistically, priorities are "To Do" items with the most urgency. But when we have a lot, how do we identify which ones have the highest priority?

> *"What is important is seldom urgent and what is urgent is seldom important."*
>
> -- Dwight D. Eisenhower

Eisenhower was a WWII five-star General, the 34th President of the United States of America, and the creator of the Interstate Highway System, along with NASA. The man was a force of nature!

Have a look at the next chart, known as the Eisenhower Matrix (see Figure 1): It is a 2x2 sliding scale matrix between importance and urgency. The idea is to correlate what is urgent and critical versus desirable or even unimportant – or more specifically, what is least important and non-urgent.

To repeat; TIME IS FINITE – so if you can only achieve nine out of ten items on your To Do list, how can you ensure that the one which drops off is the least important and CAN be dropped off, or alternatively, relocated to a scheduled time when it can get done?

As with all prioritising, this will vary from person to person. It also depends what you have going on in your life. It is a fluid movement of tasks through different times and circumstances.

For example, let's look at calling home to Mum. If you need cash from her to pay for something *today,* this phone call is IMPORTANT AND URGENT. If you want to discuss your summer holiday plans for next year, this is IMPORTANT, BUT NOT URGENT. If you want some moral support and a gossipy catch up – then bottom right: NOT IMPORTANT, NOT URGENT.

Question: In which quartile would you put your Mum's birthday?

Look at how things can move! Your answer will vary, depending on different factors, such as whether it is a landmark birthday or not; if your siblings will take action on your behalf; and if it is three months away, or tomorrow!

	URGENT	NOT URGENT
IMPORTANT	1. DO NOW! Tasks with non-negotiable, hard deadlines.	2. DECIDE WHEN TO DO IT These ARE critical items to be done, but have some time flexibility.
NOT IMPORTANT	3. MANAGE these by cutting them short, delegating, postpone or change.	4. DELETE THESE These are trivial matters that do not enhance your overall life or work.

(Fig 1) Eisenhower divided his quartiles up by describing tasks as follows. It is intended that the first tasks to be done are box 1, then 2, then 3, finally 4.

1. Urgent and important:
- Deadline driven projects which are near and have an impact. Work projects and assignments.
- Crises / Emergencies – Do these belong to you, or are you supporting someone else? Consider in which box each crisis belongs.
- Pressing problems – if you have a bone fide reason to postpone a deadline, then the email to your supervisor supersedes the actual assignment in importance.

2. Not urgent, but important:
- Documentation admin management (in other words, building long term systems to help you better manage time and motion.)
- Planning.
- Building long-term relationships.

3. Urgent, not important:
- Interruptions. This can include phone calls and emails which distract your engagement in something else.
- Routine meetings which have little consequence. (Does a proposed meeting or seminar have an agenda and clear objectives? If so, you can evaluate the urgency and your need to attend. If not – the probability is, you can excuse yourself from this one!)
- Other people's activities.

4. Not urgent, not important:
- Social / social media / gaming / TV.
- Time wasters / idling.
- Distractions.

This is a very useful tool to help you make a well-prioritised "To Do" list. FIX this image in your mind as a memory aid to ranking all additional things that come your way. You could even have a blank copy in which you put the tasks you have to do. If you're someone who prefers to scribble a to-do list quickly – prefix all tasks with 1, 2, 3 or 4 and you will know where to start!

	URGENT	NOT URGENT
IMPORTANT	1	2
NOT IMPORTANT	3	4

(Fig 2)

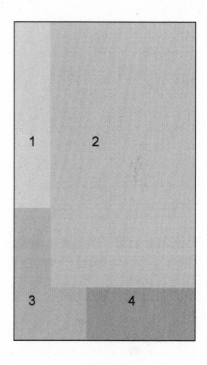

(Fig 3)

Whilst the Eisenhower Matrix is presented as four equal quartiles, successful time management will allow you to look more like Figure 3.

The frustrating thing is that just as we have organised a "running list" based on our ranking of priorities, we may have another assignment or task hurled at us which zooms in above many existing things on the list. However, knowing HOW to prioritise means it can be done in conjunction with all the other things that need doing, within the allotted time.

THREE Simple Steps to Setting Your priorities

This may sound like a lot of analysis but starting off your college life with a clear picture of where you are will allow you to reassess and regularly fine-tune and improve this difficult balance. If you can solve a small problem quickly – it is so much easier than fixing a big problem later!

Step 1: Establish how each day for a typical week is broken up currently.

By ranking the time spent on each one – your current priorities emerge.

Keep a notebook, become mindful as you track units for the key activities. Keep this simple. Suggested categories include:

- **Study:** Lecture/seminar contact time plus private reading, research, writing, revising and library time.
- **Social:** Include all non-study related contact time with friends, whether it be coffee, lunch party, or going out dancing. Also factor in planning your rendezvous, plus communication through email, social media and your phone. Relaxation counts here too: reading, TV shows, movies, videogames, and anything else you do to decompress.
- **Sport and exercise:** This might include a sports club meeting, or a solo trip to the treadmill or swimming pool.

- **Travel:** This refers to more than just the time on the bus or train but includes the walk to the station or bus stop. *NOTE: Riding on public transport offers a great opportunity for multi-tasking: use a long journey to read, plan or revise.*
- **Domestic:** Any task like doing laundry, washing, ironing, bed-changing, and housework (washing up, household cleaning and emptying bins).
- **Food:** Shopping, preparation, cooking, and finally, eating! Whether you eat a bowl of soup at home, grab a handful of nuts on the go, or sit down to a three-course meal, eating is important, and it deserves a time allocation.
- **Bathroom time:** Includes your shower, toilette, hair, shaving, and so on! Plus, trips to the toilet during the day.
- **Sleep:** The time between falling asleep and waking up.

Step 2: **Identify which things are a struggle to get done.**

At the beginning of your university life, you may not know what the perfect time allocation is, for each activity. It is different for everyone, and it is an ever-changing quantity.

After a period of observation, you will probably be surprised by some of your findings. Have you ever calculated how long you spend in the bathroom? Do you allow time for packing up your study bag, or unpacking the shopping? It is certainly not necessary that we track every minute of our time either looking back – or planning forward.

> *"I thought I did a lot of sport, but the actual time engaged is only three hours a week. The travel and "quick" drink afterwards, more than double that!"*
>
> -- Catherine G., Exeter University

> *"I never realised I needed to spend so much time on the laundry! I now know how to smooth out my clothes before and after they dry, which saves me ironing a lot of them (or looking like I slept in them!) I also never realised how long it took to make a double bed. By partnering with my roommate, we make both our beds between us – it is so much easier and saves a lot of time. The effort is worth it, sleeping in clean sheets is the smell of home!"*
>
> -- Paul L., Aston University

Step 3: After tracking, make adjustments.

After a week, take a look at your own results, and listing any additional areas you haven't made time for such as health and wellness, relationships, planning and organising for the future, communicating with home, career planning etc.

Rate each one with YES or NO in terms of your satisfaction with time spent in this area.

		Example: Satisfied with time allocated / Needs more/less	Your turn:
1	Study	Too little	
2	Social	:) OK	
3	Sport and exercise	Too little	
4	Travel	Too much	
5	Domestic chores	Bit more :-(	
6	Shop, prepare, cook	:) OK	
7	Eating	:) OK	
8	Bathroom time	:) OK	
9	Sleep	Enough at weekends, but could use more Mon-Fri	
10	Other		
11	Other		
12	Other		

You may be allotting too much time for "laundry/shopping" or too little for "sport/ study" but without knowing where you currently allow time, it is impossible to re-adjust. To allow more time for one activity you have to steal it from somewhere else! For example, could travel time be also used as reading time? If you walk or cycle, can reading be converted to listening? Can one fewer trip to the library per week save one hour return trip travel time?

REASSESSMENT and re-positioning of priorities

In order to spend more time on one of your priorities or add in time for things that you are missing out on, you have to free up some time from something else. Over an academic year, there will be pressure periods of exams, where study goes up and social must go down. Conversely, this means that being on top of your time management WILL allow you to have a wonderful birthday night out, an end of term Christmas splurge, or a weekend stay with a friend without falling behind.

Be aware of what are temporary changes and what are for the longer term. One all-night study session is an answer to an emergency, but regularly stealing time from your sleep will compromise study, health, mood and other aspects of your life. Beware! At university, sleep is often one of the first things to fall off our priority list, yet it is also one of the most important keys to wellness.

Now your PRIORITES have been identified and ranked, we will now discuss the keys to avoiding last minute time crises.

7. TIME Management Planning!

BE WARNED! Sloppiness with time management can negatively infiltrate to other areas of your life and performance. You may feel frustrated and anxious, with a feeling of never being able to catch up. Other people's perception of you may be inaccurate and unfair, as you might appear disorganised or unreliable. This may lead to relationship conflicts and missed opportunities. Some tips for avoiding this predicament include:

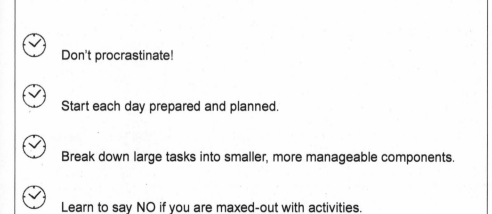

Don't procrastinate!

Start each day prepared and planned.

Break down large tasks into smaller, more manageable components.

Learn to say NO if you are maxed-out with activities.

🕐 Keep a TO-DO list and re-prioritise regularly. Keep important tasks at the top.

🕐 Combat distractions. Have techniques to stop incoming temptations to time waste!

🕐 Confine email and electronic distraction to a rigid period of budgeted time.

🕐 Allow budgeted, guilt-free breaks.

REMINDER! Time Planning for Time Management.

You cannot execute effective time management without the essential pre-step of planning your priorities and time! This seems an arduously boring thing to do, but it gets easier the more experienced you become and the more you see the results of your planning.

"Even my cup of tea and chocolate digestive biscuits tasted better, because I had achieved what I set out to do, in the time I budgeted for the task. I DESERVED my treat!"

--Emily, York University

8. ALLOWING Appropriate Time for Each Task

This is one of the key skills for time management success. Whether you are meeting a friend for a cinema visit or need to hand in an assignment on time, to execute each task thoroughly and without stress we need to make a realistic evaluation of the time needed.

Let's use a cinema trip as an example. We know the start time and can find out the length and hence end of the film. Then we know what time to book a restaurant table afterwards. Sometimes we forget to make time allowances for the less obvious bits-in-between. What is the commute to the cinema? Will there be a long queue for the bathroom after the movie? You may bump into a friend you haven't seen for a while and chat for ten minutes. You might need to find a money dispenser to withdraw cash. These are the daily normalities that we think nothing of, but could throw off your later engagements.

SARAH GOES TO THE CINEMA

The plan was for Sarah to meet Marie at the cinema. They were going to see the 7:00pm screening which would finish at 8:40pm, then go for a quick meal so Sarah could take the 9:15pm bus, and be home at 9:45pm to spend one hour finishing her reading for tomorrow's lecture.

What actually happened was that Sarah left home at 6:00pm, but just as she was leaving, her friend Marie texted to say she would be ten minutes late. So Sarah took a side road, so she could do some window-shopping, which she did until 6:15pm. She then took the bus, which was stuck in traffic longer than usual, and she arrived at the cinema at 6:55pm. Marie was there already, but the queue was huge, and they couldn't get tickets for the screening they wanted. So they went and ate (it was 7:15pm already), then went to the next screening at 8:45pm. By the time Sarah took her bus home, it was 11:15pm and she reached home, exhausted, at 11:45pm.

What was missed out? Sarah had moved her lecture prep to quartile 1 – and the possibilities are either not getting the preparation done, or reduced sleep time.

9. TRAVEL Can be a Time Waster

When travelling from A to B, we tend to give a cursory estimate like, "just a ten minute drive!" or "around 15 minutes on the bus."

We don't take into account actual and possible "add-ons":

- Walking to the bus stop / car - 3 minutes
- Putting bags in the boot / queue of people boarding bus - 2 minutes
- Passengers getting in and putting their seatbelts on - 2 minutes
- Radio and programming the GPS / map planning - 2 minutes
- Waiting in line to leave the car park - 4 minutes
- Paying for the car-park / passengers scrabbling around to find small change - 2 minutes
- Heavy traffic / road works / emergency vehicles passing by - 10 minutes
- Finding a car space at the other end - 5 minutes
- Parallel parking - 4 minutes
- Finding "pay and display" machine and acquiring ticket / slow passengers disembarking - 4 minutes
- Walking to meeting place - 2 minutes

What in theory was a quick ride has become a 40-minute period, which can initiate feelings of anxiety and create stress about being late, or actually incur physical consequences for lateness. Perhaps you can read your book on the bus and quell your anxiety, but your friend waiting may have reduced her trust capital in you and increased her perception of you being unreliable or impolite.

10. HOW to Manage Your Time, Environment and Energy

TIME - Optimum performance schedule

> *"Everyone has a different natural time pattern. We are naturally either an early morning lark or a night owl. The key to successful time optimisation is to know your best study format. Arrange that your best time of day is kept for study. Don't be overly ambitious and make your study block so big that you need to push yourself to the limit where the last minutes of your study time become un-productive."*
>
> --Winston C., Graduate of Hong Kong University (HKU)

Identify your optimum performance schedule. Small units don't mean less study.

Crunch it down!

- One student may engage for a fifty-minute study block and then take a ten-minute break. Another student may study for three fifteen-minute blocks with a three-minute stretch and walk around between each one.

- Organising your thoughts around a topic takes time too. Do not waste time jumping from topic to topic. Dedicate enough uninterrupted time for each one to avoid having to repeatedly refresh your mind and re-organise your thoughts.

- Turn off phones and social media! They are our biggest enemy when it comes to studying efficiently.

- Do some trial and error experiments to calculate your optimum study time unit. Think about breaking down study in types of study task: for instance, learning a lexical field of new vocabulary and terminology; writing an essay; reading a book; or reviewing a lesson for a test. Each of these study tasks doesn't require the same level of attention and time. The task "writing an essay" can be broken down in different blocks (finding ideas, organising them, researching the topic, and so on).

- Remember that you will find some tasks more engaging than others, so be kind to yourself and take a "worst case scenario" outlook with time planning.

You can avoid a build-up of work not efficiently done, and hence lateness at the end of the project.

- Use your breaks as a reward. If planned effectively as part of your total time, so that the study unit was engaging and achieved successfully, then you deserve that reward! However, be as disciplined with the timing of your break as you are for the study period!

- Be realistic with your rewards! 15 minutes of background reading does not deserve an hour off and a pint in the pub! If your units are small, the rewards should reflect this. You could:
    - ✓ Eat an apple and flick through a magazine.
    - ✓ Allow yourself to check your emails and social media.
    - ✓ Walk outside for five minutes fresh air.
    - ✓ Standing up approximately every 30 minutes is good advice – move around for a few minutes and focus your eyes on far away things.

When you have a long-term project that has a deadline, adjust that deadline for yourself 24-48 hours earlier than the actual one. This way you have a built in "overflow" time to deal with emergencies. Should you have no set-backs and not need the built in extra time, you can sit with your feet up and bask in the pleasure of having finished early!

Just try it once! Just once, even if it is not your habit and hard to break long standing habits of starting assignments at the last minute. The pleasure of finishing early, doing other things and relaxing is addictive!

ENVIRONMENT: "Tidy desk = Tidy mind!"

If you are studying, you are much more focused, effective and comfortable in a neat and tidy, naturally bright or well-lit environment. Choose the best environment for your study, being realistic about potential distractions!

Your own room may be small or messy, or you may just want a change of scenery. A coffee shop might be peaceful one day, but the next day may be hosting a mother and toddler coffee shop meeting! A public or university library should guarantee quiet. Studying away from home means being organised enough to take everything you need with you.

Often university accommodation is small, so you live and study in the same space. Build into your study time a realistic window to tidy your environment. Make your bed, file away papers, and clear your desk so that when you sit down to work, you only have the relevant task material in front of you. Even these small tasks can give you a sense of achievement.

Be creative with organisation. Use cut up boxes and packages, bottles and jars to store bits and pieces to keep you tidy. Decorate them if you wish!

Everyday waste items can create organised storage.

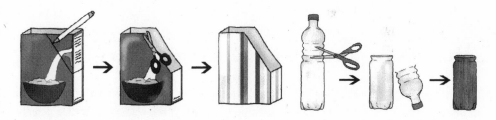

If there is a possibility that you will be disturbed by someone, put a friendly note on your door with a time that you will be available later.

Put all electronic items not essential for study away. We all know that phones EAT time!

Finish drinks and snacks, and remove all empty wrappers and dirty crockery.

When you are relaxing, your room should be a haven, but when you are studying your room should be an office. Don't mix the two! Never make your bedroom your dining room.

ENERGY: Managing and optimising YOURSELF for your work

To work well, you need to be in the right frame of mind. If you know yourself well, you know how it feels for you to be holistically WELL: Well-rested, and in a positive state of physical and mental wellbeing to study. You don't need to have a "problem" to welcome additional support that can be cheaply and easily added into your routine! You can experiment with the following wellbeing factors to see what works for you, and which you enjoy.

Energy Booster 1: Meditation

Meditation is the ability to calm your mind and find peace. You can purge your worries and feel happier. Meditation does not have to be hours long, you can have some fast, effective help in minutes.

→ **Calming & balancing three-minute fix:** Breathing slightly slower than usually, and more mindfully, inhale and exhale through your left nostril for 30 seconds, closing off your right. Switch and inhale and exhale through your right for thirty seconds, closing off your left. Then inhale through your left, inhale though your right for a minute. Inhale through your right, exhale through your left. When you breathe, breathe deeply into your belly. When you exhale, relax leaning forward onto your heart. Your left nostril controls the creative right side of the brain. The right nostril controls the rational left side of the brain.

→ **Calming & establishing distance between you and your emotions:** Inhale for five seconds, hold the breath for five seconds, and exhale for five seconds. Repeat 12 times which takes you to three minutes.

→ **Meditation Apps!** There are many internet sites offering tips and tricks to help you achieve heightened concentration through meditation, so surf around for ideas which can help you at your level. The app Headspace is an excellent starting point.

Energy Booster 2: Restful Sleep

If you're struggling with sleeping, see chapter 5.

Energy Booster 3: Aromatherapy

Aromatherapy is the art of using pure or blended essential oils extracted from flowers and herbs to resolve issues and find calm. It has been proven that these oils can influence your mood, ability to concentrate, and general well-being. Blending oils to your taste and need is a science. Like anything, you pay for quality, and some oils can get pricy. Generous relatives and friends wanting to buy you a going away gift could be steered in this direction!

Start off with just a few essentials and build from there.

For **mental clarity** (to keep you alert and enhance concentration) try Rosemary, Basil, Peppermint or Juniper.

For **relaxation and de-stressing** (especially if you need a night of refreshing, quality sleep) try Lavender, Rose, Ylang-ylang or Bergamot.

Just a few of many ways to use oils:

- ✓ Essential oils can be evaporated - simple essential oil burners can be found quite cheaply in economy stores.
- ✓ Add just a few drops to your bath water or onto your pillow for some extra luxury.
- ✓ Take an inexpensive body lotion or cream (avoid luxury brand names as you pay a premium for the brand. Baby products are a good choice as they are often free of chemicals and irritants). Add a few drops of lavender or your favourite oil and blend.
- ✓ Teas infused with a drop of oil can also add to your feelings of relaxation and well-being.

There is plenty of information about essential oil blending and usage on the internet.

11. TOOLBOX For Planning!

Of course, the greatest key to successful work is good planning and organisation. What are the best tools to facilitate optimum plans?

PLAN YOUR WORK & WORK YOUR PLAN

PLAN by term, month, week, day, even hour!

To plan effectively we need to consider time for executing short medium and long-term goals, and build in regular reviews. Your school studies will have demonstrated this to you to a certain degree. Teachers prompting you and parents not allowing you to go out because of a deadline may have seemed like a drag, until suddenly you are on your own!

Study is the reason we go to university, so planning the reading, preparation and assignments may seem like the most important aspect of life, but there has to be a balance between study and life! Remember to respect your academic and non-academic needs, yet equally remember that it is not all about socialising! Domestic chores, sleep, and sport are all part of the whole. Remember too, that networking and community service are all worthwhile activities you can seek out in your area.

When you were at school you probably had a system of planning your life. At university it has probably become more complex. Take the time to evaluate honestly how efficient, practical, and comfortable your previous life balance was. If it worked perfectly, by all means continue! But as you are now taking responsibility for so much of what was done for you, you will need an efficient system to make sure everything runs smoothly.

Tom W. graduated with a first-class honours degree in English Literature. He offers the following advice:

"Good advice I received was that for each of my three plans (long-term, weekly and daily) I needed three different tools.

i) *I had a university wall planner poster to oversee the whole year. It was a great way to visualise and slot in long term projects.*

ii) *I kept an electronic weekly planner available to me on my phone and computer. On Sunday night I printed out the next week. I kept it on the mirror next to my desk. It reminded me that, for example, if I was invited to a party – I could quickly see the impact on study and other activities already planned for the week.*

iii) *Finally, every evening I made a "TO DO" list for the next day – using a good old-fashioned notebook and pencil.*

My friends laughed at me initially, but by mid-term, I noticed that some were adopting the same or similar habits!!

Maybe I was over fastidious, but I even added an additional tool:

iv) *- An overview sheet for each assignment.*

But really, all the planning took away a lot of potential stress. I knew where I was and what I had to do. I actually enjoyed the planning process."

There are endless permutations for how you arrange your lists. Weekly / daily / monthly / and so forth. Consider your preferred planning format: paper, electronic, or some combination of the two.

THINGS to avoid when making a list

Loads of post-it notes or scraps of paper which are "half lists".

Don't feel that every item is the priority. Struggling to juggle too many priorities means they all have the potential to fall and break!

Some research suggests a daily "To Do" list should be compiled in order of importance. If a new task pops up – schedule it, in relation to its priority, rather than just adding it to the top or bottom.

You could make your "To Do" list in running order sequence. For instance, if you have lectures in the morning and also need to see the university admin office and careers adviser, listing these together will help you execute them as a package since they are all in the same geographic location: on campus. When you go to town, you can clump together the bank, chemist, library and shoe repairer, so they are executed efficiently too.

ESSENTIAL things to do when making a list

A desktop paper pad, large enough to make columns, is a great way to keep a master plan.

Long term	Term	Month	Weekly	TODAY	Notes
Renew passport June 2023	Pay fees first day of each semester	Pay rent – 4th of the month	Wednesday – put money into the shared fund for communal items such as washing up liquid	9am extra seminar Ms Lam 7pm Talk: Darwinian Theory	Dev is away all of March – his friend will be in his room and pay the electric

"Today" elements can be extracted and added to the daily "To Do" list.

Long term planning:

Legal documents: Passports, and other critical legal documents, require renewals. Because these are so infrequent, up to ten years apart, we often don't write them down. Yet they can cause problems if not renewed, and may take time to administer when you may be in a rush. Therefore don't put in your diary the actual expiry date of a passport – enter it for at least six months in advance, so you can start the application for a new one on time. Especially be aware of all expiry dates that incur a penalty if late – such as car insurance or tax returns.

Annual events: Term start and finish dates, along with exam weeks should be marked down far in advance. Even if the exact exam timetable isn't available yet, provisionally block out the window which is likely. You don't want to arrange a weekend away only to discover you need to cancel because of exams.

Medical and dental check-ups: Even though you may not have an appointment yet, make sure you put a reminder in your diary a few weeks before the necessary time, so you can get ahead and make the bookings. Vaccinations are often needed several years apart, so keep track of what you have had, what you still need, and the dates for renewal. Make sure you have allowed plenty of time to get an appointment.

Long term travel arrangements: If you study overseas and have an open-ended ticket, it needs to be scheduled into your planner with enough time to reschedule. It is a frustrating waste if it expires unused. Often, it is economical to book flights a long way ahead. Beware about procrastinating over travel, as it is very expensive to book at the last minute. It will save you a lot of money to commit to dates as early as possible!

Holiday jobs, volunteering, and internships: Next summer seems a long time away – the following summer even longer. But as the expression goes, "The early bird gets the worm." If you want the pick of best opportunities, do your research in advance and add the application due date to your agenda.

Birthdays and special occasions: Whilst the people around you are new friends and will be happy to celebrate special events with you, don't forget to make note of special days for your family and friends back home. Write birthdays in your diary in advance so you have time to post a card, or arrange a phone or video call.

> *"Every year my grandmother remembers my birthday ON my birthday! A card is always dispatched the day afterwards and duly arrives one week late!"*
>
> --Rose M.

When you graduate at the end of your studies, you will want to celebrate! Remember to give your family and friends plenty of warning so they can get organised and attend your graduation too!

Weekly:

It is an effective process to organise a "Weekly Review" at the same time each week. Review what you have done from last week – not forgetting to congratulate yourself on what you HAVE achieved. Praise is good!

> *"Every week I had at least thirty tasks on my "to do" list. By the end of the week, typically I could only cross off about a third of them. Depressingly I had to re-write the others onto the new list. Some tasks hung around for months on end and were re-written every week, causing me so much guilt!"*
>
> --Mohammed K., M.A. Engineering

> *"When I did my weekly "To Do" list, I included generic items like "Chores" or "Clean House". These were so large and vague that they never got done and hung around like a raincloud forever!"*
>
> --Lucy C., Modern Languages

A weekly planner is an excellent tool for your regular events. A time-table which encompasses study commitments, sports, social events is an easy memory aid to be able to decide whether an invitation or other one-off event is a possibility or not.

Include regulars such as:

- ✓ Immoveable events such as lectures and tutor groups
- ✓ Sporting commitments
- ✓ Regular socials – book club, debating society, choir
- ✓ A window for laundry and chores
- ✓ Time to communicate with your family/friends back home

Any gap between what was done last week, and what has not been done yet, needs re-building into the coming week or beyond schedules.

Don't put something non-urgent down for next week, if you KNOW it is not going to get done. Save it for a week when you can reasonably book the time to achieve it. You can use the Eisenhower Matrix to help you plan, prioritise, and schedule.

If you have new assignments or tasks that must be done within this week, book them into the weekly schedule early, whilst you still have big chunks of time available to do them in.

Weekly planner

Week beginning:							
	Monday	Tuesday	Wednesday	Thursday	Friday	Saturday	Sunday
Morning							
Afternoon							
Evening							

Daily tasks

A to-do list is the simplest of aids and will help you identify each item, and create a timeline for getting them done.

It should be easy to create this list, by selecting from the weekly planner the things that need doing TODAY. Add in anything not completed yesterday, IF you deem it needs doing immediately, and if it can be reasonably achieved. If not, schedule it for when you can realistically accomplish it.

Never add an item which you know will not be done today. If you can fit a trip to the post-office on Thursday when you do the weekly shop, add it in the weekly planner for Thursday, NOT the today list on Monday.

Keep in mind the Eisenhower Matrix, correlating urgent and important. For a task that needs time, don't keep putting it off until tomorrow – block out a piece of time to get it done.

Tips

- If you are a more visual learner, sketch out your schedule/to do list, or use colour coding to link subjects or themes.
- Go to sleep knowing you're prepared for tomorrow. Just before bed, consider the next day. From your weekly schedule you can prepare tomorrow's "To Do" list. First thing in the morning, review and check what you have ahead for today.
- Keep a notebook and pen by the bed! If you wake up with a nagging thought or a brainwave – jot it down!

Each task

With the help of your list of PRIORITES, you are now able to slot into the week the things you have to do.

1. Immoveable first – such as lectures, tutorials, team matches and training.

2. Next add the high urgent, important quartile one items, followed by Q2, Q3 and time left over can be the Q4 items - if you are keeping them! If you have several items in any one of the quartiles, which means they have the same importance and urgency, then rank them secondarily, by the time you think they will take to complete. As you plan your weekly schedule you can put time-heavy tasks in first. This way shorter tasks can be slotted in around existing events. You have minimised interruptions, and will be more efficient getting work done.

Each assignment

When you list each assignment, break it up into small units and stages.

If you simply write down, "Essay: 6 Hours", it gives you little information, accuracy, or scope to change or track progress. Goal setting is impossible.

Written like this:

Essay:

✓ Internet search	1.5 hours	
✓ Library documents and note taking	2 hours	(Don't forget travel time)
✓ Sorting notes / planning	30 minutes	
✓ Writing	1 hour	
✓ Review (one day after writing)	1 hour (allow for second review?)	
✓ Wait for email from tutor with answer with feedback to a question asked.	(24 hrs – or more)	
✓ Collating appendices and bibliography	30 mins	
✓ Printing and presentation packaging	30 mins	
✓ Plagiarism check	30 mins	
✓ Submission, cover email / document	30 mins	

Breaking down the process into so many steps has shown that not only does the task actually need more than six hours, but that the project will, by necessity, be spread over a minimum of several days. Useful information! Yet each component part is less daunting than the whole. You can now set realistic short-term goals, one task at time, which guide you throughout your work. Plus, any unseen problems now have time to be accommodated and addressed.

REMEMBER – Cross reference your planning with your optimal performance schedule. In other words, plan to write at your most productive time.

Let's refer back to the story of the rocks, stones, and pebbles.

Rock	Pebble	Sand
Internet search	Sorting notes / planning	Travel time to library
Library documents/note taking	Review	Printing & presentation packaging
Writing	Email exchange with tutor – Q&A	Plagiarism check
	Collating appendices & bibliography	Submission, cover email

"As you plan your list, the more small action points the better. TEN actions points will provide TEN moments of satisfaction, as each one is crossed off!"

-- Mark H., UCL

Top Tip Reminder:

Prioritise your assignments, finding the discipline to avoid just doing your favourite tasks. Start with the hardest and the most time intensive, and work towards the easiest and shortest, tasks you'll still be able to complete when you're fatigued after working hard.

12. STUDY Habits

Keeping ORGANISED saves time, and makes your study periods more effective.

We know how to take notes in class – but it is very important, immediately afterwards, to take the time to review and fill in where you have abbreviated or had to rush. You will have had to write very fast during class, and in the moment, your heavily abbreviated notes made sense. Six months later they may not.

When you revise, a string of unconnected words might not mean anything. If you don't understand your notes or the content, the best time to seek help, whether it be from peers, the lecturer, or online resources, is immediately.

Make your notes visually attractive and themed – these techniques support memory recall in both the short and longer term.

Check list for maintaining your work:

- ✓ Underline headings and subheadings.
- ✓ Use different colour highlighters for different themes.
- ✓ Rewrite any illegible portions.
- ✓ Underline important sentences and paragraphs.
- ✓ Fill in any gaps in your notes.
- ✓ Ensure that you understand all the concepts.
- ✓ Date every piece of paper – even scrap! This way you have a logical progression, which helps during revision.
- ✓ Try working with a wide margin on your page. Repeat key words in the margin to help future sifting for information. You can also use this space to add information as your knowledge base expands through further research.
- ✓ Use mind maps to summarise heaps of information. Several pages can be condensed into a half page diagram linking important information, facts and figures. Use key words in the center and develop your own symbols, abbreviations, and colour codes.

Repeatedly review your study timetable. If an unplanned event wipes out a weekend, this should not be an insurmountable problem. If the weekend had been planned into blocks, then each one can be shifted and reinserted elsewhere over the next week.

This all sounds idealistic. At the beginning of every term we intend to do exactly this. So how come we still have those pressure points and crisis all-nighters propped up with coffee and energy drinks? In the same way that a tidy room helps you focus, by keeping your files (both online and in paper form) organised, you are already ahead.

HOW to Study Effectively for Examinations

Exams should not creep up on you as a surprise! At the very beginning of your course, find out as much as you can about the exams. The most effective exam preparation technique is one that is structured across the entire year, not an all-night cram to catch up a couple of days before the exam. Questions to ask your professors or tutors to seek out from the course syllabus include:

- ✓ When will the exams take place?
- ✓ How many will there be for each module?
- ✓ How long is each exam?
- ✓ What format are the questions? – Essay, short answers, multiple choice, etc.

The more you know about each exam in advance, the easier it becomes to prepare.

"The longest journey starts with a single step."

--Chinese Adage

---

13. FOOD and Eating on the Go

In this section, there are some tips and tricks to plan your food purchases, preparation, and packaging to get the most bang for your buck, your health, and your time!

The process of planning meals need not be complicated or time consuming. Plan your eating week ahead using a simple tool like the one below. It can even be part of your weekly plan.

	Breakfast	Lunch	Snack	Dinner	Shopping
Monday					
Tuesday					
Wednesday					
Thursday					
Friday					
Saturday					
Sunday					

- ✓ Blank out any meals you are going to have away from home (for instance, if you're visiting a friend for dinner, or going out to a restaurant).
- ✓ Identify meals you may also be cooking for other people. You might invite a friend for dinner, or be on a house-share cooking rotation.
- ✓ What is the total number of meals you need to prepare?

Before you plan for the week:

- ✓ Check your fridge and list any leftovers that you need to use up.
- ✓ Itemise items in the cupboard that could be the foundation of a meal like a box of pasta, tin of chickpeas, or bag of rice.

Now the best way forward is to produce a weekly document incorporating a menu plan and a shopping list.

	Breakfast	Lunch	Snack	Dinner	Shopping
Mon	Scrambled Eggs	Couscous lunch box (make it on Sunday night)	Fruit	Fish (perishable item so plan to eat soon after shop) broccoli, sweet potato.	□ Eggs, milk □ Fish, broccoli, red pepper, sweet potato □ Couscous – tomatoes and cucumber □ Canned tuna, apples
Tues	Fruit, nuts and yoghurt	Sandwich (Keep sliced bread in the freezer)	Flapjack	Eat at the pub after rowing.	□ Ham, tomatoes □ Apples, oats, butter, treacle □ Yoghurt, nuts, strawberries
Wed	Toast with peanut butter	Classmates having lunch together in canteen.	Carrots and hummus	Spaghetti bolognaise – My turn to cook. Four people. Side salad	□ Minced beef □ Onion, garlic, tinned tomatoes, wine □ Peanut butter, carrots, tin of chickpeas □ Lettuce, cucumber, tomatoes, avocado radish, spring onion
Thurs	Sausages & eggs, tomatoes	Late breakfast – no need	Peanut butter sandwich	Chicken, mushroom, red pepper, baby sweetcorn stir fry	□ Eggs, sausages, fresh tomatoes, chicken fillet, baby sweetcorn, mushrooms, red pepper, sesame oil □ Rice
Fri	Oatmeal / porridge	Salad	Going to Jen's for tea.	Fried rice – Finish all the left overs in the fridge	□ Oats □ Salad items □ Ham
Sat	Croissant (Lie in - collect from the bakery)	Late breakfast – no need	Baked potato with cheese and chives	Going to Mark's for dinner (Put dried beans to soak for tomorrow)	□ Coffee, baking potato, cheese, chives □ Dried Flageolet beans
Sun	Porridge	Sandwiches for journey en route to match.	Get take-away meal after the match.	Home-made baked beans, fried eggs and toast.	□ Oats □ Canned tomatoes, leeks, eggs, bread
Extras	□ Washing up liquid □ Shampoo, milk, sliced bread for freezer □ Olive oil, bin liners □ Lemons				

Tips for planning and shopping:

Plan meals with perishable items for the days closest to your shop. Towards the end of your week you can have the dried beans and other storeroom ingredients. If you can manage one main shop a week, and then only need to top up with essentials such as milk and fresh fruit, you minimise the time spent in the supermarket.

Keep a sliced loaf in the freezer, then you can eat it slice by slice as you need it. This means you need never run out and always eat fresh bread, avoiding wastage. Slices thaw in minutes.

If you know you have a heavy day, chose a meal that is quick or easy to prepare, or that can be prepared the day before.

Keep a packet of long life milk in your store cupboard – this is a great standby if you run short and don't want a trip to go shopping just for milk.

Make your shopping list based only on the things you are planning to cook. While you are in the supermarket try not to deviate! This minimises your costs and avoids wasted food. **Only buy what is on your list.**

However, there can be some flexibility. For example, of you are planning a beef and vegetable stir-fry and there are no spring onions, a leek can do just as well. If the chicken is on special – go ahead and substitute it for what you had planned and save some pennies. This does NOT mean you can buy a chocolate bar or a discounted bottle of wine instead of oats and beans!

As for the chicken mentioned earlier that was on special: if you have a freezer, consider making extra portions to freeze, which will save you time later in the week.

Don't go to the supermarket to do your weekly shop when you are hungry. You may be tempted to buy items which you don't really want – they bump the budget and could be empty calories.

Organise your shopping list to tie in with the categories in your supermarket. This way, you can be as fast and efficient as possible and not get tempted or distracted.

Dairy & Freezer	Fruit & Veg	Fresh Meat	Long-life grocery items	Cleaning/ healthcare	Drinks/ bottles	Bakery
Eggs Milk Butter Cheese Yoghurt Frozen peas	Broccoli Lemons Red peppers Sweet potato Baking potato Tomatoes x3 Cucumber Onion x2 Chives Apples Garlic Carrots Lettuce Avocado Radish Leek Baby sweetcorn Strawberries	Fish Ham Sausage Minced beef Chicken	Couscous Rice Spaghetti Oats Tins & cans: tuna, tomatoes, chickpeas, treacle, peanut butter, nuts, Flageolet beans Olive oil (L) Sesame oil (S)	Washing up liquid Shampoo Bin liners Paper napkins Toilet rolls	Wine Coffee Tea	Sliced bread

14. PLANNING your Exercise

Some people value and love exercise above all else, others can take it or leave it, maybe depending on how sociable it is; others despise it! The first group doesn't need any advice – apart from not overdoing it at the cost of study! These tips are aimed at the somewhat motivated and reluctant participants. It is very easy to make excuses and allow a busy schedule to push out sporting activities.

Student days present you with a fantastic window to try out new things. Your college or university no doubt has facilities for sports that you haven't tried before – be bold and try new things. Alternatively, the local area where you are based will have additional sports facilities – often at reduced student rates. You will meet new people and perhaps find something that you become passionate about.

✓ Leave things you really don't enjoy and find the things that you do! If you played hockey at school and never liked it – drop it. If you find running repetitive, try something competitive; if football requires too many other people, find a partner and try squash. Give yoga a go!

✓ Be realistic about your level. If you fancy starting a gym workout, don't think you have to lift massive weights and run for an hour, just because the buff person next to you does! Build your level up and feel a sense of achievement as you improve.

✓ Pick activities for your timeframe. Golf takes 4-5 hours plus travel and extras, yet perhaps suitable at the weekend. Choosing skydiving or mountaineering limits you by location; so try all-encompassing and locally available options, with minimum preparation.

✓ Try to avoid sports that need expensive, specialised equipment. Try renting before you buy a big item like a saddle and realise that you are not a natural show-jumper!

✓ High impact sports are an excellent choice – try Tae Kwon Do or other martial arts. Learn to protect yourself as well as getting fit. Once you learn routines you can practice this at home between sessions.

✓ Competitions are a great motivator. Whether you are a beginner, making progress or an expert, there is a competition in your sport, at your level. Entering gives you something to strive towards and validation of your progress.

✓ If you really feel you do not have time for organised sport – think outside the box. ANYTHING is better than NOTHING! A fifteen-minute walk first and last thing in the day is a start; take stairs instead of the lift or escalator. If you walk to the bus stop, make your walk COUNT! Don't saunter, stride! Get off the bus a few stops earlier to lengthen your walk – and maybe save some pennies too!

✓ There are plenty of gadgets or aps that help you measure your exercise. This might start off as a bit of a nag but ends up being a pleasing achievement!

"I received a pedometer for Christmas; I became obsessed with tracking steps. I was so motivated to hit the target that each night I ran up and down the stairs of my four-story hall of residence until I reached it! After eight months, the wristband broke; within a week, I had stopped! I downloaded a free App on my phone, which does the same thing. Now I have increased my target! Sometimes I only need to run up and down a few times – other days it may take forty minutes!"

--Francois L., International Business

Keep moving!

✓ Going on a date? Instead of being sedentary at the cinema and piling up the calories with sugary snacks, try hiking, ice-skating, roller blading or a dance class. Anything that keeps you moving.

✓ Watching TV? During the ads, don't reach for the biscuit tin, try some home-made weights and pump some iron.

✓ Set yourself up with a homemade gym – many items around the house can be incorporated into a workout regime. Empty fabric conditioner bottles are an ideal size for weights – and they are adjustable too! Keep two old ones and fill them with sand, soil or water. Perfect for arm or leg crunches.

✓ There are plenty of exercises you can do whilst still sitting at your desk. Surf the net and try out a few until you find the one for you.

For example, to exercise your shoulders and upper back, sit tall and straight-backed on your chair, putting your feet, ankles and legs together. Engage your abs by squeezing your tummy. Extend your arms at shoulder level out in front of you, keeping your palms down. With a controlled movement, pull your shoulder blades together until they just touch. Gently relax your shoulders. Repeat five times. Keeping your arms out in the same position, rotate your arms to make eight ball-size circles with hands. Repeat the whole process several times.

15. TAKING Time for YOU

Sometimes we are exhausted because we have been working hard. Sometimes we are exhausted because we have been partying hard. The truth is that we tend to cram our timetable with SOMETHING. It is a necessary truth that you need time for relaxation!

Running a hot bath, reading a good book, calling a friend you haven't caught up with for a while, or just doing nothing are essential parts of reenergising, given the full-on timetable you execute. It is similarly important to allow transition time between activities: from the end of lessons to a social night out, or from studying till late, to peacefully sleeping.

Allow time to change gear. Music, deep breathing exercises or simple meditation can make each new mental engagement more productive. For this to happen, time needs to be blocked out on your agenda.

> *"I block out "me time" in the early evening. Even if I know that I'm going to get back online later and work, I realised that I'm a lot more likely to go to the gym, see friends, or cook myself a real dinner if I give myself half an hour "off"."*
>
> -- Dimitri B., Social Anthropology

> *"Even if I'm feeling busy, I remind myself that time away from work and the computer is energising and important. Scheduling downtime requires a combination of time management (deciding when else to get the work done), working ahead when possible (so I have more time later), and keeping a to-do list."*
>
> -- Maxine R., Hospitality Management

PLAN your social time

As with the planning for the rest of your day, week, or term, the key to providing yourself with enough social time is well organised and realistic planning. Whilst study, domestic chores, sporting, and every other aspect of your life is important – so is your social life.

University is often called the "best years of your life" and for many people, this adage is true! Enjoying your social life is all the better when you know that academic and other responsibilities are managed successfully. You need to see your friends and let off steam to maintain your balance and sanity. Don't underestimate it, but balance carefully so you CAN have it all! Your workload will seem manageable if you have something planned to look forward to. Be wary of not overdoing it and compromising the planned commitment for the next morning! If you are invited to a spontaneous social event, think carefully about the impact it will have on important planned activities before agreeing!

ENJOYING a moment each day

Don't think that university life is all about running around trying to cram as many academic things into your life-mix as possible. Be sure to include time every day when you look up from your screen or books and enjoy doing nothing and being at peace in your exciting new surroundings.

> "*I was mesmerised for ten minutes, as I watched two squirrels race around each other. It was a nice thing to do, and time well spent too!*"
>
> --Sophie P., International Finance, France

When you enter the big wide world of post-graduate work, you will look back with nostalgia at the long holidays of your youth! Your year is balanced between study and holiday for a reason. You need life balance. The long spells of holiday are intended for you to garner additional life experiences.

USING my vacation time

Vacation time is not only about holiday. It is also a time to research, review, pre-read about new topics and write your assignments. Planning the vacation time is as important as planning term time. Holidays give you something to work towards and look forward to. Get the work under control so you can manage your holiday, rather than merely spend holiday time being anxious, followed by a mad dash to get things done before term resumes.

> "*For me, travelling is relaxing and mentally enriching. I come back to carry on happier and more focused.*"
>
> --C.M.Lee., Zhejiang University

142

TERM Time

Instead of saving up all the chores for the weekend, get them out of the way as soon as possible so that FREE TIME is exactly that. Remember, that "many hands make light work", so where you can, share tasks and they can even become fun!

If you're feeling exhausted, plan a stay-cation day off. During term time, weekends are equally important for you to find a life balance. Having something to look forward to amongst the seemingly endless grind is highly motivating. Take a coach or train trip, or pool together with friends to hire a car. Going somewhere you have never been can be just the trick to get you back to work with renewed vigour and motivation!

GUILT-FREE enjoyment

If you can plan your timetable as described, using some of the pre-mentioned tools, and if you're truly going to commit to your priorities, as you identified them, then your social time will emerge by itself. Now enjoy it with no feelings of guilt or stress!

16. ADDITIONAL Add-ons for the New, Time-Managed You!

With TIME being finite and our most limiting commodity, figure out where you can overlap; listen to audio podcasts or audio books as you walk or jog; give study a social aspect if you form a group for brainstorming or research sharing. Have a homemade soup simmering away whilst you do the ironing. Some more ideas for streamlining your daily routine include:

- ✓ Get organised as early as possible. Packing your bag the evening before saves a morning rush and the possibility of forgetting something.
- ✓ Keep separate bags for each activity. If you swim once a week and play netball twice a week, keep a separate bag for each activity. Refill each bag immediately when your kit is clean, and then it can be conveniently grabbed on the run.
- ✓ Choose and layout your next day clothes and equipment so that you aren't frantically searching in the morning.
- ✓ Do laundry regularly so that you have clean, dry and where necessary, ironed clothes ready every day. Never leave clean, wet clothes or bed linen lying around – they will smell mouldy and terrible! Don't put your wet towel on your bed either – you will make both smell!

✓ Create an "out the door" mental check-list; wallet and keys, bus pass, library pass, glasses/sunglasses and other last-minute items. Designate a place to keep these together. If you always put them there, they will always be there!

If getting out of bed is your weakness, implement a range of helpful ideas:

✓ Double Alarm – Rather than roll over and go back to sleep, put one alarm next to your bed and a second one, a couple of minutes later across the room. Ensure that the sound of each is loud enough!
✓ Be realistic with your getting ready time budget. If you only need 20 minutes between getting up and going, don't set your alarm for one hour before and keep snoozing! You won't be ready in time if you only give yourself a ten-minute window to get up, get dressed, and have breakfast when in reality, it takes you 20 minutes.
✓ Be realistic with your travel time budget. When estimating the time needed to get to where you are going, don't take a "best case scenario," or even an average time taken. Allow for the worst-case scenario. If the journey takes 15 minutes – have you added on the maximum length of time between buses that you might need to wait? Have you considered the extra traffic during rush-hour? If you have back to back commitments, and you miscalculate each activity by seven to ten minutes, you will be seriously late by the end of the day.
✓ If breakfast really isn't your strong point, pack a snack or meal the night before, to have in your bag for break time. Don't leave yourself starving and at the mercy of the expensive, unhealthy options in a coffee shop.

> "*My mum used to nag and nag me to eat breakfast at 7am before I went off to school. Now I am independent, but I still just can't do it! Since I do always feel hungry around 10:30AM, I found a yummy recipe for healthy oat and protein balls. I make them on a Sunday, pack them in foil and grab a couple every morning to have with my coffee. Now we're both happy!*"
>
> --Caroline V., Singapore University of Technology and Design

Regularly refresh your mind by doing something physical or creative away from your phone or computer screen.

Watch the TV or listen to the radio while you iron. Podcasts or audiobooks can even be work related and help you study or revise! Take time to go for a digital free walk. Try locking up all your gadgets for 24 hours – or a whole weekend. How do you cope? Digital addiction is a widely recognised problem. It isn't only students who suffer; companies are starting to offer professionals "Digital Detox" training. Like all things in our life, we need to accommodate and balance alongside everything else for optimal living.

Making time for family and friends back home.

> "*When my daughter first went to college, she sent me texts and photos every hour. This slowed down after the first trimester and now if she calls – she usually wants something!*"
>
> --Mother of Emily, Brighton, UK

It is typical that you call home when you have a problem. Don't forget, though, that parents delight in your successes and are always thrilled to hear from you. You might have had a "normal" week, but this still contains lots of interest for family and friends back home, because your new "normal" is now different to theirs. Be willing to share. Remember to respect different time zones, and don't wake them up at 3am unless it is an emergency!

Chapter 3: Food Smarts to Thrive not just Survive

by Sheila Partrat,
Contributions from Dr. Jean Francois Lesgards and Denise Fair, Registered Dietitian.

"Connecting the dots between the food industry today, what's on our plate that we can't see, and what our cells need in order to thrive, and not just survive."

> This chapter is about making the connections between:
>
> ❖ The food industry today,
> ❖ What's on our plate that we can't see,
> ❖ And what our cells need in order that we thrive, not just survive.
>
> When we connect the dots, we are better able to navigate restaurants, canteens, grocery stores and kitchens to our advantage, without paying the cost in health and vitality due to less informed decisions.

Food and drink are one of life's many pleasures as well as a basic need. We make choices daily about what and when to eat and drink. Yet how much time and effort go into making these choices? The reality is that these choices will contribute to either feeding our health or even feeding an illness.

The aim of this chapter is to help us make decisions about what we eat and drink from a standpoint of knowledge. It builds skills sequentially, so read or skim, but do it in order.

1. INTRODUCTION

One of the first changes when leaving home, is going from being fed to feeding ourselves. Like it or not, understand it or not, decisions about what, when and how we eat can work for or against us. Add to that a cocktail of heavy studies, social grazing, opportunities for drinking and late-night partying, the link between cause and effect of what we consume and how we feel, are difficult to pinpoint. Nonetheless, our choices will have consequences and we alone have to live with them. They are non-transferrable!

We start with a bit of theory:

- A "bird's eye view" of the food industry, so we get a close up.] of what is on our plates
- Nutrition essentials: What we need to flourish and what happens when we don't get it.
- A look at those "traps" which are easy to fall into and their impact on our wellbeing: too much sugar or salt, or bad fats.

- Our glass: We rethink the drink and look at priorities, including alcohol, so we know our boundaries (because too much fun means the next day isn't!).
- Food and mood, and find tips to support positive stable thoughts.

Then we get practical:

- Tips for optimising balance and portion size, with self-checks for good habits.
- Know-how so we can "play by the food safety rules", because the best foods can harm us if we ignore them.
- A look at labels so we can "read between the lines" of the media and food marketing blurbs.
- Great ideas to feed yourself in a snap. Things to always have at home and easy to make meals.

Food plays a big part in our life journey, however not all food is created equally and some effort has to be put into the quality and quantity of food. The key is to understand basics, as well as to develop good habits. We don't need to analyse everything, rather to understand the basics of balance, which provides a framework for a healthy core diet as well as freedom to indulge.

So, relax, have the occasional cookie, beer or stack of fries. However, strive to consume from a standpoint of knowledge, while being mindful and having fun. In the overall picture, strive for balance in all things, including what you consume.

2. I CHOOSE my Food, then my Choices Define Me. A Closer Look

Leaving home for the first time means the responsibility of feeding yourself rests with you, and you alone. While this may seem exhilarating and freeing, as no one is telling you to "eat your broccoli!" there can be consequences. Getting some insight as to what drives food choices as well as their consequences is valuable.

We have all heard of the "Freshman 15". Weight gain tends to be the first consequence, with minor nutrient deficiencies following over time. This is partly due to the random eating that can happen when dealing with a new environment and schedule, stress, homesickness, as well as the effort necessary to make new social ties. In addition, keeping an "even keel" is even more of a challenge in a society completely saturated with food – it's everywhere. Food has become an "art", a crutch, a social tool, and an emotional outlet.

Keep in mind, however, that our choices, mindful or not, go a long way in defining us. Getting some insight as to what drives them as well as their consequences, is valuable.

WHAT is driving our food choices?

Practically speaking, you and your new roommates or friends will likely have started from a different place and with different habits. If you have lived healthily, your challenge is to keep on eating that way despite the cafeteria, little time (and maybe inclination!) to cook, a tight budget, and a lot of temptation. Alternately, starting university with less than optimum eating habits, students may not know a better way. And feeling homesick can encourage making even less careful choices.

Understanding what is driving our food choices is key to developing a solid nutritional foundation. There is no such thing as a perfect diet but stepping back and looking at what is "making" us eat the way we do, can have positive outcomes.

COMMON factors that influence our eating choices

- ✓ Finances
- ✓ Time
- ✓ Influence of friends and family
- ✓ Education and nutritional understanding
- ✓ Food availability
- ✓ Food tastes
- ✓ Cravings (such as for sugar)
- ✓ Marketing

While these can influence when and how much we eat:

- ✓ Boredom
- ✓ Loneliness
- ✓ Celebration
- ✓ Emotions
- ✓ Avoidance/procrastination

The point here is to start to become aware of what drives our selection of what, when and how much we eat. Awareness is a great start towards vitality.

3. **FROM Factory or Farm to Fork. A Look at Where Our Food Comes From**

This section brings awareness about the food we get today, helping us see what we can't always see in our food on our plates, but what our body has to deal with every single day.

PROGRESS since the 1950's: More diversity and variety

Lucky us! The range and diversity of food that we have today compared to what our parents grew up with is far superior. There are about five times more choices available now than there were in 1975 in a typical North American supermarket. For example:

- Exotic fruits like kiwi, or grains like quinoa were rarely, if ever, available.
- Few knew about gluten, nor did we have the abundant gluten-free choices.
- Milk was mostly cow's milk. There was no "milk section confusion" coming from the choices: soy, rice or oat milk, skim, 1%, 2% or 3.5%.... Milk was simply milk.

Along the way, our tastes and preferences have been scrutinised, broken down into marketable chunks and catered to, making the available choices much larger indeed. This is not necessarily a bad thing, it's just a big change. One

151

brand selling one base product can now segment the market into little chunks. For example, Pepsi-Co's freshly pulped Tropicana juice comes in more than 20 different varieties (pulp, no pulp, half pulp, added vitamin c, added calcium etc) up from just six in 2004. There could be as many as 30 in the next decade. But how did we get here?

Feeding more people, who eat more, AND want it fast!

Consider that the world population has exploded since the 1950's and collectively we eat more. The global average individual daily calorie intake has increased by approximately 25%. How? It is thanks to industrialised farming and the globalisation of the food industry which has ushered in some huge benefits, and yes, a few "trade-offs" as well.

International Data Base
World Population: 1950-2050

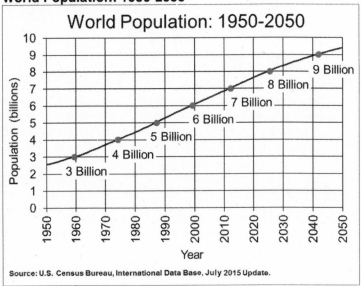

Source: U.S. Census Bureau, International Data Base, July 2015 Update.

Growth in the fast lane: how livestock today is three times the size in half the time.

After World War II, most farms in the industrialised world were diversified. They cultivated a variety of crops, along with breeding livestock. However, the demands on the food system since WWII (due in part to population increase, lifestyle shifts in Europe and North America like two working parents, commuting, busier family schedules) resulted in more industrialisation. Farmers moved away from diverse farming in favour of specialised operations that separated crops from animals.

Today, industrialised crop production is characterised by highly specialised, genetically uniform monocultures (fields planted with a single crop species over a given season, typically over a very large area).

"The beef supply chain meanwhile, is separated into distinct, industries; breeding and birthing calves, raising cattle, growing feed crops, storing and transporting grain, transporting cattle, finishing them in feedlots, slaughtering and processing their meat." [8]

The more specialised production and processing became, the more work became simplified and routine based, allowing for mechanisation of tasks. At the same time, production processes relied increasingly on resources manufactured off the farms, like agricultural chemicals, synthetic fertilizers and chemical pesticides to control crop pests. These eventually found their way to our plates which is the downside of more choice and economies of scale.

According to "Teaching the Food Systems", a project from the "John Hopkins Institute For a Liveable Future" from 1948 to 2008, the use of agricultural chemicals increased more than fivefold. In food animal production, hormones and antibiotics were also introduced to speed the growth of food animals. These new technologies made production more predictable, reliable and repetitive. Specialised facilities, including farms, feedlots, and processing plants, could work together more efficiently by adopting uniform practices and turning out products of uniform size, weight and consistency. Chickens, for example, are now grown to a uniform size so they can be quickly slaughtered, plucked and processed into meat using mechanised assembly lines."

---

[8]   Of. "Teaching the Food System | A Project of The John Hopkins Center for a Liveable Future." *History of Food*, pp. 1–9., www.jhsph.edu/research/centers-and-institutes/teaching-the-food-system/curriculum/_pdf/History_of_Food-Background.pdf.

"Chicken then and now".

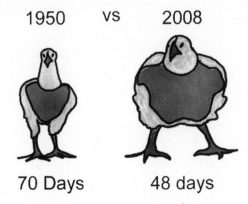

1950   VS   2008

70 Days   48 days

Ever wonder how fast food influences the food industry? Consider: Fast food only started to become an option in the 70's. Epitomised by McDonald's, fast food revolutionised the restaurant industry and changed farming and food distribution businesses from its beginnings in the '50's and '60's. At the time, outlets were scattered few and far between. The trend caught on quickly and spawned a global industry. According to a recent article in the Economist, which just takes into consideration the global expansion of the five largest US fast food chains (McDonalds, Starbucks, Subway, KFC and Pizza Hut), claims that there are now over 138,000 US fast food outlets globally.[9]

9   "Fast Food Nations." *The Economist*, 2015, www.economist.com/fastfood. Accessed 29 Nov. 2015.

A few of the hidden consequences

The industrialisation of the food system has been successful in offering consumers more choice, meeting the increasing demands while minimising labour, and often passing on the cost savings to consumers. However, it's good to keep in mind some of the consequences.

There has been an increase in substances in our foods that don't always contribute to health. Take an example of a typical plate of food.

A typical dish then and now

1950's	+2015 (assuming non-organic)
Smaller piece, limited antibiotics and growth hormone	Chicken likely with some growth hormones and anti-biotics
Tomato sauce with sugar and salt	Tomato sauce with High Fructose Corn Syrup
The vegetables will be more nutrient dense	Broccoli and potatoes will be less nutrient dense, due to industrialisation of crops

What synthetic substances can we find in our food?

Some of them can be found on the food label: *(See "Reading a label" in "Getting Practical" page 199)*

- **Fortification:** This is a good thing. Manufacturers will often add back vitamins and minerals sometimes lost during processing.
- **Added sugars:** Those which have been taken out of their original foods and added into a new food as a preservative or flavouring. Sugar in excess has a massive impact on our bodies. And it's hard to avoid, because it is everywhere.
- **Additives (food colouring, preservatives, stabilizers)** These are denoted by E-numbers, which are numbered for standardisation.

But you won't see these on the food label:

- **Pesticides on fruits and vegetables:** It's often the combination of the types of pesticides that can be damaging to health. Some produce will be exposed to over 20 types of pesticides, while others are less exposed.
- **Industrialised livestock production (meat, poultry and fish):** The conditions in which animals are raised has a significant impact on meat quality. Keep in mind that what they eat, we eat. Industrially raised animals and fish likely consume antibiotics and possibly growth hormones. Being aware of this allows us to do something about it.

4. **NUTRITION Essentials: Knowing What Will Help Us Thrive Not Just Survive**

What are macronutrients, micronutrients, and calories? What are nutrient dense foods? Why they are key to looking and feeling our best? Lastly, what are the tell tale signs when we may not be getting what we need?

NUTRITION vs. Food

How do we categorise food? What matters most? Calories? Nutrients? Fat content? While many people focus on calories, they are only PART of the equation. Calories are essential and a main reason why we eat, but we can't forget about the nutrients that food has.

To help you keep the lingo straight:

- "Substances we get from food, used by our bodies to promote growth, maintenance, and repair of tissues" → **NUTRIENTS**
- "An energy-producing potential needed to raise the temperature of one gram of water by one degree" → **CALORIE**

The food we eat supplies both calories (energy) and nutrients. All calories come from only three types of macronutrients: carbohydrates, fats, and proteins. Nutrient density refers to the amount of vitamins, minerals and trace elements that are present in foods.

OUR Three Macronutrients: Protein, Carbohydrates and Fat

ALL NUTRIENTS COME FROM FOOD, BUT NOT ALL FOODS ARE NUTRITIOUS!

Macronutrients are the structural and energy-giving caloric components of our foods. There are three types.

→ **Type 1: Protein:** far more important than commonly understood

Protein is one of the biggest contributors when it comes to making and using our bodies. It is involved in the structural part of our bodies – being the foundation of bone, muscle, organs, tissues, hair and nails. Protein is also essential for the functional part of our bodies in that it is used to make our enzymes and hormones. It is also responsible for overall body maintenance, tissue repair and growth.

Proteins are far more important to us than are commonly understood. They are found virtually everywhere in the body, and are not just needed for muscle growth. Because our bodies cannot stock the amino acids, unlike carbohydrates and fat which can both be stored as fat, we need to replenish our supply of protein every day. Most experts agree that we need approximately one gram of protein per kilo of body weight per day.

Our two main protein sources: animal and vegetable

Animal protein sources	Vegetable protein sources
Meats (beef, chicken, lamb, pork, venison, bison etc.), Fish, shellfish, Eggs Dairy products such as milk, cheese, yogurt and dairy derived protein powders like whey and casein	Soy milk and yogurt Other milk alternatives (almond, rice, hemp milks) Quinoa, corn - most grains have a small amount of protein. Hummus, chick peas and falafels Peanut butter or other nut butters Raw nuts and seeds Black, navy, red, cannelloni and butter beans, black eye peas Lentils and pulses (red, black or green lentils, split peas etc.) tofu, edamame and other soy products, vegetable textured products, vegetable-based protein powder

How do animal and vegetable sources differ?

The key difference is in their amino acid profiles, the building blocks of proteins, and the rate at which our bodies can absorb and put them to use.

Because animal protein is more similar to protein found in the human body, it tends to be used up more rapidly than those found in plants. It's also easier to reach our broadly recommended daily intake (one gram per kilogram of body weight) with protein rich food. Animal sources contain two to ten times more protein than vegetable and cereal sources.

Ultimately, it's ideal to mix both sources.

How do we distinguish the quality of protein?

✓ **How many essential amino acids does the food contain?** Our bodies need 20 different amino acids to build and repair muscle, bones, tissues and drive enzymes and hormones. We can make most amino acids we need out of using what we eat except for a few known as the essential amino acids. These MUST come from food. The first determinant of protein quality is the amount of each of these eight essential amino acids consumed, which varies widely. On the whole, animal protein sources will have a better quantity of each of the eight essential acids. Vegetable proteins will have less of one or the other.

✓ **How easily can our body absorb the protein?** If we cannot digest, absorb and utilise the amino acids in the proteins, then they are useless. Typically vegetable proteins are not as easy to absorb. Many plant-based proteins are not absorbed well by the human gut, whether cooked or raw, because of substances such as phytic acid. These 'anti-nutrients' are commonly found in grains, beans, seeds and nuts, and have been shown to block nutrient absorption.

✓ **What is the quality of fats that are associated with our proteins?** Fats can either save or harm you. As fats often "come along for the ride" in protein, it is best to become aware of the quality of fats that are associated with our proteins. Bad fats **come from** fried foods, processed meats, skin and fat of non-organic meat and poultry. Good fats come from wild fish & eggs. More on this later!

✓ **What else comes in the protein package?** We eat what our animal source of protein have eaten. We are also affected by what is in the soil in which our vegetable proteins grew. Keep in mind what we are exposed to, through the way the animal or food was raised or grown: pesticides, growth hormones, genetically modified animal feed, antibiotics, or added sodium, food colourings, preservatives, trans fats...

Amount of Protein per:

100g Lean Chicken   1 Large Egg   25g Cheese   50g Cooked Lentils   100g Grilled Salmon

28g   6g   7g   8g   22g

Top Tips for Meat and Seafood Eaters:

- ✓ Meats should be the size of a palm of your hand – no bigger.
- ✓ Choose lean meats – chicken breast with no skin, fish and beef.
- ✓ Skip the deep-fried meats. Try broiled, braised, roasted or grilled meats.
- ✓ Limit cold cuts to lean turkey, chicken or ham – avoid salami, pepperoni and limit Parma or other cured hams.
- ✓ Eggs should be boiled, poached or scrambled, limit frying.
- ✓ Try to eat protein at every meal.
- ✓ Limit farmed salmon to once per week and try to have fish or seafood at least twice per week.

Top tips for Vegetarians

In vegetable protein, generally one or two of the Essential Amino Acids will be low. We can optimise the quality of our protein intake by combining two vegetable proteins that are "complementary" to each other. A protein pairing is complementary when they are combined, they provide sufficient total protein and enough of each essential amino acid.

To optimise the quality of the vegetable protein, try mixing & matching. Vegetable proteins are inexpensive and good quality if they are combined, as they are often "clean" with good fat profiles.

Mix any of these legumes or nuts:

- ✓ Any type of bean (black, kidney, white)
- ✓ Lentil
- ✓ Nut or nut butter like pistachios, peanuts, almonds

With any of these grains:

- ✓ Whole wheat
- ✓ Brown rice
- ✓ Corn

Type 2: Carbohydrates – getting the right fuel

Carbohydrates are our main source of fuel and provide our cells with energy. It's a very diverse group, which goes way beyond the basic list of fruits, pasta, and bread. We find carbohydrates in:

- ✓ Dairy products
- ✓ Fruits
- ✓ Vegetables
- ✓ Seeds
- ✓ Legumes
- ✓ Cakes, cookies, cereals, canned drinks

Carbohydrates have been getting "a bad rap" over the past few years. Most of us will have heard that eating complex carbs is better than eating simple carbs, but food labels don't always help us distinguish between the two. The key is getting a better understanding of how carbs are classified and how they work in our bodies, so that we can tell the difference and make better choices, rather than avoiding them altogether.

Carbs are made up of fibre, starch and sugars. Fibre and starch are complex carbs, while sugars are simple carbs. **Sugars** are short chains of one on or two of the basic simple sugar molecules: glucose, galactose or fructose making them quick and easy to break down and digest thus increasing blood insulin levels. **Complex carbohydrates** like starch and fibre are longer and more complicated chains, taking longer to break down and digest and do not impact our insulin level as dramatically. This rate of absorption has a major impact on how our bodies processes carbohydrates. The key takeaway is that the nutritional quality of a food and how it will function in the body will depend on how much fibre, starch and sugar it has in it.

Avoid or embrace carbs? Start with this classification:

COMPLEX CARBS

High in Fiber
Metabolism Booster
Feel Fuller, Longer

FOOD EXAMPLES

Whole Grain Bread
Brown Rice
Quinoa
Beans
Nuts/Seeds
Oatmeal
Fruits
Sweet Potato
Vegetables

SIMPLE CARBS

Low in Fiber/Nutrients
Empty Cals Turn to Fat
Feel Tired

FOOD EXAMPLES

White Bread
Sugar, Brown/White
Fruit Juices
White Rice
Muffins
Candy
Cookies
Pretzels/Chips
Sugary Cereals

How Carbs affect our Body: the Glycemic Index of foods

The Glycemic Index ranks foods from 0–100 according to the speed at which they impact blood sugar levels in the two or three hours after eating.

High GI (70-100): Carbohydrates, which break down quickly during digestion, releasing blood sugar rapidly into the bloodstream – causing marked fluctuations in blood sugar levels.

Medium GI (56-69): Carbohydrates, which break down moderately during digestion, releasing blood sugar moderately into the bloodstream.

Low GI (0-55): Carbohydrates which break down slowly during digestion, releasing blood sugar gradually into the bloodstream – keeping blood sugar levels steady. These are often our nutrient dense foods, with unrefined carbohydrates, low fat, high naturally occurring dietary fibre, vitamins and minerals.

The Glycemic Index is one tool amongst a few to improve your control. When referring to any GI Food List, remember that the numbers aren't absolute and should serve as a guide only. The impact on blood sugar will be influenced by other factors including factors such as the ripeness of the fruit, cooking time, product brand, fibre and fat content, time of day.

GLYCEMIC INDEX CHART
Low Glycemic (55 or aBelow) High Glycemic (70 or Higher)

SNACKS	G.I.	STARCH	G.I.	VEGETABLES	G.I.	FRUITS	G.I.	DAIRY	G.I.
Pizza	33	Bagel, Plain	33	Broccoli	10	Cherries	22	Yogurt, Plain	14
Chocolate Bar	49	White Rice	38	Pepper	10	Apple	38	Yogurt, Low Fat	14
Pound Cake	54	White Spaghetti	38	Lettuce	10	Orange	43	Whole Milk	30
Popcorn	55	Sweet Potato	44	Mushroons	10	Grapes	46	Soy Milk	31
Energy Bar	58	White Bread	49	Onions	10	Kiwi	52	Skim Milk	32
Soda	72	Brown Rice	55	Green Peas	48	Banana	56	Chocolate Milk	35
Doughnut	76	Pancakes	67	Carrots	49	Pineapple	66	Yogurt, Fruit	36
Jelly Beans	80	Wheat Bread	80	Beets	64	Watermelon	72	Custard	43
Pretzels	83	Baked Potato	85	Peas	22	Dates	103	Ice Cream	60

Lowering the Glycemic Index of your meals and diet will help stabilise your blood glucose and insulin levels. Check out the difference between the sugar rollercoaster and the whole food glide.

The sugar rollercoaster vs The whole food glide

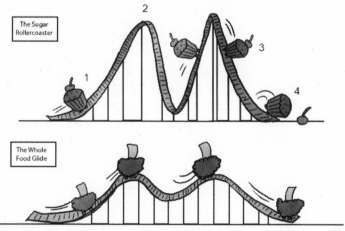

Eating sugar can take you up and down again quickly, heightening your cravings and exacerbating other issues like weight gain, fatigue, irritability, and hormonal imbalance. Over the long-term sugar wrecks havoc on your immune system, and overall health.

Sugar roller coaster:	Whole food glide
Increased blood sugar, energy, and euphoric mood	Sustained long term energy
Insulin spike	
Blood sugar falls	
Hitting the bottom: fatigue, mental fogginess, and more sugar cravings, eat sugar and up we go again!	
Long term effects: weight gain, increased risk of hormonal imbalance insulin resistance and other inflammatory diseases	

By lowering the glycemic index of your meals and diet, this will help stabilise your blood glucose and insulin levels.

Tips to lower the effect of glucose on your blood glucose levels (ultimately shrinking your waistline!)

- ✓ **Eat Low Glycemic Index Foods:** These are the foods high in fibre such as whole-wheat cereals and grains, lentils, beans and peas, fruits and vegetables. Choose brown or fibre rich bread and rice over white or refined bread rice and pasta. Avoid highly processed foods and simple sugars (candy, chocolate). For a sweetener, choose small quantities of natural honey, molasses, or raw sugar.
- ✓ Mixing carbohydrates (starches) with a protein source also lowers the glycemic index of a meal. Eat a starch or a fruit with a dairy (milk or yogurt), protein source, (meat, beans, eggs) or fat (nuts/olives).
- ✓ **Timing**: Make sure you eat every three to four hours. Never skip meals, and always have breakfast.
- ✓ **Exercise**: Following a big meal, even just a slow walk will help reduce glucose levels quickly.

Top tips for eating carbs:

- ✓ **Limit starches** (rice, pasta, bread, bagels) to no more than the size of your fist at each meal. This generally is no more than one cup.
- ✓ **Limit processed foods** such as store-bought cookies, crackers, crisps, candy, sweets, cakes, and other desserts.
- ✓ **Limit simple sugars** such as honey, raw sugar, molasses, brown sugar, maple syrup, candy, and other sweets. These rapidly increase your blood sugar and cause insulin levels to spike.
- ✓ **Nutritious carbohydrates and how to eat them:**
  - o Eating pasta? Choose whole wheat if possible and serve it al dente!
  - o Think of whole foods like potatoes, sweet potatoes, yams, squash, and pumpkin which are all good choices.
  - o Choose brown, red, or basmati rice over white rice.
  - o Limit bread consumption to one or two slices. The darker the bread, the better!
  - o Avoid Asian noodles (AKA ramen) as they are just oil and flour!
  - o If you are looking for a snack bar, choose ones with protein, low amounts of sugar and no hydrogenated oils.
  - o Try other grains like quinoa, barley, buckwheat noodles.
  - o Have whole wheat, high bran cereals with fruit or yogurt. Choose muesli with no added sugar over granola!

Type 3: Oils and Fats: they can either heal or harm – getting it right

In the words of Dr. Robert Lustig, Paediatric Endocrinologist "some fats will save you, some fats will kill you. On one end of the spectrum we have fats that are essential to life and can only be found in food, while on the other end, we have "trans fats", mostly found in processed foods which are used to increase shelf life"[10]. Our body is not equipped to break down trans fats so they just accumulate. Fats either do a lot of good, or are damaging.

Fats and oils form the basis of skin and cell membranes and create cell boundaries. They provide necessary energy, help absorb our fat-soluble vitamins A, D, E and K and are needed structurally throughout the body. In addition, we use fat as a temporary storage of fuel and we all require a thin layer to help maintain body

---

[10] Lustig, Robert H. *Sugar Has 56 Names, a Shoppers Guide*. Hudson Street Press, Published by the Penguin group A Kindle Publication, 2013.

temperature. Thus, the quality of the fats directly impacts the quality of our skin and cell membranes. If the membranes are not solid enough, toxins can pass through the barrier more easily.

❖ **Generally Good:** Unsaturated fats, which are liquid at room temperature. These are considered beneficial and are mostly found in foods from plants and fish**: nuts, seeds like pumpkin and sesame, olive oil, avocados, and (wild) oily fish. This is where we find Omega 3 and 6's.**

  o Essential fatty acids Omega 3 and omega 6, can only come from food. Omega 3 is anti-inflammatory. It is needed for growth, development and proper brain function and can be found in great amounts in wild fatty fish, walnuts and flaxseeds. Omega 6 sources: corn, soybean, safflower, and sunflower.

  o The ratio for Omega 6 to 3 is an important health fact to keep in mind. The ratio 4:1 of omega 6 to omega 3 fatty acids is generally considered optimum. In Western countries however, the ratio ranges from 10:1 to 25:1 in favour of Omega-6. This is because of the wider use of oils containing omega 6 in our industrial food supply chain. We are getting way too much Omega 6 relative to Omega 3. To keep the ratio in balance, consider reducing the Omega 6 rich foods while increasing the supply of foods rich in Omega 3. Your brain will thank you.

❖ **Generally bad:** Saturated fats, which are mostly solid at room temperature. They are found in animal products such as butter, cheese, whole milk, ice cream, cream, fatty meats, tropical plants and vegetable oils such as coconut, palm and palm kernel. Saturated fats have had some bad press in the past, associating them with heart disease. That literature has been revised recently, shifting the blame onto sugar!

  o A word about good quality coconut oil, which is saturated. It's tasty, and healthy. So even if it is on the "generally to restrict", it's by far the best of the lot. It's versatile and has many health and beauty uses at home. It has anti-viral properties, is easily digested, so puts little strain on your digestive system, stimulates metabolism supporting weight loss (if needed), and provides rapid energy WITHOUT causing an insulin spike.

❖ **To avoid: trans fats.** Oils that have been processed to make them more stable through hydrogenation. Referred to as partially hydrogenated oils, and commonly found in cookies, biscuits, margarines, baked goods, and microwave popcorn, we want to avoid these totally!

All fats are not created equal

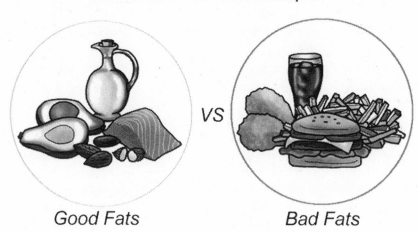

Good Fats   VS   Bad Fats

Tips for cooking with and eating fats:

✓ Use olive oils, sesame and nut oils at low temperatures and high quality canola, coconut and sunflower oil for cooking.
✓ Use small amounts of butter.
✓ Add nuts, seeds and avocado to your snacks and salads.
✓ Forget "low fat" products as the fat is often replaced with sugar.
✓ Avoid trans fats "like the plague"!
✓ Choose liquid oils that come from nuts, seeds, and fish as opposed to saturated fats, which are generally hard at room temperature. Forget fried food!

The Cheat Sheet to Macronutrient Essentials

Carbohydrates	Protein	Fats
1 gr = 4 calories	1 gr = 4 calories	1 gr = 9 calories
3 types of carbs	2 types of protein	3 categories of fats
Sugars: Found naturally in fruit, vegetables and milk. Added to many processed foods. **Starch:** Found in breads, cereals, rice, potatoes etc. **Fibres:** Indigestible parts of plants found in grains are either soluble or insoluble. Fibre is unavailable for energy because it can't be broken down. Fibre is helpful in many other ways.	Think of protein as a collection of 20 piles of Lego called amino acids, all necessary every day. Our body can make the most of what we need out of what we eat, but eight of these we only get from food. Proteins will come from **animal** (meat, dairy, fish and eggs) and **vegetable** sources (beans, lentils and tofu). The quality of protein depends on the proportion and quantity of the different essential amino acids. How easily our bodies can use them depends on how "clean" the protein is. (Avoid additives, growth hormones etc.)	**Unsaturated fats:** Liquid at room temperature. Includes veggies, nuts, seeds and wild fatty fish. Omega 3 and 6 found here. **Saturated fats:** Mostly solid at room temp. Animal origin (butter, cheese, whole milk, ice cream, cream and fatty meats) plus tropical plants and vegetable oils such as coconut and palm. **Trans fats:** Manufactured trans fats are VERY HARMFUL. Identified on food labels as "partially hydrogenated" oils. Our bodies cannot use them for energy, so they just line our arteries and livers.

What do they do for me?	What do they do for me?	What do good fats do for me?
Starch & Sugars: Provide energy. They are converted to simple sugars (mainly glucose). Glucose prompts the release of hormone insulin which circulates and gets our cells ready to take it in. (Every cell in our body runs on glucose). **Fibres:** Can be **soluble** (Dissolves to form a gel. Helps lower blood cholesterol and glucose levels. Sources: oats, peas, beans, apples, citrus fruits, carrots, barley) or **insoluble** (Promotes the movement of material through the digestive system. Increases stool bulk. Sources: Whole-wheat flour, wheat bran, nuts, beans, vegetables, such as cauliflower, green beans, potatoes)	The primary function is for growth, body repair, production of hormones and enzymes, which help to control different body functions. The secondary function: an alternate energy source if we don't consume enough carbs and fats. They also keep us well (antibody production); play a role in the thousands of chemical reactions that happen in cells; transmit signals to coordinate biological processes; and provide structure and support for cells. On a larger scale, they also allow the body to move. ***How much do I need?*** National guidelines vary, but a safe bet is to aim for 1 gr. per kg. of body weight. Elderly or sporty individuals can go up to 1.5 grams/kg of body weight. If there are known kidney issues, then reduce intake.	Taste-carriers for flavour and "mouth feel" Brain function (Approx. 60% of our brain is made of fat!) Energy source (When calories from carbs are used up, after the first 20 minutes of exercise or so, we begin to depend on fat for fuel) Support healthy skin and hair Help the body absorb and move vitamins A, D, E, and K through the bloodstream Insulation from shock and cold

MICRONUTRIENTS: Where they hide and what they do for me

Micronutrients are the vitamins and minerals that come along with the macronutrients and are essential for good health. We want to make sure that our macronutrients are packed with micronutrients.

Micronutrients are essential for every process that happens in our body. Every system requires some vitamins and minerals in order for it to work properly and keep us in good health. Some examples include B vitamins, which are needed for proper brain function; iron, which is essential in oxygen transport within the blood system; and vitamin C, Zinc, vitamin A, and copper, which are all required for wounds to heal. A complete list of these vitamins and minerals and their roles can be found in the appendix.

While vitamins and minerals are found in most foods, including meat and milk, they are concentrated in fruits and vegetables. The vitamins and minerals are what give fruits and vegetables their bright colours. Polyphenols are present in leaf vegetables (cabbage, spinach, leeks, lettuce, parsley), in tubers (onions, garlic) and fruit (blackberries, blueberries, cherries, plums, apricots, apples) along with in beverages (fruit juice, cider, wine, tea). They contribute to flavour and nutritional quality. [11]

We consider a food nutrient dense when it is relatively rich in nutrients for the number of calories contained. For example, a sweet potato is a nutrient-dense carbohydrate.

Are we getting enough micronutrients? That question is best answered looking at our own plate. Statistics suggest however, like the table below, that it's not always the case.

---

[11]   Manach, C., Scalbert, A., Morand, C., & Rémésy, A. C. (2004, May 01). The American Journal of Clinical Nutrition, Polyphenols: Food sources and bioavailability. Retrieved from http://ajcn.nutrition.org/content/79/5/727.full

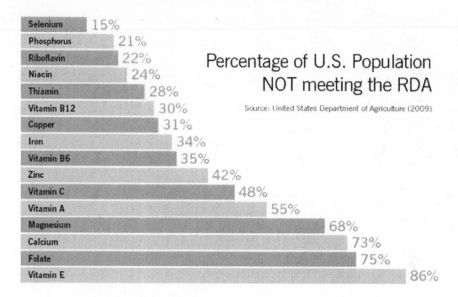

Selenium	15%
Phosphorus	21%
Riboflavin	22%
Niacin	24%
Thiamin	28%
Vitamin B12	30%
Copper	31%
Iron	34%
Vitamin B6	35%
Zinc	42%
Vitamin C	48%
Vitamin A	55%
Magnesium	68%
Calcium	73%
Folate	75%
Vitamin E	86%

Percentage of U.S. Population NOT meeting the RDA

Source: United States Department of Agriculture (2009)

Tips for improving our intake of micronutrients:

✓ Aim for three servings of veggies and two servings of fruit per day, which are full of micronutrients. You can often pick up washed, ready-to-eat fruits and vegetables at your local grocery store. Buy frozen fruits and vegetables as they are cheaper and are usually more nutrient dense as they are picked when ripe and flash frozen.
✓ Try to eat every colour of the rainbow in a day!
✓ Make sure your plate is half vegetables at meal times. Start adding vegetables to dishes: soups, stews, rice, noodles, and sauces. Remember to eat vegetables when eating out. Add a salad to your pizza or burger.
✓ Juices don't count for your fruit allotment. They are too high in sugar, even 100% natural juices!

Micronutrient Cheat Sheet: Food Sources & Signs of Deficiency [12]

Water soluble vitamins, used in small amounts by cells when needed. Whatever is not needed ends up in the toilet water

B1 Thiamine Signs we may lack: Food sources:	For energy, brain function and digestion. Possibly tender muscles, prickly legs, constipation, tingling hands, rapid heartbeat Mushrooms, asparagus, peas, cauliflower, Brussels sprouts, beans, mackerel and milk
B2 Riboflavin Signs we may lack: Food sources:	Helps turn fat, sugars and protein into energy. For healthy skin, hair nails and eyes Linked to burning or sensitive eyes, dull or oily hair, eczema, split nails, cracked lips Mushrooms, broccoli, wheat-germ, mackerel, fish, milk
B3 Niacin Signs we may lack: Food sources:	For energy, brain function, skin and digestion. Helps balance blood sugar and lower cholesterol Linked to low energy, diarrhoea, insomnia, migraines, poor memory, mood issues, acne or eczema Mushrooms, asparagus, whole wheat, tomatoes, tuna, chicken, salmon, lamb, mackerel, turkey
B5 Pantothenic Acid Signs we may lack: Food sources:	For energy production, fat metabolism, anti-stress hormone, healthy hair and skin Linked to muscle cramps, apathy, poor concentration, burning feet, exhaustion after light exercise and teeth grinding Mushrooms, broccoli, peas, lentils, tomatoes, cabbage, celery, strawberries, avocados, whole wheat and eggs
B6 Signs we may lack: Food sources:	Used in protein digestion, brain function and hormone production. Helps balance sex hormones Infrequent dream recall, water retention, tingling hands, mood issues, muscle tremors or cramps Cauliflower, cabbage, peppers, bananas, squash, broccoli, lentils, red kidney beans

---

[12] Holford, Patrick. *Patrick Holford's The New Optimum Nutrition Bible*. Piatkus, 2004. Source for: Micronutrient cheat sheet: food sources and signs of deficiency table

B12 Signs we may lack: Food sources:	Helps utilise proteins; for nerves and memory. Helps deal with tobacco and other toxins Poor hair condition, eczema, anxiety, lack of energy, constipation, sore muscles Oysters, sardines, tuna, lamb, eggs, shrimp, cheese, turkey and chicken
Folic acid Signs we may lack: Food sources:	For brain and nerve function. For utilising protein and red blood cell formation Anaemia, eczema, premature grey hair, mood, cracked lips, lack of energy and appetite Wheat germ, spinach, peanuts, sesame seeds, hazelnuts, broccoli, cauliflower, walnuts, avocado
Biotin Signs we may lack: Food sources:	Helps body use essential fats, supports healthy skin, hair and nerves Dry skin, poor hair condition, premature grey hair, sore muscles, poor appetite Wheat germ, spinach, peanuts, sesame seeds, hazelnuts, broccoli, cauliflower, walnuts, avocado, oysters, herrings, milk, eggs
Vitamin C Signs we may lack: Food sources:	Strengthens immune system, fights infection, and makes collagen for bones, skin and joints. Anti-oxidant for detoxifying Helps make anti-stress hormones and turn food into energy Frequent colds and infections, lack of energy, slow wound healing, tender gums, red pimples on skin Peppers, watercress, cabbage, broccoli, cauliflower, strawberries, citrus fruits
Fat soluble vitamins: stored in body fat (for as long as 6 months) until they are needed	
Vitamin D Signs we may lack: Food sources	Vitamin D: It maintains healthy bones by keeping in calcium Possible joint pain or stiffness, backache, tooth decay muscle cramps and hair loss Sweet potatoes, wheat germ, tuna, sardines, salmon, sunflower and sesame seeds, unrefined corn oil
Vitamin A Signs we may lack: Food sources	For healthy skin, protection against infections, immune system booster. For night vision Possible mouth ulcers, poor night vision, acne, frequent colds, dry skin, diarrhoea Carrots, watercress, cabbage, squash, sweet potatoes, melon, pumpkin, liver

Vitamin E Signs we may lack: Food sources	Protects our cells. Also an anti-oxidant, helps us use oxygen, improves wound healing, fertility and is great for skin
	Lack of sex drive, exhaustion after light exercise, easy bruising, slow wound healing and varicose veins
	Sweet potatoes, tuna, salmon, unrefined corn oil, sunflower seeds, sesame seeds

Minerals and trace elements required in small amounts. Minerals tend to be required in milligram (mg), trace elements in much smaller amounts - microgram (µg) quantities. Some are found only in a few foods, so it's important to vary the intake. Main minerals include: Calcium, Chloride, Fluoride, Iron, Magnesium, Phosphorus, Potassium, Sodium, Zinc. **Trace elements**: Copper, Chromium, Iodine, Manganese, Molybdenum, Selenium

5. SIMPLIFY Life with the "80% Nutrient Dense, 20% Relax" Rule

We all know that life isn't textbook perfect and that there is no such thing as a perfect diet. There has to be room for flexibility. That's the beauty of an 80/20 rule. A beer and pizza night with your university club; a caramel mocha latte during a coffee date with a friend; or a delectable chocolate candy bar during stressful exam revision, are all instances of "treats" that can be part of your diet, just not a majority of it.

A good rule of thumb is to consume 80% "nutrient dense" food, keeping 20% for the empty or "ugly" foods/drinks, like the occasional splurge on processed or fast food meal.

Three steps to keep in mind during a relaxed and budget friendly trip to the supermarket:

Learn to evaluate food/drinks by placing them in one of three groups

- ✓ **Real and nutrient dense:** These are most "real foods" that undergo little or no processing. Foods that look like they came from the farm.
- ✓ **Moderate:** These are in between foods that have had some processing but still retain some health benefits. Think of it like a scale between the nutrient dense/clean and the ugly foods. Pasta, homemade cookies, refined oatmeal, or white rice.
- ✓ **Ugly or harmful:** Highly processed foods with added fat, sugar and salt. High or low in calories, they take away from health. Fast food burgers or a pile of sweets.

Then get the priorities in order:

✓ Aim to make 80% of what we eat come mostly from the "nutrient dense" pile with some moderate or in between foods.
✓ Restrict the "ugly category" to about 20%. This is the splurge on processed or junk foods, or the overly sweet treat that we just have to have. No big deal once in a while!

Finally, observe and adjust.

We learn a lot when we tune in to what our bodies are saying. After all, when we eat, we are either filling our bodies up with healthy fuel, or feeding our bodies garbage that will make us feel terrible in the long term!

Top tips to make the 80/20 rule work for you:

80% nutrient dense 20% go easy

✓ Saturday night is party night? Eat / drink wisely during the week, then Saturday you don't need to think about it so much!
✓ Dinner is your thing? So you eat wisely during the week and splurge a bit for dinner from Thursday through Saturday evening.
✓ In exams? It's not the time to forget about eating correctly. You'll pay the price in energy and focus.

6. **THREE Common Traps: Food with Added Sugar, Extra Salt and Bad Fats**

While it is fairly easy to sort out which foods would be listed as unhealthy, there might be a number that would surprise you. The foods in the 20% bucket are going to be mostly processed, but how do you distinguish them?

✓ Long list of ingredients, of which some can be questionable
✓ Contains added sugar (as opposed to the natural sugars in fruit or glass of milk)
✓ Often high on bad fats (trans fats or partially hydrogenated oils)
✓ Added salt
✓ Presence of food colourings

Let's take a closer look at why we want to limit sugar, bad fats, and salts to the 20% bucket. Then, in "Getting Practical", we'll build up the 80% bucket with great budget friendly foods.

SUGAR, the "Cereal Killer".

Sugar, the "Cereal Killer". It's everywhere!

For decades now, the damaging impact of sugar on health has been underemphasised. In contrast, the harmful impact of cholesterol and fat has been pointed out excessively. Since the 1950's, the Sugar Research Foundation (SRF) has paid millions of US dollars to "dish out" questionable information based on questionable studies. This has been exposed recently in the famous JAMA (Journal of American Medical Association) and was subsequently featured in the New York Times Newspaper in the article "How the Sugar Industry Shifted Blame to Fat".[13]

But we probably didn't need a newspaper to shine a light on our own reality. Most of us are aware of the damaging impact of sugar. Physiology often drives behaviour, most know this intuitively as most will have experienced unreasonable cravings. Sugar is hard to avoid and consuming sugar drives the consumption of sugar.

According to Dr. Lustig, American paediatric endocrinologist at the University of California and author of *"Fat Chance, The Bitter Truth About Sugar"*, as well as the YouTube video *"Sugar: the Bitter Truth"*, which went viral with over five million views, "The negative effects of sugar on our bodies are staggering. Sugar alters our hormones so we don't register hunger the way we normally would, making us eat more and it affects our liver in the same way that alcohol does". [14]

Worldwide, we overload on sugar, and the industry supports it. It is produced in 113 countries and is often supported by subsidies. Consumption has unsurprisingly tripled in the past 50 years while world population has slightly more than doubled.

Currently the global daily average sugar consumption ranges between 50 and 125 grams per day, between two and five times the World Health Organisation recommended daily intake. See the chart below for examples on a national level of daily sugar consumption.

---

[13]   O'Connor, Anahad. *How the Sugar Industry Shifted Blame to Fat.* 12 Sept. 2016, www.nytimes. com/2016/09/13/well/eat/how-the-sugar-industry-shifted-blame-to-fat.html.

[14]   Lustig, Robert H. *Sugar Has 56 Names, a Shoppers Guide.* Hudson Street Press, Published by the Penguin group A Kindle Publication, 2013.

	USA	UK	France	Australia	Hong Kong
Current average daily consumption	126 grams or over 30 teaspoons	93 grams or over 23 teaspoons	68 grams over 17 teaspoons	95 grams or over 23 teaspoons	53 grams or over 13 teaspoons
WHO recommended daily limits	25 grams per day or 6 teaspoons (1 teaspoon of sugar = about 4 grams) *Note: The daily limits refer to sugars that are manufactured and added by cooks/consumers, as well as honey, syrup, fruit juices and fruit concentrate. See definition below.*				

The WHO are not singling out the naturally occurring sugars. It's the added sugars that are problematic. Out of the 600,000 items in the North American food supply chain, 80% have added sugar. Even though this statistic is North American, the issue is not restricted to the Americas. Added sugar is everywhere:

- ✓ Yogurts
- ✓ Boxed cereals
- ✓ Sauces
- ✓ Canned fruits and vegetables
- ✓ Beverages
- ✓ Breads, baked goods
- ✓ Baked beans

At best, these foods provide empty calories. We all know that they should be limited. In reality however, reducing can be a challenge.

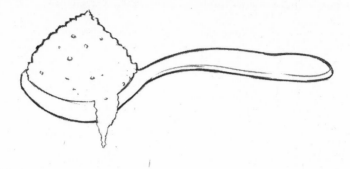

Why it's easy to indulge in excess

It's easy to consume sugar in excess without even dipping into the sugar bowl. To illustrate the point, below is a true story.

"While visiting my hometown I invited two new students for breakfast. Both were looking forward to studying at the local university so we met at a local coffee shop close to campus. We were all hungry, so ordered between us a decent supply of food and drink: chai tea latte, blueberry muffin, two orange juices, a cafe mocha, a cappuccino plus two of my favourite Montreal bagels with cream cheese.

The only available chairs were at a shared table, with a young mother and her two girls who both looked to be under seven years old. The mother had a cappuccino with a blueberry muffin. Her girls shared a hot chocolate and a reduced fat banana chocolate chip cake. No water.

With a background in nutrition and a plethora of books supporting my prediction, it was only a matter of minutes before a meltdown ensued. As predicted, the little girls soon experienced a case of the *"sugar crispies"*: Reeling between the urge to run around, cry, and laugh with a certain aggression. The mother was apologetic about their behaviour, and seemed unaware of its' cause. Just as predictable, was that it would be our turn next. We soon experienced our own "sugar high": Thirst, a little fatigue and a head buzz, but as adults we are able to manage it a bit better.

The table below gives a breakdown of the amount of sugar each of us consumed: between once and three times the maximum recommended daily sugar intake by the WHO. However, this was no Christmas brunch. It was an average coffee shop gathering."

How much sugar did each individual at the café consume?

	Orange Juice	Chai Tea Latte Tall	Bagel and Cream cheese	Café Mocha Tall	Cappuccino	Blueberry Muffin	Reduced fat Banana Chocolate Chip Cake (39 grams)	Tall Hot Chocolate (32 grams total)	Total Grams & approx. # teaspoons of added sugar
Me	12		5		7				24gr/ tsp.
My Friend	12	32				30		1	74 grs. / 18 tsp.
My Friend	12		5	26					43 grs / 11 tsp.
Mom					7	30			37 grs / 9 tsp.
Child							19	16	35 grs / 9 tsp.
Child							19	16	35 grs / 9 tsp.

Why eating sugar drives us to eat more sugar:

Like the story above, have you ever had a bowl of sweet cereal for breakfast, then felt a "mid-morning energy slump" which prompts you to reach for a sweet "pick me up"? This is why….

SUGAR ADDICTION
THE PERPETUAL CYCLE

1. YOU EAT SUGAR
- You like it, you crave it
- It has addictive properties

2. BLOOD SUGAR LEVELS SPIKE
- Dopamine is released in the brain = ADDICTION
- Mass insulin secreted to drop blood sugar levels

4. HUNGER & CRAVINGS
- Low blood sugar levels cause increased appetite and cravings
- Thus the cycle is repeated

3. BLOOD SUGAR LEVELS FALL RAPIDLY
- High insulin levels cause immediate fat storage
- Body craves the lost sugar 'HIGH'

However, not all sugars are the same. There are different types of sugar with a few similarities and important differences:

- All sugars are carbohydrates and contain about four calories per gram.
- Most sugars are made of simple one-molecule sugars: glucose, fructose & galactose.
- Glucose is a primary fuel, virtually every cell in our body can break it down then use it for energy.
- Sucrose or common table sugar is roughly half glucose and fructose.
- Too much fructose, which can only be used by the liver, can have devastating effects on the body. It can cause fatty liver, increase blood pressure and free radical damage and promotes the build of visceral or organ fat (think muffin top).

The problem is that fructose is hard to avoid. It makes up approximately ½ of the content in both standard table sugar and High Fructose Corn Syrup (an industry standard). So what can we do about it? Cut out anything that says High Fructose Corn Sugar (or HFCS) and reduce sugar generally by following "three steps to tame the beast" which will help you reduce, and even kill, sugar cravings.

Three steps to Tame the Beast. Tips to reduce and kill the cravings

Step 1: Get familiar with the number of tsp. of sugar consumed daily.

These examples serve as a guide. Observe for a week to come up with a daily average. Results are in range? Excellent! On the high side? The tips below will help to reduce.

We are not concerned about naturally occurring sugar in whole foods. Dried fruits and fruit juices are not found naturally, so they need to be counted. counted. 1 teaspoon of sugar = about 4 grams. WHO recommends six teaspoons per day for women and nine teaspoons for men. It is best to check the packaging to be sure of its sugar amount.

Breakfast

- ❖ Look on the cereal box under "added sugars" and calculate.
- ❖ Fruit juice: a glass of orange/apple juice is four to five teaspoons alone.
- ❖ Calculate the sugar or honey added in coffee/tea.
- ❖ Yogurt with added sugar? There is often three to five teaspoons per 200 ml tub!

Lunch, dinners and snacks

- ❖ Just one can of a non-diet soft drink has approximately nine teaspoons.
- ❖ Dried fruit is a culprit! A mini pack of sultanas has six teaspoons.
- ❖ Sweets pack a huge sugar punch: One Mars Bar has seven teaspoons, a 125 gram block of chocolate has 14, and ice-cream has two to four teaspoons per serving.
- ❖ Tomato sauce, BBQ sauce, and mayonnaise typically contain one to two teaspoons per serving.

❖ Alcohol is fermented sugar, and there is the equivalent to three teaspoons per standard drink.

Once you've estimated your number of teaspoons per day, multiply the teaspoons by four to get number of grams per day.

Step 2: Get to know the signs of too much sugar.

With high blood sugar levels (like after eating a sweet breakfast), you may experience:

❖ Thirst
❖ The need for frequent urination
❖ Excessive hunger
❖ Dry mouth
❖ Fatigue
❖ Blurred vision

Step 3: Get practical!

❖ Look at the label: aim for no more than five grams of sugar per 100 grams serving.
❖ If one of the first three ingredients is sugar, no matter what it is, it's a dessert! Skip it!
❖ Watch Dr Robert Lustig's "Sugar: The Bitter Truth" on YouTube. It will make any sugar addict think twice!
❖ Increase the protein to keep your blood sugar more stable. Replace a high glycemic shake with a low glycemic shake (note the recipes below).

High Glycemic Milkshake:	Low Glycemic Milkshake:
1 frozen ripe banana + ½ cup cow's milk + vanilla ice cream + chocolate syrup	*1 frozen ripe banana + ½ cup unsweetened vanilla almond milk + 1.5 tablespoons unsweetened cacao powder + 1 tablespoon almond butter (crunchy or smooth)* It makes you feel fuller for longer! Better slow release energy and tastes just as good!

SUMMARY: Sugar Consumption

Sugar is produced in 113 countries and is often supported by subsidies. We consume 50 to 125 grams per day, two to five times more than the WHO recommendation. In fact, the WHO recommends limiting added sugar to 25 grams or six teaspoons for women and 36 grams or nine teaspoons for men.

Sugars are carbohydrates, contain about FOUR calories per gram and are made of simple sugar molecules: glucose, fructose & galactose. Sucrose or common table sugar is roughly half glucose and fructose.

Naturally occurring sugars are not problematic. They are found in whole, unprocessed foods, such as milk, fruit, vegetables, and some grains. Added sugars are those that are removed from their original source and added, usually as a sweetener or as preservative. Avoid these.

Eating sugar, often leaves us wanting to eat more sugar. It alters our hormones so we don't register hunger the way we normally would. The Glycemic Index ranks foods from 0–100 according to the speed at which they affect blood sugar levels in the two or three hours after eating. Substituting low & medium GI for high GI foods will positively impact health.

Fructose is found in table sugar, fruit juices and processed foods, often labelled High Fructose Corn Syrup or HFCS for short. The body does not easily utilise it, so breaking it down is tiring. It does not increase insulin or leptin, which limits the sensation of satisfaction, enticing us to eat more. It is not easily metabolised and makes us fat.

FATS and oils: Good, bad or ugly

Refer to Chapter 4 *Nutrition essentials: knowing what will help us thrive not just survive*, the section on oils and fats for details. In a nutshell:

- ✓ **Unsaturated fats:** Generally healthy. They are liquid at room temperature. Sources include veggies, nuts, seeds and wild fatty fish, where we find our Omega 3 and 6.
- ✓ **Saturated fats:** Mostly solid at room temp. Animal origin (butter, cheese, whole milk, ice cream, cream and fatty meats) plus tropical plants and vegetable oils such as coconut and palm and are best restricted.

✓ **Trans Fats: Manufactured trans fats are VERY HARMFUL**. Identified on food labels as "partially hydrogenated" oils. Our bodies cannot use them for energy, so they just line our arteries and livers.

It is more about "which" than "how much".

✓ Aim for 30% or less of your total calorie intake from fat.
✓ If eating grain fed meats and farmed fish as opposed to organically raised, avoid the fat and skin, this helps avoid toxins, which like to hide in the fat.
✓ Increase the omega 3's (from wild oily fish, flax seeds and their oil, walnuts). Try introducing good quality flax seed oil in the diet, or ground up flax seeds. Need a snack? Include walnuts. Coat them in dark chocolate (over 70%) if you want, just don't bake them, as the oils will be compromised.

Eliminate altogether industrialised trans fats. Reminder: If it says, "partially hydrogenated" on the label, don't buy it!

FATS: The Good, The Bad, & The Ugly

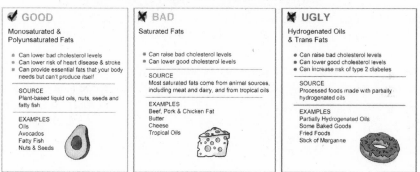

✔ GOOD	✘ BAD	✘ UGLY
Monosaturated & Polyunsaturated Fats	Saturated Fats	Hydrogenated Oils & Trans Fats
● Can lower bad cholesterol levels ● Can lower risk of heart disease & stroke ● Can provide essential fats that your body needs but can't produce itself	● Can raise bad cholesterol levels ● Can lower good cholesterol levels	● Can raise bad cholesterol levels ● Can lower good cholesterol levels ● Can increase risk of type 2 diabetes
SOURCE Plant-based liquid oils, nuts, seeds and fatty fish	SOURCE Most saturated fats come from animal sources, including meat and dairy, and from tropical oils	SOURCE Processed foods made with partially hydrogenated oils
EXAMPLES Oils Avocados Fatty Fish Nuts & Seeds	EXAMPLES Beef, Pork & Chicken Fat Butter Cheese Tropical Oils	EXAMPLES Partially Hydrogenated Oils Some Baked Goods Fried Foods Stick of Margarine

SALT: We get an ocean but need a puddle

Most of us consume too much salt. Since 2004, every May 17th is dedicated to the World Hypertension Day, a day to raise awareness about high blood pressure around the world. One of the leading causes for high blood pressure is consuming excess salt. Like sugar, it's easy to have too much.

Our salt habits: It's not about the shaker.

Salt is widely used in commercial foods as a flavour enhancer and preservative. Ready-made meals; processed meats like bacon, ham and salami; cheese and salty snacks or food consumed frequently in large amounts (e.g. bread) ALL contain a huge amount of salt.

Salt is also added to food during cooking (in the form of stock cubes, soy sauce and fish sauce) or at the table (e.g. table salt).

Michelin-starred chef, Marco Pierre White, explains, "An individual's palette is normally established during childhood. By the time we become an adult we have already acquired a strong taste for salt, which can result in us eating more than we need."[15]

How much salt do we actually need to consume?

Salt, or sodium chloride (NaCl) is a mixture of sodium and chloride. We need only a small amount of sodium to conduct nerve impulses, contract and relax muscles, and maintain the proper balance of water and minerals. Too much sodium can lead to water retention and other issues like high blood pressure, heart disease, and stroke.

According to the WHO, most people consume an average of 9–12 grams of salt per day or just around two teaspoons. WHO recommends keeping salt intake to less than five grams per day (one teaspoon). On food labels, sodium is sometimes listed separately from chloride. WHO recommends getting about 2.3 grams of sodium (chloride making up the rest of the 5 grams). [16]

Prepared and processed foods such as pizza, cold cuts and bacon, cheese, soups, and fast foods typically contain high levels of salt. Condiments also may contain sodium. One tablespoon (15 millilitres) of soy sauce, for example, has about one gram of sodium.

---

[15] Hypertension Nutrition / Diet Marco Pierre White Supports Global Call To Action To Reduce Dietary Salt Intake And Improve Heart Health On World Hypertension Day. (2009, May). Retrieved from http://www.medicalnewstoday.com/releases/150596.php

[16] "Salt Reduction." *World Health Organization*, World Health Organization, www.who.int/mediacentre/factsheets/fs393/en/.

Everyday High Salt Foods

Breads & Rolls	**Cold Cuts**	**Pizza**
Foods that we eat several times a day, like bread, when added up, can increase the sodium count significantly.	Cured meats and cold cuts. One serving of six slices can contain as much as one half of our daily recommended sodium.	Pizza. It's heavy on sodium. Looking to cut down? Limit the extra cheese, peperoni and load up on veggie toppings.
Poultry	**Soup**	**Sandwiches**
Chicken: BBQ? Roast? Sodium levels vary, but keep this on the radar screen if you are trying to reduce.	Canned soup or noodles in a cup: Typically, high on sodium even if total amounts will vary.	Deli sandwiches. Between the bread, meat and cheese, the sodium count mounts up.

SUMMARY: Salt consumption

Keep salt intake to less than five grams per day (one teaspoon). Aim for 200mg or less of sodium per serving. If a food keeps well in the fridge for days or weeks, it's a tip that the sodium content is high.

Exchange luncheon meat, bacon, hot dogs, sausage and ham for fresh meat. Limit salty snacks. Keep potato chips, salted nuts and most cheeses to the occasional treat rather than your daily diet.

When cooking and at the table, try using citrus fruit, herbs and spices instead of salt to enhance flavour. Limit sodium-laden condiments; soy sauce, salad dressings, sauces, dips, ketchup and mustard. Limit pickled foods like relish, sauerkraut and pickles, which are usually high in sodium. One pickle can have 500mg of sodium!

7. MY glass: Rethinking Drinks

Water? Milk? Glass of juice? Cup of tea? Coffee? Latte? Chai tea latte? Beer? Vodka tonic? It's all part of daily life. Below is a handy breakdown to better prioritise everyday drinks, in the "good" category, and identify occasional drinks, which fall into our "ugly" category.

OUR first priority: Water

We all know that water is essential to life. In fact, about 60% of our body consists of water. As the expression goes: "We can live for two minutes without air, two days without water and two weeks without food". Why is water so vital? It forms the basis of our complete body, including blood, digestive juices, perspiration, and urine. It regulates our body temperature, lubricates our joints, protects and moistens our organs and tissues and is used to remove toxins from our bodies. By doing all of these functions we lose a lot of water every day, making it essential that we replenish our supply.

Interesting facts: Body water content is higher in men than in women. The older you are, the less your bodily water content will be. Most mature adults lose about 2.5 to three litres of water per day. An air traveller can lose approximately 1.5 litres of water during a three-hour flight. The amount of water we need depends on our body size, metabolism, the weather, the food we eat and our activity levels.

How much water do we need?

- According to the Mayo Clinic, we need about 3.7 litres of fluids for men and about 2.7 litres of fluids for women per day. Given that about 20% of our recommended intake is covered by fluids from food, the rest comes from drinks. If you factor out other water containing drinks, a good rule of thumbs is still 1.5 to two litres of water per day. [17]

How do we know if we are getting enough?

• Check the colour of your urine. It should be a light yellow. When eating a lot of protein or fibre, or if suffering from constipation, vomiting or diarrhoea, we need a higher fluid intake.

What happens if we are not getting enough water?

A few of the early signs of dehydration are thirst and dark-coloured urine. This is the body's way of trying to increase water intake and decrease water loss.

Other possible symptoms which are reversible when drinking more fluids:

✓ Dizziness or light-headedness
✓ Headaches
✓ Tiredness
✓ Dry mouth, lips and eyes
✓ Passing small amounts of urine infrequently (less than three or four times a day).

Different types of drinking water

Here are a few types of water we come across every day:

Store bought bottled water

Distilled: Water that has been boiled then condensed from the steam that the water produces. Distillation kills microbes and removes the chemicals. Great for small electric appliances as you won't have the build-up of minerals. Not meant for drinking.

---

[17] "Water: How Much Should You Drink Every Day?" *Mayo Clinic*, Mayo Foundation for Medical Education and Research, 6 Sept. 2017, www.mayoclinic.org/healthy-lifestyle/nutrition-and-healthy-eating/in-depth/water/art-20044256.

Purified: Water from any source that has been treated to remove all the pathogens and chemicals with a smaller amount of solid particles permitted than mineral water.

Mineral: Ground water that naturally contains a designated amount of dissolved solids or minerals.

Sparkling: Water that contains carbon dioxide in an equivalent amount as when it came from the source. It may be lost, then re-carbonated during processing.

Spring: Water that is derived from an underground source or formation from which the water flows naturally to the earth's surface.

Tap water or P.W.S (public water source):

Supplied by the municipality and distributed through indoor plumbing, the water is processed through a municipal filtration system, then chlorine is added before leaving, to keep it potable *en route*. Tap water is often considered to be drinkable although water quality issues can occur. Many households use some sort of purification system like water filters.

Why drinking filtered tap water is a great option:

- ✓ Cost effective: You will need to buy the best quality water filtration system you can afford, but it is well worth it!
- ✓ More environmentally friendly: Just look around at the excess of plastic water bottles!
- ✓ Fewer toxins from plastic: When using filtered tap water, you avoid the chemicals from the plastic bottle that will leach into the water.
- ✓ Economical: Invest in a quality reusable water bottle, preferably stainless steel or protected glass and a simple cartridge filter system to filter water from the tap.

MY glass: Non-water beverages

While water is the best thing we can drink, it isn't very "exciting" and there are many other tastier options out there. The best thing for our health is water. Having moderate amounts of other drinks is fine, but don't make them your go-to beverages.

✓ Enjoy milk, coffee and tea no more than once or twice per day.
✓ Flavour water with mint, lemon, ginger lemon grass etc. Avoid sweetened cordials because of the sugar content.
✓ Enjoy sodas, bought juices, sweetened coffees or teas, ice teas, vitamin waters and sport drinks occasionally, and no more than a couple of times per week. The empty calories have a minimal effect on improving your health and some are even detrimental to your health.

Getting to know the hidden sugar content in everyday drinks.

The hidden sugar content in every day drinks

Soda
227 calories   14 tsp

Vitamin Water
125 calories   8 tsp

Energy Drink
240 calories   15 tsp

Juice Drink
305 calories   17 tsp

Water
0 calories   0 tsp

ALCOHOL: Little known facts minus the morality

Alcohol can be considered either a tonic or a poison. It's the amount that makes the difference. Mankind has been drinking fermented beverages for over 10,000 years.

It's only when drinking responsibly that it can be a tonic. Of course, it's our choice to drink or not, and when to stop.

Refraining from consuming alcohol means fewer calories, less toxicity, and a clearer tomorrow! It's the ONLY responsible thing to do when you are driving. It's also an opportunity to observe a bunch of people who are drinking socially, which can also bring its own form of amusement!

<u>If the choice is to drink, keep in mind:</u>

- ✓ Alcohol is absorbed through our stomach and small intestines. Because food slows down the rate of absorption, alcohol will affect us more quickly on an empty stomach. It flows through the body via the bloodstream reaching the heart, brain, muscles and other tissues very quickly – even within a few minutes.
- ✓ Our bodies can't store alcohol. The liver, which is responsible for breaking down all toxic substances, breaks it down. Our ability to process alcohol depends on various things, like age, weight, sex and our daily habits.
- ✓ Our body breaks down alcohol at a rate of roughly one standard drink per hour. Because it takes time to break it down, when we drink more than about one unit of alcohol an hour, it will build up our blood alcohol concentration.

One Standard Drink

12oz. Beer	5oz. Wine	3oz. Fortified wine	1.5oz Liquor
5% alcohol	10-12% alcohol	16-18% alcohol	40% alcohol

What is "too much", and what happens when we get there?

As we drink, alcohol passes into our bloodstream, then ethanol (the active compound of alcoholic beverages) can pass through the blood-brain-barrier and thus interfere with all the brain's activities. If we drink faster than one standard drink an hour, alcohol will start to flood the brain. Fortunately, alcohol gives warning signs at each level of penetration into the brain so, if you spot the signs, moderate your drinking, or stop altogether.

Classic warning signs:

- ✓ Feeling giddy or less inhibited
- ✓ Starting to lose the thread of what you're saying, or slurring your words
- ✓ Unsteady on your feet
- ✓ Starting to see double

Alcohol doesn't affect our body instantaneously. It builds up. Leaving a party just below the legal limit can mean being over the limit 20 minutes later.

Respecting our limits

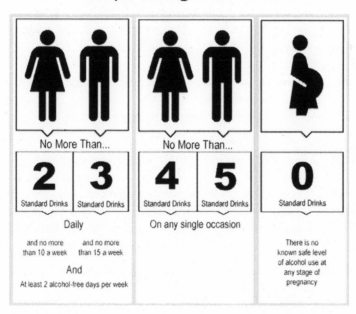

Source: "Alcohol." *Nidirect*, www.nidirect.gov.uk/taxonomy/term/708.

Hangover Helpers[18]

- ✓ B and C Vitamins get depleted when you drink. Vitamin B helps eliminate alcohol from the body. Stock up on natural sources or consider supplements.
- ✓ Magnesium also gets depleted when you drink. Because it is an anti-inflammatory, it can help reduce a hangover. Some magnesium rich foods include:
  - o Spinach — one cup: 157 milligrams (40% DV)
  - o Chard — one cup: 154 milligrams (38% DV)
  - o Pumpkin seeds — 1/8 cup: 92 milligrams (23% DV)
  - o Yogurt or Kefir — one cup: 50 milligrams (13% DV)
  - o Almonds — one ounce: 80 milligrams (20% DV)
  - o Black Beans — half a cup: 60 milligrams (15% DV)

SUMMARY of good drinking habits

Water is our first priority. Learn the signs of dehydration, and what happens when we get there. Drinking filtered tap water from home is a great option for many reasons.

Number one choice is water. Number two choice is tea and coffee. Number three choice is unsweetened milk and soy beverages. Last choice is diet beverages and sugary sodas.

Learn what alcohol does to the body and how to establish limits, then what to do after having over-indulged.

---

8. GETTING Practical: Bringing it all Together on a Plate

This section aims to give you a guide to optimal proportions between carbohydrates (starches, veggies, fruits), proteins and fats. Doing this limits the tendency to go off on a tangent. This gives us is a great start towards ideal weight, better skin and better energy. Think of it as a solid keel on your boat which helps keep it on course for optimal living.

---

[18] Sources: Alcohol: Balancing Risks and Benefits. (2016, April 12). Retrieved from https://www.hsph.harvard.edu/nutritionsource/alcohol-full-story/#intro

BALANCE, proportions, the 80% bucket and our plate

Carbs? No carbs? Vegan? High protein? What will keep me healthy? The key to being healthy and having a healthy diet really is balance. When we balance our diet we don't need to focus too much on getting specific vitamins or minerals. If you balance your plate everything else just falls into place.

1. Follow the 80/20 rule.
2. When making your choices see that your plate is balanced.
   i.   Half of your plate should be mostly vegetables and some fruits.
   ii. A quarter should be carbohydrates.
   iii. A quarter should be protein.
   iv. Add a glass of water or milk and a thumb size portion of fats/oils.
3. Lastly, go for variety, try not to repeat the same foods more than three to four times a week. It's essential for getting adequate micronutrients.

And presto, you have it balanced, with no need to over analyse what you are eating. It is that simple!

A well balanced plate

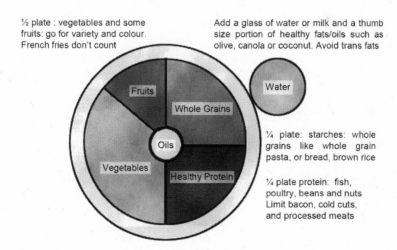

½ plate : vegetables and some fruits: go for variety and colour. French fries don't count

Add a glass of water or milk and a thumb size portion of healthy fats/oils such as olive, canola or coconut. Avoid trans fats

¼ plate: starches: whole grains like whole grain pasta, or bread, brown rice

¼ plate protein: fish, poultry, beans and nuts Limit bacon, cold cuts, and processed meats

Portions without distortion

While it is important to stick to the right proportions, portion sizes are also important! We have definitely got into portion distortion over the years, with many meals being served easily double the recommended portion size. In fact, plate sizes have increased incredibly over the years, so make sure that plates are no bigger than 10-inches.

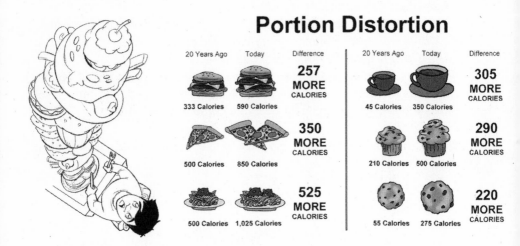

Portion Distortion

20 Years Ago	Today	Difference
333 Calories	590 Calories	**257** MORE CALORIES
500 Calories	850 Calories	**350** MORE CALORIES
500 Calories	1,025 Calories	**525** MORE CALORIES

20 Years Ago	Today	Difference
45 Calories	350 Calories	**305** MORE CALORIES
210 Calories	500 Calories	**290** MORE CALORIES
55 Calories	275 Calories	**220** MORE CALORIES

Tips to keep your Portion in Proportion

1. **Eat mindfully.** By practising mindful eating, we start to listen to our body's cues such as hunger and satisfaction. In doing so, we also enjoy the flavours and textures while eating and are satisfied with smaller portions. We have all sat down in front of the TV with a snack, only to look down and realise the food is gone. We often don't even remember eating it and then we want more because we have hardly even tasted it.
   - ✓ Never eat while distracted. That includes watching TV, or being on the computer, iPad or phone.
   - ✓ Always eat at a table – never eat while standing at the counter or on-the-go!

2. **Slow down.** When we eat fast, we tend to overeat. Our stomach takes time to tell our brain that we are full, but we often miss these signals until we are stuffed!
   - ✓ Use a timer or reminder card by your plate to make you remember.
   - ✓ Eat with your non-dominant hand.

✓ Use chop sticks or other tools that might slow you down.
✓ Use smaller utensils and take smaller bites.
✓ Drink water with meals; it cleanses the palate and slows the meal process down.
✓ Chew! Digestion starts in the mouth, and our stomachs don't have teeth!

3. **Plan your meals.** If we don't plan, we tend to eat on the fly and often have little time or desire to look for healthy options making it hard to stick to that 80/20 Rule.
   ✓ Try and roughly plan meals. It can be done each morning, or weekly.
   ✓ Have easy back-up meals. *(There are some quick meal suggestions at the end of the chapter!)*
   ✓ Always have a good snack on hand, like trail mix or a granola bar that contains only wholesome ingredients. (Make sure sugar isn't one of the first three on the list of ingredients.)

4. **Eat regularly.** For most of us, that means every three to four hours. Leaving it any longer, you risk getting hungry. It's much harder to make good choices when your tummy is rumbling.

5. **Make eating social.** You should be confident in your own nutritional choices. Just because your friends are only eating salads, or conversely, subsisting mainly on fast food, doesn't mean you have to copy them! That being said, it is a wonderful experience to get together with a bunch of friends, and designate one night a week where you all go to one person's house and take turns cooking for everyone. Not only will you expand your cooking horizons and try new foods, but you'll make eating into a celebratory, social time, not something to rush through.

HOOKED on Junk? Simple Solutions

We all fall into that junk food rut sometimes. A muffin and sugary coffee at breakfast, burger and fries at lunch, and pizza and beer at dinner can easily turn from a one-off guilty day to your routine. That kind of eating will catch up with us sooner rather than later, and leave you feeling lethargic and fatigued. Some simple solutions:

- ✓ Don't change the general food category, just upgrade everything you eat. Kraft macaroni & cheese or ramen can be substituted with pasta and tomato sauce. Soda pop can be substituted with a zero-calorie, unsweetened fizzy seltzer water.
- ✓ Slowly start introducing one great quality food at a time. For instance, buy organic eggs and one colourful vegetable.
- ✓ Incorporating more healthy protein (whether it be lean meats, nuts, or yogurts) will make it much easier to reduce your sugar intake, as you'll have slower release energy.

✓ Congratulate yourself for all the efforts you are making! Remember, you don't have to get rid of all the delicious foods you love the most, just ensure that you're nutritionally balanced.

9. GETTING Organised: My Life, My Home and My Food

Here are a few tips to ensure you make financially and nutritionally savvy choices. From reading food labels to shopping on a budget, it's all here!

NAVIGATING the grocery stores to our advantage

What should we know to navigate the grocery stores and kitchens to our advantage?

<u>Reading Food Labels</u>:

If your food has a label, chances are that it's processed and you are going to want to know what's in it. Comparing food labels is an easy way to make smart decisions between two similar items. Also, marketers know how to fool you with misleading claims, but the food labels (and ingredient lists) never lie!

Food labelling is fairly harmonised, and in most places in the world, uniform labelling has been agreed upon. Here is what you will find on a food label:

List of ingredients: Ingredients are ordered by volume in decreasing order. If sugar or hydrogenated oils are some of the first ingredients, chances are it's not a healthy choice.

Serving size: Nutritional data is listed either per 100 grams or ml or according to serving size. Pay attention to the size as well as how many servings there are in the package, then do the maths and figure out how many servings you are consuming.

Calorie or energy content: Measured in kilocalories (kcal or commonly, a "calorie") or kilojoules (one kcal is equivalent to approximately 4.2 kilojoules). This measurement shows the total amount of energy, rather than evaluating its function within the body. Calories should be evaluated in light of the associated micronutrients

Total fat: If most of the fat content comes from the healthy unsaturated fat (see section on fats), you are good to go. If the fat is mainly saturated and/or the product has trans-fat, it is not a healthy choice. If there are any "partially hydrogenated oils" in the list of ingredients (trans-fats)- it is best to avoid. Keep away from products that have more than 20 grams total fat per 100 grams serving or more than five grams saturated fat per 100 grams serving.

Total Carbohydrates: Look for at least three grams of fibre per serving. As for keeping track of sugar, the term "sugars" doesn't distinguish between naturally occurring sugars (like lactose in milk or fructose in fruit) and added sugar (like high-fructose corn syrup or brown rice syrup). The best approach is to check the list of ingredients for how high sugar comes in the list. Keep an eye out for palm or inverted sugar, and any type of sweetener or syrup. A red flag is ingredients ending in "ose", like fructose or glucose, since these are added sugars if they are listed as a separate ingredient. Aim for five grams of sugar or less per 100 grams serving.

Proteins: The average daily protein requirement for most people would be about one gram of protein per kg of body weight per day.

Salt: Aim to keep salt intake to less than five gram (5000 mg) per day or one teaspoon. Foods that are considered low sodium will have less than 200 mg of sodium per serving.

Vitamins and minerals: The Daily Value (DV) is the amount of each nutrient that is considered sufficient for most healthy adults. A food that contains anywhere from 10 per cent to 19 per cent of the DV is considered a good source of a nutrient.

Best before date: This is the manufacturer's estimate of when the premium quality may start to deteriorate and isn't necessarily when food should be discarded. You can often cut off parts of produce that look brown, but should practice more caution when it comes to meat products.

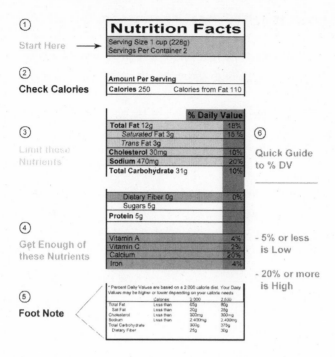

Nutrition label

Source: Understanding Food Nutrition Labels." *American Heart Association*, healthyforgood.heart.org/eat-smart/articles/understanding-food-nutrition-labels.

Some misleading terms:

All Natural: This generally means no added colours or artificial flavours, but there is no regulation on it. Surprisingly, it can be used as a label on most products.

No Added Sugar: This doesn't mean that a food doesn't contain sugar, as the basic ingredients may have naturally occurring sugar. It just means that there is no sugar added.

Sugar Free: Sugar-free products have less than 0.5 grams of sugars per serving, but they still contain calories and carbohydrates from other sources. Sometimes they have been sweetened by other harmful chemicals.

Organic? Where does it fit in? What it means to me?

Organic means that the product has been produced without any use of pesticides, harmful fertilizers, sewage sludge, radiation, or antibiotics or growth hormones.

This label varies across the globe. In the US for example, if a product has a USDA label that says organic, 95% or more of the ingredients must have been grown or processed without synthetic fertilisers or pesticides.

Organic livestock often have a better fat profile and less exposure to antibiotics, growth hormones and pesticides used during production. Organic plants, vegetables, fruits, cereals and grains have had less exposure to pesticides and often better nutrient value.

Guidelines to optimise shopping:

✓ Do ONE big food shop each week. This will prevent you spending extra money in convenience stores and takeaways. Top up the perishables such as milk and fruit.

✓ Prevent impulse purchases in the supermarket by making a shopping list.

✓ Supermarket own-brand products are usually cheaper than branded goods.

✓ Keep an eye on "use by" dates. A marked-down item is only a bargain if you use it!

✓ Keep a stock of meals and ingredients in the freezer for those moments when the cupboard is unexpectedly bare. Sliced bread kept in the freezer means you never need to waste any. You can defrost a couple of slices at a time, when needed and within a few minutes they will thaw.

✓ Only buy food for the meals you're planning on enjoying at home.

✓ Plan and buy packed lunch ingredients for cheaper meals on the go.

✓ Buy seasonally, and buy staple items in bulk.

✓ Chocolate is ok if it contains over 72% cacao. This will only have about 10% sugar, and has micronutrients including magnesium (relaxing). By contrast, milk chocolate often has more than 50% sugar!

✓ Foods in their natural state are best and the most nutrient dense option out there!

✓ Organic eggs are reasonable, nutritious, and delicious.

✓ Go for whole grain foods, and beans.

✓ Aim to buy foods with five or fewer ingredients, of which all of them should be wholesome.

✓ Make sure you recognise the names of the ingredients. Are they natural or additives?

Ideas of budget items for students to consider:

✓ Grains
   o Whole grain crackers (wheat crackers, rice cakes)
   o Whole grain cereals (no sugar added granola and muesli)
   o Whole wheat tortillas or pitas
   o Brown rice
   o Couscous or cracked wheat (only needs to be left to sit in hot water to cook)
   o Whole wheat bread

- o   Oatmeal or porridge packets
- ✓ Dairy
  - o   Milk
  - o   Naturally unflavoured yogurt
  - o   Cheese (hard, soft, feta)
  - o   Cream cheese
- ✓ Protein
  - o   Cans of tuna and salmon
  - o   Cans of beans (chick peas, black beans, baked beans)
  - o   Eggs
  - o   Non-sweetened peanut butter or other nut butters
  - o   Nuts and seeds
  - o   Dried or instant lentils/rice cups
- ✓ Produce (fresh & frozen)
  - o   Frozen meats
  - o   Fruits and Vegetables
  - o   Canned fruit in juice
  - o   A few pieces of fresh fruit – they last longer in the fridge (except bananas!)
  - o   Dried fruits
  - o   Ready to eat veggies - carrots, snap peas, cherry tomatoes, snap peas, cucumbers
  - o   Frozen vegetables and fruits
  - o   Edamame (quick and easy to prepare)
- ✓ Snacks
  - o   Protein bars (check the sugar content first. If sugar is one of the first 3 ingredients, put it back, it's a dessert!).
  - o   Ingredients for salsa and hummus

TOP TIPS for optimising the quality of what we eat on a budget:

- ✓ If possible buy organic for what you consume most. You drink one litre of milk per day? Consider making it organic.
- ✓ Limit fat and skin on meats, as toxins can be stored there.
- ✓ Wash all fruits and vegetables before eating because pesticides are mostly retained on the skin. Soak leafy vegetables for 30 minutes.
- ✓ Be aware of the "dirty dozen" produce which is notorious for collecting more pesticides. If your budget can stretch, go organic or else, wash it, peel it or cook it!
  By contrast the "Clean15" are normally freer from chemicals.

DIRTY DOZEN & CLEAN 15

Dirty Dozen:
Apples
Celery
Tomatoes
Cucumber
Grapes
Nectarines
Peaches
Spinach
Strawberries
Blueberries
Bell Peppers

Clean 15:
Onions
Avocado
Sweet Corn
Pineapple
Mango
Sweet Peas
Eggplant
Cauliflower
Asparagus
Kiwi
Cabbage
Watermelon
Grapefruit
Sweet Potatoes
Honeydew Melon

Food to avoid!

- ✓ Soft, sliced white soft bread.
- ✓ Foods where sugar is one of the first three ingredients. It's a dessert!
- ✓ Chocolate that is less than 70% cacao.
- ✓ Processed luncheon meat, bacon, hot dogs, industrial sausages, ham, or fish. Exchange it for fresh meat, eggs or fish including in a tin.
- ✓ Anything with partially hydrogenated oil (trans fat alert!) or high fructose corn syrup.
- ✓ Be cautious with grain fed meat and farm raised fish. They contain lots of Omega 6 which we want to reduce.

Here are some common additives that lurk in processed foods. If you see these substances listed, beware!

Substances to avoid	Why? What does it do?
Colouring Tartrazine (E 102)	Mildly carcinogenic
Colouring Azorubine (E122)	Induces hyperactivity
Colouring Brilliant Black (E 151)	Mildly carcinogenic
Colouring Sunset Yellow (E107)	Disrupts endocrine activity
Colouring azorubine (E122)	Disrupts endocrine activity
Colouring Ponceau 4R (E 124)	Alters cognitive functions
Colouring Patent Blue (E131)	Induces allergies
Colouring Brown HT (E155)	Induces hyperactivity
Additive Aluminium (E173)	Toxic for neurons
Additives sulphites (E221-E228)	Induces a range of adverse clinical effects in sensitive individuals
Propylene glycol (E1520)	Avoid for babies as well as for older people
Flavour enhancer Glutamate (E621)	Toxic for neurons
Parabens (E126 and E127)	Disrupts endocrine activity
Artificial sweetener Aspartame	Potentially carcinogenic
Sweetener High Fructose Corn Syrup	Turned DIRECTLY into fat
Partially hydrogenated fats	Our body can't break it down
Pesticides on fruits and vegetables	High-risk (must wash or peel)

FOOD Safety Tips

The best foods can be harmful if we are not aware of and respectful of the rules.

Refrigerator management

- ✓ Promptly refrigerate or freeze perishable leftovers. Illness-causing bacteria can grow in perishable foods within as little as one hour, unless refrigerated. In hot weather, that window of time can even be reduced.
- ✓ Keep the fridge at a safe temperature - 5°C or below. With your flat mates or roommates, it is worth investing in a mercury-free fridge thermometer to keep on the bottom shelf above the salad drawer. Check the temperature once a week, ideally first thing in the morning. Make sure the door seal is intact and keep the fridge door tightly closed. The temperature will quickly rise if the door is left open, often because of an inefficient seal.
- ✓ Don't overfill the fridge. This can stop cool air circulating freely keeping the foods properly chilled.

When to throw food out

- ✓ You can't always tell by looking or smelling whether harmful bacteria has started growing in your leftovers or refrigerated foods.
- ✓ Use refrigerated leftovers within three to four days.
- ✓ Swollen or rusty can? Throw it out!

Tips for reheating

It's a shame to waste leftovers, indeed sometimes you cook larger amounts to deliberately have meals prepared in advance. Either way, it is so important to remember to refrigerate them promptly and reheat properly.

Never reheat food in a plastic container. If it's going in the microwave, choose glass. Heat on the plastic will release some of the nasty toxins in the plastic right into the food. When reheating leftovers, be sure they reach 165°F / 74°C. You don't actually need a food thermometer – but the rules of thumb are:

- ✓ Reheat soups and sauces in a saucepan by bringing them to the boil. The first bubbles you see do not necessarily mean that the whole mass is hot through. Stir.
- ✓ When reheating, ensure there is enough liquid to keep food moist. Liquids can be added without impairing the flavour – consider water, stock, tomato juice, unsweetened coconut water or milk. A lid to keep food covered also helps to keep moisture in.

✓ It is best to thaw food thoroughly before reheating. Caught out and in a hurry – you can do this from frozen but be vigilant that your food, especially poultry, pork and rice (prone to diarrhoea inducing toxin - Bacillus Cereus if left at room temperature for too long) is hot through.

✓ For solid food, such as meat, use a metal skewer which you push to the center then withdraw and feel by touching against an area of delicate skin such as the inner wrist or top lip. Only eat when hot.

Food safety and food groups

Fruits and veggies: Most fresh fruit and vegetables last around a week, less if they have been washed. It is recommended to wash just before eating. Use soft or overripe fruits and make a fruit compote. Stick ripe (peeled) bananas in the freezer to use in a smoothie.

Meat, poultry or fish: Fresh meats do not last long in the fridge. Cook thawed meats within two days of buying. After cooking, meats can last in your fridge for seven days.

Bread: Bread should last three to six days after purchase. If you aren't a big bread eater, keep sliced bread in the freezer.

Dairy: Yogurts and milk can generally be eaten a day or two after their expiry dates. Cheese lasts a long time before it goes mouldy. Make sure to store in an air tight container.

Frozen foods: They should be defrosted once only. Once defrosted, prepare or eat. If you return from shopping, put your food that needs refrigeration immediately in the fridge and frozen foods in the freezer.

Pantry foods: These usually last a long time. Keep an eye on the best-before dates. Make sure to store foods in a cool, dry place and that the package is firmly closed.

GOT a freezer? Here are the guidelines

Efficient freezing will save you time and money

✓ Buy in bulk and freeze raw portions such as chicken thighs individually.
✓ Make dishes such as lasagna so you can freeze cooked portions that then just need heating up.
✓ Freeze component parts of a dish if there are leftovers so you don't waste them, and can use them again. For example, stock or béchamel sauce.
✓ Put your sliced loaf in the freezer. Each time you want toast or a sandwich just use a table knife to loosen the number of slices needed. They thaw in minutes; your bread is always fresh and you never have any waste.
✓ Try not to squish things as they freeze. It will make defrosting easier!

This minced beef is divided up into portion size sections before freezing. Use a Ziploc bag and a ruler to separate. You can then break off as many portions as you need when you are going to cook.

✓ Freeze liquids in portion size bags so you can use as you need.
✓ Freeze fruit such as strawberries and blackberries on a tray, then once frozen slip into a bag. Now you can take a handful whenever you want.
✓ Make sure things are wrapped carefully for the freezer – with minimum air pockets. This minimises "freezer burn", which does not affect food quality, but can alter colour and appearance.
✓ Apart from plastic bags and plastic film, re-useable plastic boxes can be used in the freezer. Remember to leave some space at the top – as liquids expand when frozen.
✓ NEVER use glass in the freezer – it will shatter!

"Can it be frozen?"

YES	NO
Raw Meat, poultry	Salad greens
Cooked dishes	Raw vegetables for salads, sandwiches – red peppers, green onions, endives
Raw egg white (use Ziploc bag)	Eggs in their shell
Milk	Cottage cheese, sour cream, cream in general, yogurt
Vegetables – raw or blanched. Make into useable size pieces so you can use up as you need. Good freezing vegetables – cauliflower, broccoli, pumpkin etc.	Cooked vegetables
Bananas about to go off – Peel first – then use frozen in a smoothie or to make banana bread.	Glass jars or bottles
Coffee and herbs can be kept in the freezer to maintain flavour – good idea for over the summer break.	

Tips for Defrosting

Bread can be toasted from frozen, or soup can be gently but thoroughly warmed through from frozen. For larger items, you need to wait until your food is fully defrosted before cooking. If you take a chicken breast and cook before defrosting – the outside will appear done, but the middle may still be luke-warm and even carry salmonella.

Small items will defrost quickly. Have a cup of tea and wait!

The microwave offers a defrost programme. This can be effective for medium items – to get the defrosting started off. The problem is that the microwave works from the middle of the food outwards – so by the time you see the outside starting to thaw, it is over thawed in the middle and may have even started to cook.

The most effective defrosting comes down to PLANNING! Take out food from the freezer with enough time for it to thaw in the fridge. Large, solid items such as a turkey take up to 24 hours, but small items such as sausages take about four hours.

Place defrosting items in the fridge in a bowl or plate to catch the drips.

Freezer and defrosting – the bottom line:

✓ Portion before freezing, and wrap carefully.
✓ Label everything with a permanent marker. Include contents and date frozen.
✓ Buy when cheap and store for later!
✓ To avoid things sticking together, freeze small items in a single layer on a baking sheet first, and then move frozen pieces to a bag for storage. This can include fresh berries, or a multi pack of sausages or chicken pieces. Freeze in twos or threes, so you can take out a portion size at a time.

EATING out- Stay in the driver's seat

✓ Ask for water with your meal, and skip the pop or juice.
✓ Skip the bread and butter that are offered before your meal.
✓ Listen to your body, eat slowly, savouring every bite and monitor how hungry or full you feel.

For takeaway / takeout options:

✓ Choose bread-based options like wraps, kebabs, souvlaki, or hamburgers.
✓ Avoid deep fried and pastry options.
✓ Ask for extra vegetables and salad.
✓ Limit high fat, high sodium sauces and toppings like cheese, fatty meats, and mayonnaise. Be sure to ask for the sauce or dressing on the side so you can choose to have less.
✓ Skip the fries.
✓ Don't upsize unless it's with a side salad.

At a restaurant:

✓ Consider asking for an entrée sized or a smaller serving.
✓ Think about asking for extra vegetables or salad with your meal.

✓ Don't hesitate to ask for modifications or additions to your meals. If it comes with fries, ask for a salad instead. No vegetables? Ask for a side order.

✓ A salad can be a good entrée choice if others are ordering entrees. Ask for dressings and sauces to come separately.

✓ Order the soup as an appetizer, a broth soup, avoid the heavy cream soups.

✓ Choose a lean piece of meat, skinless chicken or seafood. Avoid fried, battered and crumbed choices; instead choose steamed, pan fried, braised, poached, baked, roasted or grilled.

✓ Skip the skin or fat in meat or poultry, that's where the toxins hide!

✓ Finish with fruit or share a dessert.

10. THE Bottom Line: Top Tips for Best Food Choices Today... and Tomorrow

1. Increase the quantity of quality protein to at least one gram per kilogram of body weight.
2. Reduce the added sugars, especially with drinks.
3. Eat the rainbow of vegetables and fruit every day.
4. Increase the foods with Omega 3 (wild oily fish), walnuts, flax seeds and their oil and decrease the foods with Omega 6 fatty acids.
5. In a grocery store, avoid any food with a label with the ingredient "partially hydrogenated oils" (they are trans fats) or High Fructose Corn Syrup.
6. Buy organic if you can, especially for what you eat/drink most of. If you cannot afford organic meat, avoid the skin and fatty pieces, as this is where toxins are.
7. Keep balanced: divide the plate in quarters, half for veggies and fruits, a quarter meat/protein and a quarter carbs.
8. Watch the 80/20 rule. 80% keep to the nutrient dense; 20% of the time, relax the rules.
9. Watch for portion distortion.
10. Stay hydrated. Get enough water and beware of the colour of your urine.
11. Be mindful. Acknowledge what you eat.
12. Enjoy your food and drink, it's part of the adventure of life!

Chapter 4: Entertaining, Life's a party!

by Rachael Desgouttes

1. INTRODUCTION

It sounds so grown up to host a dinner party, yet even if you love going out, entertaining at home ticks so many boxes. You can create whatever atmosphere you want – a cosy and romantic soiree, a birthday celebratory meal, or a night in with a bunch of friends to watch a major sporting event.

Entertaining Comes in all Shapes and Sizes!

You have control over the source and quality of the food you serve and the price you pay for it. Home cooking is always more economical than restaurants – even fast food! As you increase the number of people you cook for, this becomes even more apparent. On some occasions you may wish to treat your friends, for others you may consider agreeing to share the costs. Communicate clearly, so that you never leave someone with an expense they weren't expecting. Alternatively, you could plan a "potluck" party, with an item for each person to bring: cheese / salad / dessert.

2. MAKING your evening memorable and special

The world is getting more and more casual in its approach to communicating and arrangements, but don't let that stop you making your gathering official or formal! An invitation shows your guests the effort you are investing in the occasion. It obliges them to reply, which is not only courteous but essential for your planning and budgeting. The invite is also a reminder, for your guests as to the time and place, theme or dress code, price (where appropriate) and if they need to bring anything.

Setting a clear time of arrival means that you can cook, tidy round, get changed and be comfortable in an organised way. This is so much better than a mad rush if the doorbell rings early, and you are not done! If you sent the invite very early, a small text reminder the day before is a good idea – reminding your guests about the details. For example, "Looking forward to seeing you tomorrow at 8. 3rd floor, Flat B. Bring a photo of yourself as a baby and a good appetite." There are now so many digital tools which can help you manage and track your guest list and easily remind your friends – and all for free!

3. PLANNING

As with so many things we undertake, the key to successful entertaining is PLANNING. Make a check list as you plan your event. Some examples:

Food: If you need avocados to ripen, you may need to buy them four days in advance. Soft perishable fruit such as raspberries may need to be bought immediately before the event.

Equipment: Renting wine glasses might need seven days' notice. If you don't have enough crockery, cutlery and glassware, either borrow or use disposable – the most environmental being wooden. Rental is available through restaurants and wine shops. Sometimes this service is free if you have bought something. Beware clauses about damages. Allow enough booking time to avoid disappointment, especially at busy times such as Christmas. Check carefully the expectation for returns - clean or used, and the date and time. Compare the cost and convenience with disposables or even cheap home stores sometimes have offers that make buying the best option. You can lend on to future party hosts too.

Furniture: Do I have enough chairs for everyone to sit? Buffets and barbeques mean people stand and move around. Cushions could make the floor an option, and wooden wine crates with a cushion make a good improvised seat. Use your imagination!

Cooking equipment: Making a casserole for eight people needs a much bigger pan than warming a tin of soup for yourself! Choose your menu to suit what you have. Cooking "en papillotte" means making packages of food in greaseproof paper or foil. Easy cooking, no extra equipment, looks beautiful when served and minimal clearing up!

Decorating: Home-made decorations can be as creative and elegant as bought commercial ones. Uniformity is always a good look, so the same flower or ribbon on each place setting, or three matching jam jars filled with flowers can look great. It takes just a little imagination to set the tone you are looking for.

4. MENU Planning

Even if you are already a proficient cook, keep your menu simple. Three courses – a starter, main and dessert are perfect. Try some homemade appetisers, which can be passed around and make the pre-dinner drinks sociable and relaxed. Some crudité (raw chopped vegetables) and hummus or other dips are perfect.

Keep two out of three courses cold, (or just warm with a few minutes in the oven) so that they can be pre-prepared, and there is no stress over critical timing.

Avoid items such as steaks which need cooking to everyone's taste. If you are six people, and everyone has different preferences, you will have a difficult time juggling the timing of all of these, not to mention the vegetable or side dishes.

Choose an item that is time tolerant – for example a casserole in the oven will still be good, kept at a low temperature, even if you are half an hour late eating.

Cook a recipe you have tried before. However – think carefully when you multiply up portions for groups. Doubling or quadrupling quantities is a quick calculation – cooking and oven times are not always a direct multiplication.

Simmering times for soups and stews will remain the same but will take longer to reach a simmering point from cold.

Ask your guests about any dietary requirements they have before they come. It is a nightmare to serve up a heavy meaty dish, only to discover you have a vegan and a vegetarian in the party. One party planning trick is to think of a vegetarian meal, then treat your meat addition as a side dish. This way you guarantee there is something for everyone.

5. BEING the Perfect Host

If people don't know each other, your responsibility is to find a common interest to start them off. As the host you need to ensure everyone is engaged, not feeling shy or left out. If a couple of people know each other, don't allow them to huddle in an antisocial corner, but introduce someone new to them, perhaps pointing out that they share a common interest. Identify friends who are outgoing and will help to get the atmosphere going. You could find some game ideas from the internet which could help to break the ice.

6. SAMPLE Menu with Recipes

Sample Menu	
Pre-dinner:	Hummus with nachos and vegetable crudité, cheese straws
Starter:	Buffalo mozzarella and tomato salad. Garlic bread.
Main:	Fish en Papillote or Coq au vin.
Dessert:	Apple, marzipan and almond tart.

To make **cheese straws** - use sheets of cool, defrosted frozen puff pastry on a greased / non-stick baking tray. With a knife tip, slice into strips. Brush with beaten egg, then sprinkle with what you want: poppy seeds, different cheeses - parmesan and gruyere are good- paprika, olive tapenade. Carefully lift one end of a straw, whilst the other end remains on the baking tray. Twist a couple of times and replace. Do this for all the straws. Cook in a hot oven. Serve hot, warm or cold depending on your cooking plan and timing.

Hummus with nachos and vegetable crudité is a crowd pleaser. It is possible to buy excellent hummus in most supermarkets, but making it yourself is very satisfying. Drain a can of chick peas and mash (electrically if you have a tool, using a masher or fork if you don't) with some finely chopped garlic, olive oil, juice of a lemon, paprika or ground cumin. You can add a teaspoon of tahini (sesame paste) but this is quite expensive and not to everyone's taste. Garnish with a drizzle of olive oil and paprika. For variety, you can even add in a mashed avocado or a teaspoon of garam masala. Try some chopped coriander or some finely cubed or mashed beetroot for a stunning colour.

Now make an interesting platter of lovely coloured raw vegetables. Think cucumber, red and yellow peppers, celery, carrots, radishes, small florets of cauliflower, spring onions, cherry tomatoes, fennel, green beans, etc. Get creative with your presentation!

Nachos or tortilla chips come in different shapes and flavours, it is best to choose oven baked healthy ones. Don't put them on the same platter as the vegetables though, as the moisture will make them go soggy. Try toasted pita bread strips too.

Tomato and mozzarella salad is a visually pleasing dish showing off the Italian flag. Either make a large sharing platter, or present on individual plates. Slice large tomatoes and layer alternatively with thin slices of buffalo mozzarella. You could also add avocado for extra luxury. Sprinkle with fresh basil leaves that you can tear with your fingers. At the last-minute serve with olive oil and balsamic vinegar, salt and pepper. You could put these on the table so people can add what they want, and the balsamic colour does not spoil the look of your salad.

Look at the price of fresh cut basil, against a pot of basil in soil. The soil pot will grow again and again with a daily dose of sunshine and water. For cut basil, stand the stems in a glass of water and put on the window sill. They will shoot roots and continue to grow either in the glass or a pot of soil. Basil smells delicious!

Garlic bread is delicious as a side order for pretty much anything, Make garlic butter by leaving 100g of butter to get to room temperature or soft enough to beat. Chop half a head of garlic and a generous handful of parsley very finely. Mix butter, garlic and parsley, season well. Slice up a baguette. Spread garlic butter onto each slice of bread. Wrap re-shaped baguette in foil. Bake for approximately 15 - 20 minutes in a hot oven before serving.

Coq Au Vin (Chicken and Wine Casserole) is hearty and surprisingly easy. The juiciest cut of chicken is the thigh, but drumsticks or breast work too. Into a large Ziploc bag, or a big bowl, add three tablespoons of flour plus your seasoning. This can be salt, pepper and some herbs or spices of your choice. Add the chicken and shake or mix until coated.

On medium heat, add chicken to an oiled saucepan a few pieces at a time and brown on the outside – this takes about two minutes on each side. Remove. Keeping the pan on a gentle heat, fry a chopped onion until it is soft, not coloured. If you wish, you can add lardons or cubed bacon or garlic.

Add the chicken back to pan, with (optionally) some sliced carrots, mushrooms, red pepper and other vegetables of your choice. Pour a whole bottle of red wine into the pot, and about half the same amount of water or stock, enough until all the ingredients are covered. Not keen to use wine? You can replace the wine using the full amount of stock. Top up with bunches of herbs to add flavour. Of course you would have to give your dish a new name!

Add some seasoning, a bay leaf, or some thyme along with salt and plenty of pepper. This can be simmered on the stove or in the oven (170 degrees C) for 50-80 minutes.

To make a real "one pot supper" you can add chopped or new potatoes 30 minutes after starting and add fresh or frozen peas a few minutes before serving. Alternatively make some mashed potato and serve with whatever vegetables you choose.

Fish en Papillote has to be the easiest dinner party cook of all times – all the work is done in advance.

Cut foil or greaseproof paper into about 30cm squares. Basically the fish cooks from the steam created in the parcel which also cooks the vegetables. You may want to grease the paper by rubbing some olive oil on the cooking side.

In each parcel lay out some base vegetables - a raft of French beans, or asparagus, thinly sliced fennel or kale. Hard vegetables like carrots or potatoes need to be cut into small pieces. Soft vegetables such as zucchini can be in bigger chunks.

Place a piece of fish onto the vegetables. Salmon or a white fish are excellent; then season and flavour - you can run wild with ideas: pesto, olive tapenade, cherry tomatoes, anchovy puree and capers. Season well.

Close up the parcels. Lift up all four corners making a bag. Just before sealing, add a little liquid. One spoonful is enough. Water, stock, tomatoes or a good option is a tablespoon of white wine. Twist corners and edges together to create a sealed packet.

Bake at 180 degrees C for 12-15 minutes, depending on the density and size of the piece of fish. Check it is cooked by opening the parcel and pressing the fish. If it feels firm to the touch, give it a little longer. Now serve. It looks lovely served in the parcel. Couscous is a lovely accompaniment to soak up the lovely juices you have made. A green salad works too.

> *"This is what I called BLOKE COOKING. I learnt how to cook to impress whilst at university but have still cooked this weekly ever since. The varieties are endless - and I still appreciate no mess!!"*
>
> --Mike, Newcastle University

Apple and Almond Tart is a great recipe to have up your sleeve because everyone enjoys something sweet at the end of a meal. This easy tart can be prepared in advance and can be served cold or just warmed slightly.

Take a sheet of puff pastry and cut in half lengthways. Brush the long edges with egg, then fold over a one-centimetre line, sticking it down to make a border. Roll a packet of marzipan thinly and cut into strips which you arrange over the centre of the pastry.

Thinly slice up three large cooking apples. Peeling them is optional. The tart looks lovely with skin off or on, so long as you arrange in a neat pattern to fill your tart frame and cover the marzipan, you will be all set. Dust the top with icing sugar and bake at the top of a hot oven for approximately 20 minutes, or as the pastry packet instructs. It is ready when the edges have risen and are golden. Sprinkle with sliced almonds. Delicious served with cream or vanilla ice cream. You can also substitute the apples for fruits such as apricots or cherries, but nothing too watery like melon or pairs.

7. HOME Cooking

Home cooking does not have to be time consuming or overly challenging. This section will give you tips and tricks for food management that take into account student limitations – a tight budget, limited time, and limited equipment. You can eat well whilst mainly avoiding fatty, sugary, or fast-foods. Here's how to replace them with items that are easy, economical, tasty and healthy.

Cooking for one can be lonely. It can also get pricey, as supermarkets make bulk or "family size" purchases cost effective. By buddying up with your housemates, you can make a rota for not only the chores, but include the shopping and cooking too. This way you can have one or more nights "off" when a meal is cooked for you, and you can enjoy a sociable, economical meal instead of a lonely plate!

By learning a few basic culinary techniques, you will have the flexibility to adapt many recipes. The recipes in this section can be cooked up in a flash. Of course, don't forget to ask your friends and family to contribute their tips and recipes.

TIPS and reminders

The mantra in Time-Management equally applies to food management. To optimise your budget, time, AND wellness: *Plan what you eat, and eat what you plan!*

If the local newspaper or supermarket offer discount coupons, take advantage. Save some cash. Also, keep an eye out for when the supermarket marks-down perishable items and plan to shop to take advantage of this.

Be aware of sell-by dates. Rotate your fridge so you eat in date order. Whilst the fifo (first in, first out) principle is important, sometimes you may find a reduced item with a short shelf life – this could need to move to the front of the queue.

Non-perishables can be saved for your end-of-the-week recipes. Plan your weekly menu following the logical order of consumption; fish first, then meat, then pasta and legumes at the end of the week.

THREE Core Recipes

1. Stock / bouillon / broth

This is easy and cheap to make, yet very nutritional and the basis for nearly all soups and sauces. Although the process seems long, there actually isn't much work involved, it is simply a matter of simmering the stockpot until done. I make a batch every week, and can use it as a base for so many other dishes. There are no essential quantities, just put in what you have, fill up with water, and simmer gently with the lid on, on the lowest possible heat. Ideal simmer time is two to four hours.

Base stock – vegetables only

- ✓ One or two large onions, cut in quarters – keep the brown skin on, it adds colour to the stock
- ✓ Two to four carrots cut in half – no need to peel, but wash off soil
- ✓ The outer tough stalks from a head of celery – cut roughly into chunks to fit your pan
- ✓ The dark green leaves from the top of a couple of leeks washed thoroughly

OPTIONAL EXTRAS: choose your favourites from the following selection:

- ✓ a couple of bay leaves
- ✓ a few whole black peppercorns
- ✓ herbs as desired – fresh or dried, garlic, lemon rind

✓ chilli adds spice – cabbage adds robustness, and spices can make it exotic!
✓ *NOTE: You may also add these items for your final dish.*

<u>Chicken, beef and fish stocks</u>

For chicken stock, take all the above ingredients and add chicken bones. These can be raw – a chicken carcass, just pieces, or even a whole chicken. You can even keep the wing tips and neck if they come with the chicken! Alternatively, use cooked bones (for example, bones left over from a roast).

To make beef stock, ask a local butcher for beef bones, which he may give you free of charge. You could roast or fry them first to maximise the flavour. A teaspoon of vinegar in stock made with bones helps to leech out even more goodness.

To make fish stock, the bones should not boil for more than 20 minutes or else the taste will be sour. So, start off the vegetables and twenty minutes before finishing, add the fish bones and head. Prawn peelings, raw or cooked, also make a great stock for a flavoursome soup or risotto.

For all stocks, strain liquid through a sieve lined with a piece of cloth – ideally a piece of muslin, but a clean tea-towel will do. You can eat the chunks of vegetable, especially carrot and onion, which are soft, sweet and delicious. The celery and leek can get a bit tough. Stand in a tall Tupperware and keep in the fridge once cool. The fat will rise to the surface and can be removed easily.

2. Béchamel or white sauce

This is an easy recipe that can be used as a base for creamy soups and sauces.

Melt a knob of butter (30 grams approximately) in a pan, then add enough flour (about 1.5 - 2 tablespoons) to make a "roux." This is a ball which has the consistency of play-doh!

Whilst continually whisking to avoid lumps forming, add 500ml of milk a little at a time – or until it is the consistency you require, depending on what you are going to use it for. Bring to the boil and simmer gently for five minutes. Add seasoning to taste and your choice of flavour:

- ✓ Add grated cheese for a sauce for pasta – such as macaroni cheese.
- ✓ Make a little thinner (as desired) with extra milk and add to pureed vegetables for a soup – try cauliflower soup; broccoli and cheddar soup; flaked fish and parsley soup; stilton and walnut soup; sweetcorn, with crab or clams for a sweetcorn chowder.
- ✓ Add plenty of chopped parsley for a sauce for ham or gammon, fish or boiled eggs, steamed or roast vegetables.

This recipe, with slightly less milk, is also the topping for a croque monsieur (toasted cheese and ham sandwich), a lasagne or moussaka. This can also be used for the bottom layer of a fish or chicken and mushroom pie. Try a topping of mashed potato. When you have perfected a béchamel sauce, look for a cheese soufflé recipe (which uses béchamel) and have a go!

3. Spaghetti bolognaise

Here is a basic recipe that is quick and easy and can be used as the basis for many other dishes. Vegetarians should not miss out, so an equally delicious version can be used by meat eaters and vegetarians alike.

Meat lovers bolognaise

- ✓ one chopped onion
- ✓ three cloves of garlic
- ✓ olive oil
- ✓ an optional glass of wine, red best but white is fine too
- ✓ 150g minced beef
- ✓ a large teaspoon of dried oregano
- ✓ one tin of tomatoes
- ✓ salt and pepper
- ✓ tablespoon of tomato puree

Note – All these quantities are flexible depending on the sizes sold at your supermarket and your personal preferences.

Fry the onion in some olive oil, and after five to six minutes, add the beef. When it is browned all over add everything else. Simmer for 40 minutes, season well. Serve on pasta, a baked potato, rice or use in a lasagne, layered with pasta sheets and béchamel sauce.

Hearty veggie bolognaise

- ✓ 100g (approx.) each of shitake and white mushrooms
- ✓ three cloves of garlic
- ✓ one chopped onion
- ✓ olive oil
- ✓ half a tin of lentils / chickpeas
- ✓ optional glass of red wine
- ✓ one red and one green pepper diced
- ✓ large teaspoon of dried oregano and thyme
- ✓ one tin of tomatoes
- ✓ salt and pepper
- ✓ tablespoon of tomato puree

Sauté the onion, garlic, then add all the other ingredients. Summer gently for 30-40 minutes. Season well and enjoy! This can be used in a vegetarian lasagne, and as a pasta, rice or potato sauce. Experiment adding your favourite vegetables too.

Chilli

Follow either of the bolognaise recipes above, omitting the oregano and adding instead a fresh chopped chilli and a teaspoon of chilli flakes as you fry the onion. 10 minutes before serving, add a can of drained red kidney beans. Serve with rice or a baked potato. Top with grated cheese.

SOME Favourites

Here is a selection of favourites and essentials our team has put together. You will notice that for most of these recipes there is a huge amount of choice and flexibility – as there is in most recipes. Allow your preferences, seasonality, price and sense of adventure be your guide!

There's also room for you to add your favourites! Ask your friends and relatives to give you recipes for the dishes they make that you love.

1. Cheer for Chia!

Not so much a recipe as a collection of goodies that are assembled and soaked the night before, so that your breakfast the next morning is ready to go!

- 50g whole oats
- 1 tablespoons chia seeds. These can be pricey, but are worth the spend as they will keep you feeling full up all morning
- 180ml milk - any dairy free alternative is fine, but avoid sweetened ones
- Your favourite fruit /nuts chopped up – try apple, banana, raspberries, sultanas / apricot / almonds / grated coconut etc
- Juice of half a lemon
- Half a teaspoon of cinnamon (optional)

Put all items in a portion-size plastic tub or re-used jam jar, put on the lid and shake. Chill overnight to allow to swell. Before eating, sweeten if desired with honey.

2. Hooray for Pancakes!

These mean different things to different people. My family makes thin crepes for breakfast when someone has a birthday. The French are happy to eat them every day!

- 180g plain flour
- 3 eggs
- 300ml milk (almond or other non-dairy options)
- 100ml water

Put flour in a large bowl. Make a hole in the middle, into which you add eggs. Start to whisk, incorporating the flour. As it thickens, slowly add milk mixed with water. Keep whisking until all lumps are gone. Let the batter settle in the fridge for at least half an hour.

Use a lightly oiled frying pan, keeping a piece of kitchen paper to spread the thinnest smear of oil before each pancake. Butter is traditional, but tends to burn easily, and adds calories. Over a medium heat, pour a small amount of batter into the pan, quickly rotating it around to spread out the mixture as thinly as possible. Fill any gaps with a little extra batter. Work quickly. When pancake slides in the pan, flip to cook the other side. Serve with jam, chocolate spread or simply sugar and lemon.

3. Homemade Baked Beans

Great for breakfast, or in fact any other meal of the day. Once you have tasted this recipe you will never go back to the sugary canned ones. Easy to make, this just needs time and planning. Use a can of flageolet beans – or better and cheaper is to soak your own in a container of water over night. The next day, boil for 1.5-2 hours. Perhaps a weekend job! Experiment with other beans too. Follow the instructions for soaking and cooking times. Similarly adjust the sauce flavours to make it your own. Each time we make this, it varies!

- I finely chopped onion or washed leek
- Olive oil
- ½ teaspoon paprika
- 3 cloves garlic
- 1 tin tomatoes
- 1 tablespoon tomato puree
- (optional extras – teaspoon of curry powder and 50g sultanas)

Gently fry onion or leek in olive oil, add a teaspoon of smoked paprika. Add garlic, tinned and puree tomatoes and beans. Simmer for 30-40 minutes to let the beans absorb all the flavours. Serve on toast with a fried or poached egg on top.

4. Amigos! Mexican Soup

We invented this recipe when we had some red peppers starting to get a bit wrinkly. Cumin is a favourite flavour.

- 3-4 Peppers Use two red for colour and sweetness, the others can be any colour
- 2 onions
- 2-3 teaspoons ground cumin
- 1 – 1.5 teaspoons of chilli powder
- 250gms soaked and rinsed kidney beans – or one drained can
- four, large fresh or one can of tomatoes
- 750ml chicken or vegetable stock

Roughly cut up peppers and onions. Fry together until softened, then add ground cumin and chilli powder. Add kidney beans, and tomatoes. Save some pennies by buying a tin of whole plum tomatoes. Chop – or rather mash them yourself with a wooden spoon. Finally add chicken or vegetable stock, - or just enough water to cover. Simmer for 20-30 minutes before whizzing with a food wand or blender. Season.

This is a whole meal, and can be served with a selection of traditional Mexican toppings: – choose a mixture from tortillas, chopped avocado, sour cream or grated cheese. You could also add some shredded chicken, which has been pan fried with garlic.

5. Anything Risotto!

Don't tell an Italian, but risotto is dead easy to make. Don't believe the hype about stirring in one direction only, blah! If you have rice in your cupboard, (Arborio is traditional, but any will do,) mixed with anything flavoursome, you are never far from a tasty meal. Be adventurous with flavours you add to your risotto!

Risotto Ratio Rules. Rule of thumb is 1:3. That means whatever you measure for your rice, you will need three times as much liquid. Stock is the most traditional, but you can use milk in a chicken and mushroom or creamy risotto; or even water so long as you add plenty of flavour. Up to a third of your liquid can be white wine. A vegan option is a risotto made with a generous amount of pesto sauce, plenty of vegetables and water.

- 1 onion or a whole leek
- 30g butter /ghee / coconut oil
- 100g rice
- 300ml liquid – stock / wine
- Your choice of flavours
- Herb / spice / seasoning

Dice onion or leek and gently fry in butter. Add the rice to the pan. Stir gently to coat it before adding the liquid. You can add other flavours here – herbs such as sage for robust flavour, dried but rehydrated mushrooms for an earthy flavour, small cubes of pumpkin, etc.

Add the liquid and simmer gently for 30 to 40 minutes depending on how crunchy or al-dente you like your rice. Stir as needed to stop the rice sticking.

Just before serving you could add a handful of spinach and stir as it just wilts, then serve sprinkled with a generous amount of parmesan cheese, of which a vegan option is available.

6. Sophie's Stir-fry Special.

"I grew up in Asia and love Asian flavours. I was not allowed instant noodles because of the chemicals...so I make my own! The first year of uni, I lived on stir-fry, but never tired of it, because it's always different!" My essentials: *garlic, ginger, spring onion, chilli, light soy sauce, Thai fish sauce.*

Stir frying is a fast and healthy way to enjoy one-pan cooking. You can add anything you fancy! No wok? Use a frying pan. Prepare and chop all ingredients before starting to cook. Each item should be bite-size and never need cutting when served. Make sure the oil (such as corn oil) is really hot before adding your ingredients. To create a Chinese flavour, add a few drops of sesame oil. Build up the pan with your choices in the order of how long they need to cook:

1. **Longest time**: onions, leeks, thin strips of chicken or meat (8-15 mins).

2. **Medium time**: red / green peppers, mangetout / snow peas, broccoli, ginger, garlic, prawns (2-3 mins).

3. **Noodles**: keeping all ingredients moving. Add soy sauce and flavours of choice. Be gentle if you add salt, as soy sauce is already salty.

NOTE on NOODLES – there are 100's of types of noodles; dried, fresh, with or without egg, different flours – rice, wheat, mung bean to name a few. They come in different widths, lengths, and flavours! Follow their instructions, usually pouring boiling water over them to loosen, then add to your stir fry. They cook for a further one to two minutes while soaking up your flavours.

4. **Fast, last minute items**: bean sprouts, tofu, spring onions, baby sweetcorn, mushrooms, peas (one minute – enough to heat through.)

5. **Garnish**: chopped coriander, sesame seeds.

7. Over-night Packed Lunch Couscous

My French pen pal taught me how to do this, and I have never looked back. Dead easy, no cooking, healthy and really delish.

To your Tupperware lunch box, add the following:

- 3 tablespoons dry couscous. (Yes! Straight out of the packet – no cooking needed!)
- 1-2 tablespoons olive oil
- The zest and juice of a whole lemon
- Half a cucumber chopped up into small cubes
- 1-2 large tomatoes finely diced
- Salt and pepper

Then let you imagination take over: choose a selection of whatever you enjoy from, but not limited to; beetroot, goat's cheese or parmesan, Greek yoghurt, fresh mint chopped, frankly - any vegetables, fruit or nuts!

Leave in the fridge overnight for the magic to start. The vegetables will create juice which will swell the couscous. Yet, in the morning if it seems a little dry still, add a few teaspoons of water or lemon juice, it will be ready by lunchtime.

8. Quick Ratatouille

This classic combination of eggplant, courgette (zucchini), tomato and onion is divine! Many French recipes give the instruction to fry all the parts separately before combining. This takes a lot of time, and soaks up a large amount of oil.

Instead: Chop equal amounts of all aubergine, courgette and onion. Add a generous teaspoon of herbs de Provence, and four cloves of chopped up garlic. Fill with enough tinned tomatoes to cover, and simmer gently for 25 minutes. Add some tomato puree to thicken the sauce if necessary.

Optional extras – mushrooms or red pepper – whatever you fancy.

Served sprinkled with grated cheese, and crusty bread this is a quick and tasty, low calorie meal.

9. Helen's Banana Bread.

Bananas always seem to ripen at a different speed, and you end up with either not enough or too many. You can freeze them, peeled first. Indulge in this delicious banana bread. It is really a cake – but calling it a bread makes it seem less decadent!

- 3 mashed bananas
- 1.5 teaspoons of baking powder
- 110g butter
- 200g sugar
- 3 eggs
- 180g plain flour
- 0.5 teaspoon salt
- Optional extras: chocolate chips, chopped dates, vanilla essence, nuts etc.

Mix together the butter and sugar with a wooden spoon. Add the eggs and the mashed bananas. Mix in everything else. Pour the mix into a greased (or silicon) loaf tin. Bake in a pre-heated oven180° for 55 minutes.

Allow to cool (if you can) before serving. Keeps well for several days.

10. Chocolate and Pistachio Biscotti.

Because these are dry, they keep well for a couple of weeks in a Tupperware box – if you can resist them!

- 100g plain flour
- 50g caster sugar
- 1 tsp baking powder
- 40g shelled pistachios
- 40g chocolate – either chips for baking, or a bar of dark chocolate chopped up finely with a knife
- 1 medium / large egg
- 1 teaspoon of cinnamon (optional)

Combine all the ingredients in a bowl and mix well to form a slightly sticky dough, which you can gently knead on a floured surface. Roll into a long sausage shape about 4 cms wide.
Bake for 25 mins160C/Gas 4.
Cool, then cut into slices about 1cm/½in thick. Put slices flat on the baking tray and bake again for 5-10 minutes. (Dipped into coffee is best!)

11. Crustless Quiche

Do you want the taste, flexibility (lunchbox) and convenience of a quiche, but without the hassle of making pastry AND all those calories? Four portions. Freezes well.

Whisk four eggs with 375ml milk and 100g of self-rising flour.

Grease an oven proof dish and scatter your filling ingredients - which is approximately 150g of the "stuff" you want in your quiche – examples include ham, cubed bacon lardons, smoked salmon, broccoli florets, sliced mushrooms or tomatoes, goats cheese etc.
150g of grated cheese – choose something with a strong flavour such as mature cheddar.
Salt / pepper plus seasoning of your choice –e.g. dill for fish, oregano or herbs de Provence for vegetables, parsley and coriander go with everything, crushed red pepper flake etc.
Pour the egg mixture over the top and bake in a pre-heated oven at 180°C for 35-40 minutes until golden. Can be eaten hot or cold in your lunchbox.

12. Sheila's Protein Balls

The fastest, no cook, yummiest, energy fired, healthy snack on the planet. Keep in your fridge and you will never want a cheap candy or chocolate bar again!

INGREDIENTS:
50g of chocolate protein or whey powder
60g of smooth peanut butter
100g rolled oats
60ml of coconut cream + 30ml of coconut water. Open a tin of coconut milk – use the solids from the top and some water from below.
6 dates or dried apricots chopped up roughly but finely with a sharp knife.

Mix the whole lot together with a wooden spoon in a mixing bowl, then roll into balls with your hands. Chill in the fridge for at least half an hour, and roll in cocoa powder before serving.

These make a great gift for friends too!

13. My favourite! A recipe for

_____

Given to me by_____

14. My favourite! A recipe for

_____

Given to me by_____

15. My favourite! A recipe for

_____

Given to me by_____

16. My favourite! A recipe for

_____

Given to me by_____

8. ALCOHOL: What Strategy?

The pressure to drink is part life for most students. Nonetheless, not every student actually WANTS to drink. Religious, allergic or personal reasons, such as experience with a family member who has an addiction problem, are all valid reasons to avoid alcohol. In addition to this, wanting to keep a clear head for an important event the next day or wanting to preserve budget (alcoholic drinks can easily as much as double your restaurant bill) are all valid reasons that must be respected. As mentioned in chapter 3 on Food and Health, drinking is a choice, not an obligation.

SAYING NO

If drinking is *NOT* your thing, either as a one off, or a permanent philosophy; yet you feel a pressure that you are being coerced to partake, here are some helpful strategies:

- Have a glass of fizzy water, with ice and a slice of lemon. Nobody is to know that it's not a gin & tonic.
- Be aware of the tendencies of your friends and the types of parties you go to, and gravitate toward those where you don't have to swim "against the current".
- Try saying "no thanks" in the mirror a few times before you have to say it in a social situation. It will make it easier.
- Carry around a glass (of wine, beer, etc.) so nobody will single you out. You don't have to drink from it.
- The occasional white lie. Taking antibiotics or prescription medicine disallows alcohol. Claiming to be on "Dry January" – or any other month can help to deter a persuasive pal.
- Alcohol is packed with calories, so being on a diet is a good excuse not to drink.

THINKING Maybe

Alcohol is part of your life. In the US, the legal age to drink is 21, and in the UK 18. If you are legal and open to drink alcohol, ask yourself why you want to drink.

- You should never be answering, "to get drunk".

- Alcohol may give you confidence and act as a social lubricant – but remember; excess can cause you to say too much, do foolish things, and make a fool of yourself. You could quickly end up with a negative reputation, which takes considerably longer to shake off.
- To fit in with a social group. Make the conversation the focus of the evening, not what is in your glass.
- Know your own personal limits. If you need to take transport to get home at the end of the evening, don't leave yourself in a situation where your safety is compromised because you are muddled or uncoordinated.

Here are some strategies to manage that choice optimally and conscientiously.

- Get informed: Read about the effects of alcohol on your body. Read the "alcohol section" in the food/health chapter.
- Be really careful about the effects of cheap alcohol on you, your body and yes your reputation. Wasted means just that ... wasted.

CHOOSING a drink

- If you NEED a drink, you may have a problem. Dependency may creep up without you noticing. If you drink every day or can't cope without a drink, seek some help. Alcoholics Anonymous is a global organization, so look for your local meeting.
- For those that choose to drink, here is a section on how to appreciate wine, written and contributed by wine expert and wine author Wendy Narby. Wine has been around from for millennia, and is a part of the culture and lives of many. This section is by no means here to promote wine, but rather to educate those who are interested to take an objective look not just at wine, but also at alcohol. It is also intended, that when you choose to have a drink, your selection is based on the right reasons, and that you can say "yes" or "no" with equal comfort.

9. THE Pleasure of Wine by Wendy Narby

Students and alcohol are often linked together with negative connotations. But it doesn't have to be this way. Wendy Narby, wine expert and author of "Bordeaux Bootcamp" presents a comprehensive introduction to wine, introducing the art of an ancient and complex commodity and what can become the pleasure of drinking.

Wine is basically fermented grape juice. Ripe grapes contain sugar that is converted into alcohol via yeast. Similar fermentation also converts apples into cider and cereals into beer. The large number of regions that produce wine, their different soils and climates and the different varieties of grapes that are used to produce it, explains the wide range of wines available.

Spirits are made when these wines are distilled, concentrating the alcohol. Wine is about 80% water, 12-15% alcohol and the remaining percentage includes the polyphenols or plant extracts, mainly from the skins and pips that give the wine it's colour, flavours and tannins.

The riper the grapes, means the more sugar, and hence more alcohol. New world wines from hotter climates nearer the equator are often higher in alcohol than cooler climate wines like Germany and Alsace for example. The higher the altitude, the cooler the climate, the fresher and lower the alcohol level in the wine tends to be.

To appreciate wine, we usually proceed through three stages: sight, smell and taste. It's not about wine snobbery, it's more about understanding what is in the glass and more importantly whether you like it or not. Understanding what you like prevents disappointment and possibly expensive mistakes when choosing wine. YOU decide what you like, so don't be told by anyone else what wine you should and shouldn't like. Don't be afraid to experiment and try new wines - you might discover a whole new passion.

The tools of the trade

Wine bottles are usually 75cl, which gives six generous, to eight glasses of wine. Heavier bottles imply a more expensive wine or a bigger bolder wine or a bigger marketing spend. There are half bottles, magnums (two bottles,) and so on - up to a Melchior which is 18 bottles - you'll need a hand pouring that one!

Wine glasses come in all shapes and sizes and do affect the way a wine tastes, but you really don't need different wine glass shapes for different wines. Ideally a clear glass with a stem, so you can see the colour and heat from your hand won't warm the wine up. Ideally the bowl of the glass should be wider at the bottom and narrower at the top, to trap in the aromas. One regular wine glass will be fine for any wine including bubbly.

How to taste wine

- ✓ Don't fill your glass too full, about one third, this will allow you to swirl the wine in the glass without getting it down your shirt!
- ✓ Tilt the glass over a white surface, look at the colour and density - which means how easy it is to see through it.
    - o A young red wine will be purple in colour and will become more ruby red and eventually tawny and browner with age.
    - o A young white wine will have greenish tinges when young becoming more yellow and then also brownish with age.
    - o Normally less intensive wines (less easy to see through) will age more quickly than other deeper, darker, more purple wines. Most wines you find on wine and supermarket shelves will be ready for drinking.
- ✓ Legs or tears are when the wine sticks to the side of the glass. Different ingredients of wine (water, alcohol, and sugar) have different surface tensions so they stick to the side of the glass in different ways when mixed, creating this phenomenon.
- ✓ The smell, called a "bouquet" when there are lots of different aromas, is important too.
    - o Put your nose in the glass above the wine. You should smell anything from fruit (it's made from grapes after all!) to spices, woody notes or on older notes you might even smell leathery or mossy notes.
    - o Then give your glass a swirl and smell again. Moving the glass around allows more air to come into contact with the wine so it releases more aromas - it should smell stronger and perhaps more complex.

✓ Taste
  o Areas on your tongue are more or less sensitive to different sensations of sweet, sour and bitter. Different people are more or less sensitive to different tastes, especially bitter, which is why we all like different things.
  o Taste, flavour and smell are interwoven. Try tasting with a nose clip on and you will hardly taste anything!
✓ Wine has mouth feel, a sensation on the palate.
  o Does it feel round? Soft? Smooth? Astringent?
  o Does it leave your mouth dry or does it make your mouth water?
  o Compare what water feels like swirling around your mouth - it's different.
✓ Tannins are what give a wine body. If you want to understand the difference between acid and tannins - put some lemon juice in some water – that's acid. To understand what tannins feel like, leave a tea bag in a mug of hot water and swirl that around once it's cold.
✓ We talk about the "attack of the wine", this is the first sensation - usually fruit; then the mid palate - you start to get the notion of "mouth feel" - acidity, grip (tannins), smoothness, and then the finish - describing the final sensation or impression. This might sound technical as a beginner but this is how you can develop your skills.
✓ Finally, there's length. This means the length of time the flavours and sensations stay in the mouth after you have swallowed the wine (or spat it out if you're a taster).

How to drink wine

The traditional way of drinking wine is with food. The lovely complexity of wine is enhanced by food, and food is enhanced by wine. Matching food and wine is a complex subject that many books have been written about. Generally, the lighter the food, the lighter the wine and vice versa.

Importantly, eating while drinking wine slows down the alcohol absorption into the blood stream.

Grapes and place

Historically, wine production started in the Mediterranean, spreading North through Europe, and now wine production is established throughout the world. There are thousands of varieties of grapes, grown across many continents in many different climates, that give us an exciting world full of wine choices.

The colour (red, white or rosé) of wine depends on the skin of the grapes. Next time you eat a black grape look inside, only the skin is coloured, the flesh is clear. If we press the juice throwing away the skins and ferment it, we'll end up with white wine. If we want to make red wine we have to keep the skins in contact with that juice during fermentation - this allows the colours, flavours and tannins to seep from the skin into the juice and finally the wine.

You can make white wine from red grapes by removing the skin - as they do in Champagne for example. You can't make red wine from white grapes. Most rosé wines are made from keeping the grape skins in the juice for just a short period of time, or we can add some red into white wine, again as they do in Champagne.

Sweeter wine has more residual sugar, meaning not all the sugar in the grape juice has been fermented into alcohol.

A sense of place or a sense of fruit?

Old World or European wine production tends to be identified by place: Bordeaux, Burgundy, Rhone, Mosel, Rioja Chianti, and so on.

New World wines tend to be identified more by the grape varieties: Pinot Noir, Cabernet, Shiraz, Riesling, Chardonnay, Sangiovese, and so on.

It's not that the Old World doesn't use the same varieties, it's just that the New World prefers identifying their wines using grape varieties instead of location, believing it's easier for the consumer. Also the Old World tends to blend different types of grapes together rather than using just one type (although some places, like South Africa or California, will talk about their Bordeaux or Rhone Blends).

When reading labels, New World wine labels may be easier to understand once you have a feeling for which types of wine you enjoy. Old World labels will tend to mention place over varietal.

Hotter climates, closer to equator tend to produce wines with more alcohol from riper grapes. Northern vineyards wines show more acid, known colloquially as wines that are more "fresh". A Merlot or a Pinot grown in a hot climate will be sweeter, riper, more concentrated, and often more alcoholic wine than if it is grown in a cooler climate.

Wine makers themselves also have their own preferences and styles. If you get interested, you can start following wine makers and before you know it, you'll be hooked on this fascinating world that encompasses, geography, history, culture, agriculture, personalities and of course, pleasure.

How to buy wine

Ask the expert. This is useful advice in any walk of life. Never be afraid to ask, there's no such thing as a stupid question. People are normally happy to share their passion, and wine store staff, wine waiters, and sommeliers are a passionate bunch!

When asking for advice, put a cap on your budget. Tell your adviser what you have already tried and liked, or disliked, and tell them what you want the wine for (a party, a dinner party, a gift, casual dining, and so on).

The key to choosing wine is knowing what you like and knowing your budget, so choose a wine retailer and get to know them. If they're not friendly or helpful move to another one, and don't let them intimidate you. The wine world is full of young and passionate people, so find your wine tribe. Supermarkets tend to buy on price rather than passion.

A quick guide to the most common varietals

White:
Sauvignon Blanc or Pinot Grigio: citrusy, aromatic & fresh
Chardonnay: often more powerful from the New World when produced from stone fruit, but can be crisp and light such as Chablis
Riesling: fresh and aromatic, but can often be slightly sweet

Red:
Merlot: fruity, easy drinking
Pinot Noir: light and fresh with more power from its traditional home of Burgundy
Malbec: ripe fruit, often chocolatey
Cabernet: dark fruit, more powerful tannins, apt to age well

Vintage

The year on the label indicates the year the grapes were picked: September/October in the Northern Hemisphere, February/March in the Southern Hemisphere.

Look out for the percentage alcohol labels – a higher alcohol percentage is not always better!

"Mise en bouteille au chateau" (bottled at the chateau or estate) is normally a sign of quality, meaning the wine has been bottled at the place of production rather than being shipped around the world as bulk and bottled at the point of consumption.

How to store wine

The average time lapse between buying and drinking is a couple of hours and as a student you're unlikely to be building up a wine cellar. But, if you have a few bottles you are saving for a special occasion, pay attention to the temperature. Cool and constant is ideal, over the cooker or the fridge is not.

Store bottles horizontally if they are stoppered with a cork, it keeps the cork moist and stops it drying out, which would let air in. Vertical won't hurt a screw cap. Keep it in the dark away from vibrations.

Be aware, smaller bottles age more quickly than larger.

Don't become a wine snob - there's nothing more boring, and as said, there's no right or wrong. Just because it's more expensive doesn't always means it's better. But avoid really cheap wine, once you've counted the price of a bottle, a label, the cork (or screw cap - we love screw caps) taxes, transport, and retail margins you need to be paying enough to ensure that there's money left over for the content - drink less, drink better.

How not to get a hangover

Drink less – obviously! You may find that once you start paying attention to what you are drinking, taking time to smell, swirl and taste you will tend to drink less and possible better. If you drink less, you can afford to drink better. Joy! The other key is to eat as you drink your wine.

Remember to drink water, at least one glass for every glass of wine. Headaches associated with hangovers are exacerbated by dehydration that drinking alcohol brings, as your body tries to dilute the alcohol. Help it!

How much is too much?

Working out safe levels of wine (or any alcohol) consumption is a minefield. Some experts don't think there is any safe level and that alcohol is a poison: affecting the liver, being a trigger for certain cancers, and impacting other health issues. And that's before we even touch on the social problems of alcohol abuse. Then again, there is an argument that alcohol itself, and also other ingredients in wine, with moderate consumption can be health enhancing and possibly a social lubricant.

Recommended levels of alcohol consumption depend on which authority you consult. Consult the web for guidelines of your country of residence. For example:

- **British** National Health Service Guidelines advise maximum 14 units of alcohol for men and women, spread over one week. A small glass of wine (125ml) is considered 1.6 units so that's just less than nine small glasses of wine per week, or 1.3 bottles.

- **U.S.** Guidelines are about the same but give men a green light to drink double the allowance of women: one drink per day for women and two for men. What constitutes "a drink" is also fairly fluid, pun intended. In wine terms, one drink is defined as five fluid ounces of wine (12% alcohol), which is about 150ml, almost a bottle and a half a week.

Over the week is the key - binge drinking your whole allowance on Friday night is not part of the plan. They also recommend a couple of booze free days a week.

It obviously depends on what you drink, beer has a lower number of units per serving and spirits higher. It also depends on your own physical state; we are not all created equal faced with alcohol consumption. How alcohol affects us depends on our age, size, sex and health, our body mass, fat to muscle ratios, liver enzymes. When and how quickly we drink; whether it is with food or on an empty stomach, also effects how quickly we absorb alcohol.

Oh! - The fact that you feel fine when drinking and never get a hangover is not necessarily a good sign.

How to know if you have a problem with booze?

Awareness of your habits, feelings and reactions is a major life skill in all areas. Drinking is no different.

The **CAGE** questionnaire below is a good place to start - ask yourself these questions:

C Have you ever felt you should cut down on your drinking?
A Have people annoyed you by criticising your drinking?
G Have you ever felt bad or guilty about your drinking?
E Eye opener: Have you ever had a drink first thing in the morning to steady your nerves or to get rid of a hangover?

If you answer two with a "yes", you merit a rethink. If you think you may have a problem - get help. You are young, it's easier now than it will be later when bad habits are much more difficult to un-learn.

Final word

This short guide is a vast over simplification of a fascinating world. If you would like to know more, there are many classes, both online and in the real world. Sharing with likeminded people adds to the pleasure.

10. TIDYING Up

You might not be in the mood to clean up after the party, but you will thank yourself the next day if you complete these tasks before heading to bed!

- ✓ Put a splash of water in the red wine glasses to stop them staining.
- ✓ Put heavy, greasy pans in hot water to soak.
- ✓ Don't soak a chopping board or other wooden implements – they will warp.
- ✓ Put any leftover food in the fridge so it can still be enjoyed the next day.
- ✓ Put any scraps of food in the bin and empty it to avoid insects and other scavengers.

> *"Because our flat had a large living room, parties always seemed to be at our place. I can't say we do ALL the washing and tidying up immediately (!)... but I do always clear the space by the kettle and leave a clean mug ready – so I can stagger into the kitchen next day and start off with a strong coffee!"*
>
> Tiffany, Leamington Spa

Chapter 5: Domestic Engineering

by Rachael Desgouttes

1. KEEP a Clean and Tidy Life!

It is an old cliché that students "exist" in a filthy pigsty rather than a home. Have you seen the hilarious 1980's TV sit com "The Young Ones"? If not – take a peek!

It can be a shock to leave the comfort of home, where so much was done for you, possibly without you even realising. Now you have to do it all yourself. Don't panic! A small amount of time, effort and money can keep your home clean, neat and tidy, making a safe environment for you to live and work both physically and mentally.

One mother told another "After a whole semester away from home – my son hadn't changed his sheets once!" Her friend replied, "Oh, I have fixed that – I put twelve bottom sheets on at the beginning of the term, and my son just has to peel one off each week."

Whilst 12 bottom sheets may be a cunning quick-fix, it still isn't hygienic or economical. Instead, this chapter will contain some basic and savvy tips for maintaining a clean and aesthetic living space.

2. WHY Bother Clean?!

So, now you are responsible for everything domestic, including things you may not even have thought about! Washing, cooking, changing your bed, safety, security, and hygiene, now all fall on your shoulders. You are not alone! Your new roommates will become your support network and you will gain plenty of confidence and experience from sharing your new independent lifestyle.

Whilst cleaning may have always magically happened at home, you may have never considered why we actually do it! There are many reasons;

- Our 'feel good' factor and self-respect. You may not realise how much comfort we take from a clean home – but when your surroundings become a mess, you may start to miss this feel good factor, and crave a clean space!
- Respect for your roommates and friends. (If you want your roommates to be equally thoughtful, clean and respectful, you must treat your shared space the way YOU want it to be treated. Set an example!)
- Our health. In the kitchen, a lack of cleanliness can lead to gastroenteritis, norovirus, or salmonella. In the bedroom, lack of hygiene creates the danger of bed bugs or carpet fleas, which cause bites, rashes and allergies.
- Satisfaction and achievement! Finish a pile of ironing and pat yourself on the back.

Cleanliness is a major contributor to keeping your environment SAFE; If your home is clean, you eliminate hazards, including being at risk from fire; cuts and grazes from sharp (or worse, blunt) objects and infection; cross contamination of foods which can make you sick; bed bugs; and other infestations and allergens.

> **Never underestimate how important it is to wash your hands! As soon as you arrive home, before preparing food, before eating, and after going to the toilet, thorough hand washing is critical! This means at least one minute of scrubbing with soap before rinsing. Pay attention to under the nails.**

3. CLEANING Products

Whether you live in student halls, a hostel, a shared flat or house – this is your home.

It is not necessary to fill your cupboard with a large array of expensive, branded products. If you look along the shelves of a supermarket cleaning department, and listen to the advertisements on TV, you could end up with a dozen different products for each different area and surface.

Regular cleaning means you avoid a build-up of dirt, germs and lime scale, which can become much more difficult to get rid of if left to their own devices. Regular cleaning really is a time saver in the long run.

A good cleaning kit can be made with a few inexpensive items:

- **White vinegar:** Available in all supermarkets, cheap to buy, multiple uses.
- **Bi-carbonate of soda:** Cheap, environmental, non-toxic and effective. Less abrasive than a cream cleaner, yet just as effective.
- **Fresh lemons:** Can be bought when getting old and reduced in price. Home made cleaner can keep in a spray bottle for weeks.
- **A bottle of Eucalyptus or Tea tree oil**: Can be found inexpensively in health shops.
- **Basic washing up liquid / soap detergent.**
- **Dishcloths:** These can be made from worn out towels cut into useable squares. These can be washed in the washing machine and re-used for a long time. Sponges and foam squares have a limited life and can harbour bacteria – especially in a warm environment. Each one must be kept for a specific task - don't mix the toilet cleaning sponge with the washing up sponge! They need renewing regularly. Depending on usage – a week is about the maximum life.

White vinegar	Bicarbonate of soda	Fresh lemon	Tea Tree or Eucalyptus Essential Oil
Why do we use it?			
Very cheap to buy, this mild acid has many uses: As a general cleaner, especially for cutting through grease For descaling lime scale build up, for example in the bath, kettle etc. For deodorising such as cleaning out a smelly drinks bottle, your curry-filled lunch box, the fridge or even a pair of old smelly shoes or flip flops.	Try to find a bulk purchase, as small packets can get expensive. Mixed with water, this alkaline solution is excellent for a wide range of tasks: • Dissolving dirt and grease • Lifting stains from carpets and removing marks from surfaces without scratching them • Cleaning sinks and drains • Neutralising strong odours Bicarbonate of soda can be used to deodorise the fridge. Keep a small, uncovered pot with a tablespoon of bicarbonate on the bottom shelf of the fridge. Replace it regularly as it gets damp – weekly / bi-weekly.	You don't need organic, Italian, waxy skins. The cheapest lemons still contain citric acid, which does the cleaning magic! Lemons are great for: • General surface cleaning in all rooms • Avoiding a build-up of dirt on the inner walls of the microwave which will affect its performance and taint your food, also cleansing stale smells • Neutralising smells in plastic food containers	Worth the investment – but look around and online to find the best price. Using only a few drops at time, it goes a long way! *(Good gift idea!)* Eucalyptus gives a lovely fresh fragrance to your home, but also adds vital anti-microbial properties. You can put several drops into pretty much everything: soap, laundry detergent, mop water, toilet cleaner, window cleaner, and so on.
For smear-free glass cleaning – windows, shower doors. 		• Cleaning metals such as copper and brass, including eliminating rust spots • Scrub stubborn stuck-on food off dishes	Eucalyptus oil is effective for removing spots from carpet, clothes and basically every fabric you have! It even gets gum off shoes! Test a small area of fabric first, especially synthetic, to ensure the oil doesn't react with fabric.

How do we use it?

Bad smells → Mix in a ratio of one part vinegar, 9 parts water. Either use from a spray bottle or use as a solution to soak items with tougher stains or nasty smells. 10-15 mins is enough for everyday deodorising.

Lunch boxes → For your thermos flask, lunch box or other plastic containers, if you have garlic, curry or other smells (or if they have been forgotten for too long!) you can soak them in this mixture to eliminate the smell. Extreme cases can take up to 12 hours! Soak then rinse thoroughly.

Showerheads & kettles → For clogged up showerheads - dunk them in a bucket or tub of undiluted vinegar. For kettles, fill and leave overnight. Don't boil however, as vinegar will froth up and go everywhere. Rinse the kettle thoroughly, fill with water and boil before re-using.

Taps/faucets → To descale taps, soak paper towels in vinegar and wrap around tap, cover with plastic bags. Hold in place with an elastic band. They'll look brand new.

Getting out stains → Sprinkle directly onto a wet dishcloth to use as a general cleaner all around the home when you need a slightly abrasive rub to get rid of caked on residue. For tough stains, add a little water to a tablespoonful of powder, make a paste. Smear it onto the stain; leave for 20 mins before rinsing off.

NOTE: There's an old wives' tale, that to stop red wine staining, you can add salt. WRONG! It will just make it worse. Flush the area with bicarbonate of soda water. Dab with kitchen paper.

Freshening → Put bicarb of soda, into a spray bottle filled with warm water. Shake well. Allow to dissolve and cool before use. This product can be keep indefinitely. Add just a couple of drops of essential oil as an excellent way to freshen fabric, furniture or your clothes.

Washing clothes → Pour a cup of juice into half a bucket of water and soak very dirty items overnight before washing.

Home scents → Add a few slices to a bowl of water and microwave on high power. If your house needs deodorising, boil up a pan of water with lemon slices.

Surfaces → Squeeze a lemon into hot water. Use with a cloth that you wring out thoroughly. Or, simply cut the lemon up and wipe over the inner surfaces. Rinse with clean water.

Post-holiday hack → When you have been on holiday, or you have not used items or gadgets for a long time – such as coffee makers, or blenders – run lemony water through the system to get them in tip top condition again!

All-purpose spray → Mix two drops of Tea Tree or Eucalyptus oil with two cups of water in a spray bottle. Limitless shelf life. It has a lovely freshening effect as a laundry/ironing spray.

Combatting mildew → To beat strong smells of mildew, soak items overnight in the solution, then air for a few days for the tea tree oil smell to subside.

Hand cleaner → If the chain came off your bike and you are covered in grease, Eucalyptus is an excellent cleanser and degreaser to remove grease and grime from your hands. Use neat and rub into skin before washing off thoroughly.

Excellent as an antiseptic or disinfectant wipe down, or on mould or mildew. Spray, leave for 20-30 mins, and then rinse off with soapy water.

Toilet → Half a cup of white vinegar followed by a couple of tablespoons of bicarbonate of soda put down the toilet will fizz up but clean the toilet nicely. When fizzing stops it can be flushed away. 	**Sinks & drains →** For sinks or drains, pour 100g of bicarb followed by some boiling water down the sink or basin. A weekly task. **Bathroom fixes →** Shower curtains are breeding grounds for germs. Keep a spray bottle of solution in the bathroom cupboard; quickly spray down after each use.	**Cutting board cure →** From time to time, rub a cut lemon over your wooden or plastic chopping board. 	*NOTE: As well as cleaning, Eucalyptus is one of the most powerful forms of natural medicine. See the First Aid and Medical chapter.* Eucalyptus 

4. HOUSE Management – One Room at a Time

As you read this chapter, try to list the tasks that need doing, along with the frequency. See if you match the suggested Task Schedule at the end of the chapter! Of course, it is only a guideline, and will vary depending on the number of people sharing, how long you spend at home, the frequency with which you cook, clean, shower, and so forth.

KITCHEN

The kitchen is often the focal point of a home. Especially when it is shared, it is vital to manage it effectively.

Fridge Management: Arguably the most important piece of equipment in the home, apart from keeping your fridge clean, there is an essential protocol for food storage.

It is important to prevent germs cross contaminating other foods such as from raw foods to cooked foods.

Fridge Temperature: It might seem too obvious to say, but the fridge should be cold! In rented or student accommodation, fridges are often old and may not function well enough. Ask your landlord to service or renew. A fridge thermometer can be bought cheaply to ensure you food will be stored properly and hence be safe.

Temperatures between 5°C and 63°C are known as the danger zone because bacteria can grow on food to a point where it can make you ill. Keeping food correctly chilled in the fridge slows down the growth of bacteria. Here are some cool rules to keep foods safe:

- ✓ **Ensure your fridge is at 5°C or below.** Place a mercury-free fridge thermometer on the bottom shelf above the salad drawer. Check the temperature weekly, ideally first thing in the morning before people have been in and out of the fridge getting milk and affecting the temperature. Don't rely on the fridge's own calibration scale to know that you are safe.
- ✓ **Keep the fridge door closed tightly**. The temperature will rise if the door is left open. Make sure the rubber seal is intact. This piece of rubber is folded and creased, it can crack and deteriorate with age and is an area that can harbour mould and bacteria. Pay attention and ask your landlord to renew if necessary.
- ✓ **Don't overstock** the fridge, as this can stop cool air from circulating freely and the fridge may not keep the foods properly chilled.
- ✓ **Don't put hot food** in the fridge as this can raise the fridge temperature, and cause condensation – which may drip and damage other food in the fridge.

Food Safety

- Keep dairy products wrapped and/or in containers on the top shelf of the fridge.
- Keep all cooked meats and leftovers, wrapped or in sealed containers on the middle shelf.
- Keep all raw foods, including meat, fish and poultry wrapped and in sealed containers on the bottom shelf so they don't touch each other or drip.
- If you are defrosting something, place the frozen item into a bowl and put the bowl on the bottom shelf. That way it cannot drip contaminated juices onto something below.
- Store leftovers in the fridge within two hours of cooling after cooking. Eat them within three days. Only reheat cooked food ONCE. If not eaten after reheating, throw away.
- Keep fresh vegetables in the vegetable draw. If one item is damaged, it will spoil other items, so use produce as quickly as possible.

- Wrap herbs and salad in kitchen paper to absorb moisture and keep longer.
- Take mushrooms out of plastic, or they sweat and rot. A brown paper bag is best, or in a glass/china bowl.
- Rotate your food items such as eggs so that you always eat the oldest first. If you keep taking the freshest, you may end up with a very smelly rotten egg experience which is NOT pleasant! If you keep eggs in a rack in the fridge door, always add new to the right, take from the left and shift along leftwards as you use!
- For homemade food, it is a good idea to keep a marker pen handy and label the lid with the date that the food was made or frozen. This will help you decide when it is past its prime.
- Dry goods also need regularly checking. Items such as pasta and flour could harbour weevils which will multiply and infest your cupboard if not cleaned away.
- Bread is tricky because we often can't see mould growing on it until it is quite advanced. To avoid wastage, sliced bread can be kept in the freezer and taken out a slice at a time, as needed. A bread bin is ideal to minimise moisture spoiling your bread, but for this, a plastic box will suffice. Be careful not to keep adding more and more bread on top of old crumbs as the spores will spread. If your bread has mould, it isn't enough to just cut away the mouldy bits. It could have spread to inside the bread. Dispose of the bread and wash the container thoroughly, making sure it is absolutely dry before placing new bread inside.
- If you are using canned food or drink, make sure you wash the top of the can before opening. You don't know where it has been stored before you bought it – best case scenario it will be dusty, but it could have rat's urine or other toxic nasty elements. If you don't use all the contents at once DO NOT store the remainder in the can. Decant into a plastic box, or a dish covered with Clingfilm.

---

1. TOP SHELF

Keep dairy produce and delicate items well wrapped on the top shelf. *NOTE: Lidded yoghurt pots are excellent containers to keep and reuse.*

Do not keep perishable food in the refrigerator door. With frequent door opening the temperature fluctuates and may spoil fragile items such as pâté or butter.

2. HIGH SHELF

Cooked meat and prepared food such as quiche should be on a high shelf. Mushrooms do not like plastic. A paper bag is best, or just an open bowl.

---

3. LOW SHELF

Raw meat, fish, and especially poultry may drip and cross-contaminate so must be stored on the lowest shelf.

If you are defrosting a raw frozen item, place it in a bowl or on a plate otherwise it will drip.

4. CRISPER – bottom shelf / drawer

Raw vegetables and fruit keep best here. Put heavy vegetables such as cauliflower and cabbage at the bottom and light items such as salad on top. Wrap delicate greens in kitchen paper to absorb their "sweat" and keep them dry! Dry produce keeps longer.

Be sure to check at least twice a week that items are still fresh – a bad item will turn other items bad.

5. DOOR

"Fifo" = first in, first out. Find a system to rotate your eggs, if you add new eggs to the rack, shuffle along the old, so you always take from the same end.

Milk is often kept in the door because the cartons are tall, and because it can also pick up odours of other items in the fridge. Ensure consuming in date order and well within the recommended date.

All items should be wrapped and stored separately. Environmentally, the safest way is a glass bowl covered with a plate. Second choice is a selection of reusable plastic, lidded boxes. Plastic wrap is the last choice, yet sometimes necessary.

Kitchen Surfaces

Ensure food preparation surfaces are hygienically cleaned after every use. Keep a bottle of one of the cleaning products in the previous table handy, and spray the surface with a designated cloth.

Use separate chopping boards for meat (including fish and poultry), and vegetables/salad. Wooden boards can harbour bacteria, so plastic is best. To clean, keep a brush or abrasive sponge and scrub thoroughly with your vinegar spray. Add a teaspoon of coarse sea salt, which gives abrasiveness to your cloth and which can then penetrate and clean grooves made by your knives.

Wash and dry your hands after handling high-risk foods such as raw meat, chicken or eggs.

Washing-up

Contrary to popular belief, the sink and the draining rack are NOT cupboards, even temporarily!

Don't leave piles of washing up in the sink. It will have to be done sometime – and the longer you leave it, the harder it becomes as food dries on, and the more germs can fester. Leftover food scraps can also attract various unwanted guests in the form of insects or even rodents.

Brushes, sponges and tea towels are a haven for bacteria. Wash them regularly or clean with mild detergent and warm water, or a capful of white vinegar, after each use. Renew from time to time. One washing up sponge is not intended to last a four year study programme! A weekly change of sponge is not extravagant.

Never leave a wooden board or wooden spoons to soak in water as they will warp. If you have used your oven, as it cools down, you can dry wooden equipment inside.

Floors

Clean floors regularly to remove visible dirt with warm water and a product described. A kitchen floor is often greasy so needs a degreasing detergent such as lemon or vinegar.

Two buckets for mopping – one with solution and the other clean water for rinsing – is the perfect scenario. Both buckets should be cleaned and disinfected after each use. Soak cloths in lemon or vinegar solution. However, if you only have one bucket, don't think you can skip the rinse part. Whatever you have used to degrease the floor, you will need to rinse away, along with all the dirt you have dissolved.

If soiled with vomit, urine, or other unsanitary substances, the floor should be cleaned using disposable cloths or kitchen paper with warm water, then disinfected. You can make a solution of vinegar stronger – with a ratio of one part vinegar, two parts warm water. Make sure the floor is dry before allowing people back in the kitchen.

Oven

I have yet to find a commercial product sold to clean your oven which is not highly toxic, especially to asthma sufferers. Skin and eyes are also sensitive to these corrosive products.

Luckily, a weekly de-grease means it will never reach a situation of needing such a dramatic product. Turn the oven on to a very low light, which will help melt any fatty build up on the walls, bottom and even top of the oven. Then your regular degreasing home-made product will allow you to clean it effectively.

Old food or grease not cleaned up will burn and smell, plus taint the fresh food you are cooking. If dirt does build up, your oven can be more thoroughly scrubbed with a solution of equal parts of salt and bicarbonate of soda, with just enough warm water to mix into a paste.

Overall, if you have an oven, keep it clean regularly: each time you use the oven, wipe it clean as it is almost cool.

Dish cloths and sponge cleaners

Cloths harbour germs. The warmer the weather, the faster those germs will multiply and your cloth becomes a ticking time bomb of disease. In a research program by the UK Centre for Disease Control, kitchen cloths came 4th in the list of surfaces which have the highest number of germs per square millimetre – following the toilet bowl, toilet floor in front of the bowl, and kitchen drains.

Disposable cloths, regularly changed, are the safest choice, yet not the best environmental choice. Reusable terry towel dishcloths are next best, but at the end of every day, leave them to soak in a fresh bucket of solution. You can also throw them into a laundry cycle.

Keep different cloths for different tasks. You don't want to use the toilet cloth to wash your coffee cups!

Bacterial spots you may not have thought about!

These often-forgotten areas need building into your scheduled cleaning programme. The more frequently done – the less the build up!

- ✓ Taps, handles, light switches, toilet flush handle or lever in the bathroom/ toilets
- ✓ Microwave buttons, refrigerator door / handle
- ✓ Garbage bin, inside and out, plus the floor around the bin
- ✓ Phones – land lines and mobiles, plus remote controls, computer keyboard and mouse
- ✓ BBQ's and outdoor cooking areas – clean immediately after use, and dust before use

"Happy, Clean Kitchen"

BATHROOM

Germs can be passed from person to person, but especially in the bathroom. They pass indirectly as we touch unclean equipment and surfaces. Cleaning regularly will help prevent germs spreading and keep your home hygienic. Bathroom cleaning is not a pleasant task – but it has to be done!

Some general bathroom cleaning tips:

- ✓ Buy some rubber gloves to execute unpleasant tasks.
- ✓ Take it in turns, and plan a chore rotation. When it is your turn, dig deep and do it thoroughly!
- ✓ In order to maintain a consistent standard, it is a good idea to put a check list on the wall, allocating frequencies and a rota of who cleans when! If necessary implement sanctions for anyone failing to comply!
- ✓ If your bathroom is carpeted, it is a good idea to buy a mat shaped around the toilet stem, so that it can be regularly washed. That way, your bathroom remains clean and you don't have to pay for new carpet when you leave.
- ✓ Make sure you unplug the bath, shower and basin drains of hair and other solids. Each person needs to be vigilant, each time they use equipment. A flood will compound your problems.

Lavatories

Use a lavatory cleaner and brush every few days, but each individual is responsible for leaving the toilet clean for the next person. When deposits are left in the bowl after flushing, clean with a toilet brush, then flush again keeping the brush under the fresh running water. Regularly clean brush with disinfectant, and be careful not to allow a puddle of water to collect in the brush container.

Keep the lavatory seat, handle and rim clean by using one of the cleaning products in the cleaning product table.

Baths, basins and shower trays

You should hygienically clean, and then dry, baths and basins frequently using a product listed before. Alternate days is fine unless a large number of people are sharing the same facilities. If so, it becomes critical to plan who and when will clean.

- ✓ If someone is ill and using facilities, use disinfectant and clean thoroughly on a daily basis.
- ✓ Be particularly vigilant if the toilet is close to the bath or shower.
- ✓ After a holiday break, allow some water to run through the system before using it.

Towels

Towels should be changed every three to four days. As described below in the toothbrush section, urine can spray 25cms, so ensure your towel storage is away from the toilet, even in your room if necessary. Towels need to dry thoroughly after use before folding, to avoid smell. Aim to have clean towels twice each week.

Soap and other toiletries

Don't share items that come into direct contact with intimate parts of your body – such as deodorants, bars of soap, or any brushes. To avoid having a shelf full of everyone's different things, consider liquid soaps in plastic dispensers that everyone can hygienically share (which need to have the spout cleaned regularly).

YOUR TOOTHBRUSH – This really deserves a little section of its own!

Think about where your toothbrush could pick up bacteria:

- **Your own mouth:** At any given time, there are 100-200 species of oral bacteria living in your mouth. In an unbrushed mouth, there can be as many germs as a dirty bathroom floor.
- **Hand germs:** If you store your toothbrush next to the bathroom basin, it can get contaminated from splash when hands are washed: Whatever you are washing off your hands, is getting splashed onto your brush.
- **The toilet:** It's a ghastly thought, but when you flush the toilet with the lid open, bacteria and viruses falling from toilet spray remain airborne long enough to settle on surfaces throughout the bathroom. Studies have found that diarrhoea-causing bacteria from a lidless flush can fly as high as 10cms above the toilet.

If your brush drops to the floor, the five-second rule does NOT apply! It comes into contact with toilet spray particulate that has settled there, plus other dirt and infections that have been brought in on people's feet or shoes.

Protect your brush!

- ✓ Don't use plastic containers – not being allowed to dry out between uses encourages mould to grow. If you store other people's toothbrushes in one container, bacteria can spread from one to the other if the heads touch. This can be disastrous if someone is sick.
- ✓ It is a good idea in shared accommodation to keep your own brush AND toothpaste (the nozzle can transfer bacteria from brush to brush) in your room and take it with you to the bathroom each time you need it.
- ✓ Clean your brush bristles after each use by dipping the bristles into clean water with a few drops of Eucalyptus oil.
- ✓ Replace your brush approximately every three months – not just to keep it hygienic, but to ensure it is doing its job to protect your teeth and not scrubbing away your gums!
- ✓ Never EVER share your brush!

BED changing and other laundry

We spend up to a third of our time in bed, so it is worth the effort to make it a safe, clean, hygienic and comfortable place to be. It is a pleasure to fall into a freshly laundered, sweet-smelling bed. How can we achieve this?

When you move into new accommodation, you want the mattress to be as clean as possible before you start. Minimise potential allergies by reducing dust mites. Use a hose attachment on the vacuum cleaner to clean up as much dust as possible. For small spots or stains, use some bicarbonate of soda, moistened with some water. Make sure to leave it to dry THOROUGHLY before dressing the bed. These small steps will improve your health, and best of all, help you sleep better.

In addition, consider a mattress protector, which has two main values – hygiene and delicious comfort! Remember, they also need washing – perhaps monthly.

> *"It seemed like a strange gift to ask for, but the mattress protector I received for Christmas was amazing! I felt safe knowing I had a clean barrier under my bottom sheet, but best of all – it was padded, and so comfortable that I slept like a baby!"*
>
> Rachel C., Southampton

The frequency of laundering bedsheets is optional, but try to aim for once a week. Choosing a regular spot in your timetable means that you get into a routine and it isn't forgotten. Make it a fun activity by sharing with a friend and doing two loads together! Listening to music, audio books, the radio, or podcasts will make this chore into a fun activity.

Wash in warm water, and the more you can avoid harsh chemicals in washing powders and conditioners the better. Whether air drying or tumble drying, make sure the sheets are *completely* dry, or else they will smell and harbour mould. If you have two sets, you can rotate them, and leave the set not being used somewhere warm to dry out. Ironing sheets is cumbersome but has its rewards. If you are disinclined to iron, fold neatly immediately after drying with someone to help if you can. Smoothing out the fabric will help to make sheets feel fresh when applied to the bed.

Fitted bottom sheets with elasticated corners seem hard to fold – but not so! Take one pointed corner and insert it into the opposite corner, making a crease for the border that lies around the mattress edge.

Pillowcases often suffer from oil and sweat. To avoid spoiling your pillow, there is no need to spend money on fancy pillow protectors, but instead it is a good idea, and more economical, to double up and put two cases on each pillow. Pillows themselves need washing from time to time – once a term/semester should be enough. At the end of the academic year, wash or dry-clean them (according to the instructions on the label) before packing them up for the long vacation. This will stop mould or bacterial growth. Before storing, make sure they are absolutely dry, and "plump" them up to avoid lumps forming. Store in clean, dry, heavy-duty plastic bags, which you must seal carefully.

Duvets, blankets and quilts also need periodic cleaning – ideally every six to eight weeks. Follow the instructions on the label. If it is a feather duvet, or woollen blanket it will probably need dry-cleaning. Be careful not to get it wet, as this will create lumps, and uneven warmth.

Looking after your duvet and pillows is an investment, but in return they will last longer and serve you better.

Other Laundry

The symbols on the label of a garment can be extremely confusing. Try to get in the habit of asking the sales assistant about cleaning when you buy any garment. If not, you'll have to learn to decipher the label.

A number represents the maximum temperature. The cooler the wash, the more environmental it is, and the less likely to shrink. Yet a hotter wash is more likely to remove smells from items like sports and gym kit. Underwear, towels and household linen can be washed at 40C/100F. Sweaty sports cloths can go up to 60C/140F.

Anything with an X through it means – don't do it! An iron is obvious, a triangle represents bleach, a circle in a square is a tumble drier. A hand in a bowl means hand wash.

Your washing machine and dryer may have parts that need removing and cleaning or emptying – such as fluff in a dryer. Look carefully. Not doing this regularly will affect the efficiency of the machine. Even if there isn't a manual available, you can look up your model on the internet for information.

Essential Symbols

1   Wash on a low temperature – not more that 30C/80F
2   No bleach
3   Tumble dry with no heat
4   No Ironing
5   No dry-cleaning

Other things to be aware of with respect to laundry include:

- ✓ Wash your hands after handling dirty laundry.
- ✓ Be aware that many fabric softeners contain heavy metals. Research a natural alternative.
- ✓ NEVER leave your wet laundry in the washing machine after a cycle. Remaining germs will multiply rapidly. Your washing will smell by morning. If you can air dry, this is the best option for the planet, and if possible, a few minutes in a tumble dryer will take away the crunchy crispness that is not pleasant for your towels after they've dried in the sunshine.
- ✓ Don't mix colours. Whites and colours should always be separate – especially non-colourfast items such as denim jeans. Red is a common staining colour – it runs out of clothes and will tint your whites pink. Black can make whites change colour to a dirty-looking grey.

Ironing

Rare are the people that find ironing a therapeutic activity! However, some things need to be done. Many modern fabrics available today do not need ironing, but if you are going for an interview or have a special occasion, then ironing is imperative. There are many "how to" videos on the internet showing you how to iron. These are just a few tips to minimise your ironing burden!

→ Some washing machines have an option for no-iron or anti-wrinkle. Choose this if available!

→ Don't overload your machine – this will allow the clothes to move around freely and not be over scrunched.

→ If you are planning to iron, don't dry your clothes more than necessary – this will "fix" creases. It is a balancing act to get it just right, as under-drying can cause clothes to smell of mildew. Over dried clothes – especially from a drier, are crisp and wrinkly and need ironing. Spray with a mist of water (with a drop of essential oil if preferred) to make the task much easier.

→ Hang up laundered clothes as soon as possible to minimise creasing. Don't put damp clothes on wooden hangers, as they may stain fabric.

→ A steamer is an alternative piece of equipment to an iron, but another expense. The principal of steaming, however can be achieved by hanging creased items in the bathroom whilst you shower. It is not perfect, but helps, especially fabrics that are synthetic.

→ Smoothing your clothes at the right time can remove a lot of creases! If you hang clothes on a washing line, smooth them thoroughly before hanging them upside down. I often see t-shirts with little "peg bumps" because they have been hung from the shoulders not the bottom hem! Once they are dry, smooth them out and immediately fold them up neatly. Clothes out of a tumble drier must be fully dry, then they can be smoothed and folded to remove creases. The pressure of your hands is a miracle worker! This can work for T-shirts, casual wear, items with artificial fibres, denim and items that won't be seen – such as pyjamas and tea towels!

The right way up!

If you wash delicate woollen clothes, these cannot be hung on a line, as they will droop and dry out of shape. A tumble dryer may shrink them. Place a clean towel somewhere flat and warm, and lie out the garments to dry slowly but without damage.

Sequins and bling on a garment make it impossible to iron – but you will still want to look unrumpled for a party or even graduation. Be sure to get it washed and dried at least a week in advance of the event week and hang it so it is full length. As mentioned previously, you could also put the sparkly garment in the warm steamy bathroom whilst you shower which will help the creases to fall out.

If your iron is dirty then the sticky gunk on its surface will stick to (and possibly ruin) your clothes as the iron heats up. Iron cleaning products are available in the supermarket, just follow the instructions. Iron a piece of newspaper first to check the iron is clean and leak free.

LIVING Areas

Bedroom

To avoid spillage and staining, food smells, and fallen crumbs attracting insects, avoid eating in your bedroom or study area.

If you study in your bedroom, you need to make the difference between the two activities, sleeping and studying. Don't sleep with papers and books strewn all over the place – and similarly, don't try to work with underwear and socks everywhere. *See more in the chapter about time management.*

Be a minimalist. Whilst you are studying you are probably living in temporary accommodation. You may need to move out each summer – or worse, each holiday. You need your home to be almost portable, but certainly manageable.

Have a regular tidy up and clean out. Challenge yourself to do one of the following actions for every object in your bedroom:

- ✓ Put away
- ✓ Throw away
- ✓ Sell
- ✓ Give away to a charity shop

Investment in some storage containers is a good idea, but these don't need to be costly.

Keep summer / winter clothing and equipment such as fans / blankets separately and tightly packed away when not in use.

Communal Living Areas

Who doesn't want to live in a pleasant environment? Whatever your budget and environment, it is possible to improve it by keeping it clean and tidy, and hence healthy.

Carpet and Soft Furnishings

Regularly vacuum your carpets to minimise dust mites and hence allergic reactions or skin sensitivities. Weekly is ideal.

Periodically clean carpets and soft furnishings.

Sprinkle the carpet with bicarbonate of soda last thing at night and leave until the morning, when you vacuum it up. The carpet will be fresher and cleaner. Monthly is a good guideline. If you rent your property, ask your landlord to carry out such a clean before you take possession.

At the end of the academic year it is a good investment to clean by steam cleaning. These machines can be hired, or you can call a professional company to do it for you. It's worth cleaning regularly, because if you do not keep a regular cleaning schedule, or you make a mess of the carpets, you may be obliged to pay for a deep clean at the end of your contract or lose your deposit.

Dust regularly, such as daily or alternate days. It keeps the house clean and healthy without needing lots of chemicals. Clean ledges and surfaces with suitable products. *(see Cleaning Product table).*

Pets

Typically, students don't have pets because of the cost and responsibility - especially over the long holidays. However, some like to keep a hamster or other small animals. Some cleanliness tips for pets, whatever the size:

- ✓ Always wash your hands after touching animals and their food, litter trays or other equipment.
- ✓ Don't keep pet food with human food.
- ✓ Keep separate dishes and tin openers for your pet.
- ✓ Change straw, or other bedding and clean and refill water containers regularly.
- ✓ Ventilation is necessary to allow smells to evaporate.
- ✓ If you go away for a weekend or holiday break you have an OBLIGATION to make sure your pet is looked after.

5. TIMETABLING All Those Chores

Making a timetable and rota should ensure that the tasks get done! It also allows you to share equally the load between users. You know who will do what and when; plus, each person is individually accountable. It sounds draconian, but if everyone shares their part from the beginning, the formality of the rules can be relaxed!

Hygienic cleaning in high germ areas such as the kitchen and bathroom should be ongoing each time they are used, plus a periodic deep clean. Overnight one bacterium can multiply to 6 million. Think of an unwashed sponge after a week!

When you are under the stress of a heavy workload and are trying to fit in lots of different things, give each task a time goal – and then try to beat it! For example – if you have half an hour to cook a meal – try to do it in 20 minutes. Shirts to iron – set a goal of 10 minutes per shirt and be done in under an hour.

More examples:

A family favourite dinner is ratatouille topped with melted cheese. Most recipes instruct that you pan fry in oil, first the chopped onions, then courgette, then eggplant. No need! Chop up all the vegetables, add a tin of tomatoes, herbs and garlic - bring them to the boil, then simmer on a low heat for 30-40 minutes. This saves not only time but calories too! PLUS, if the batch made is big enough – then another meal is taken care of too!

Start the washing up and be determined to finish it all, plus a kitchen wipe down, in no more than 10 minutes! If you can do it – allow yourself a reward!

Share the tasks in your weekly plan – If someone is "on duty" for cleaning and needs to be away, they need to renegotiate with housemates for a swap. Assign specific days for weekly tasks. Perhaps all clean at the same time on Monday evening; or one person cleans each week on Saturday morning. If someone misses their turn, they might have to double next time!

From this plan, a shared area rota can easily be agreed upon and drawn up, allocating tasks fairly, with consideration for each other's activities. It assumes that bedrooms are managed personally, and on-going cleaning will be done by each individual as timetabled.

Domestic Chore Planning

Daily	Weekly	Occasional	As needed
Kitchen			
Fridge: • Clean up spills immediately • Good fridge management and rotation of "FIFO" – First in, first out – especially eggs and milk	Fridge: • Throw away out of date food before next big shop • Disinfect handle	Monthly fridge: • Empty shelves and clean • Refresh bicarbonate of soda	End of year: • Clear out all foodstuffs and clean cupboards, microwave and fridge • Leave kitchen as you would hope to find it!
Oven / microwave – Wipe clean after each use		Deep clean	
Wash the dishes – 10 minutes after every meal			
Bathroom			
Toilet – each person as needed	Toilet – Deep clean	Shower curtain (see the label. Can it go in the washing machine?)	
Basin – each person as needed	Deep clean		
Bath/shower – each person as needed	Deep clean		
Floor – spot clean by each person as needed	Wash (hard) vacuum (carpet)		
Bedroom / study			
Make bed	Change and wash bed sheets	Curtains	

	Laundry – Pick a regular – unmissable spot in the week. For instance, Tuesday 7.30 – 9pm during TV programme		
	Living Room		
Clear away all mugs, plates etc. Wipe down table surfaces. Put away your personal items	Vacuum the carpet / wash the floor, dust all hard surfaces.	Clean behing the radiator; under and behind the sofa.	If the air con is inefficient – wash the filters.

Domestic Chore Rota

	Monday	Tuesday	Wednesday	Thursday	Friday	Saturday	Sunday
Washing up	Julie	Paul	Vikram	Mei-Ling	Chris	Vikram	own
Hoover Living Room						Julie	
Bathroom deep clean						Paul	
Kitchen floor						Vikram	

6. ESSENTIAL Safety

Most students now have valuable equipment, especially electronic items. This makes student homes a hotspot for burglaries, as each student living in the house will most likely own a laptop, mobile phone and maybe a TV.

Safety and Security Tips

Keep all external doors and windows locked. It is also a good idea to lock your personal space. Whilst you may trust your roommates, there may be other people coming and going whilst you are out. Be extra attentive if you are going away for a few days or more.

Keep valuables (laptops, cameras, mobiles phones) out of sight. Never leave your laptop on the desk by a window, especially on a ground or low floor.

Don't leave your house keys near the front door/downstairs or lying around. Never lend them to anyone. Be careful not to have spare sets of keys floating around. Number all sets, and ensure that if anyone leaves the accommodation, they return theirs.

Net curtains might not be fashionable. But they stop people observing what you have inside especially downstairs, and in a house which fronts onto the street. Especially in the dark and when you have the light on, it is necessary to close curtains. With no nets or blinds, be particular about closing curtains at dusk when you put on the light.

Avoid having valuables in the house, but of course your passport and other valuables need to be stored. A small lock box, hidden away is a help but never a fool-proof insurance against a determined housebreaker. Consider taking out insurance for any expensive valuables, or even a bank safety box to store exceptional valuables. Some universities offer such a service – particularly for overseas students.

Whist you may be keen to turn off lights as an economy when you're not home, a night light left glowing creates an impression that someone is home, which might deter an intruder.

Don't leave the packaging from new expensive equipment such as a computer or TV in the bins outside. This is an advertisement to a thief of your new precious goods.

Fire Safety Tips:

- Turn off electrical appliances such as the oven, iron, anything that generates heat when you are going to be out of the property.
    - o Leave on the fridge though! Don't be tempted to leave electrical appliances on standby.
- Check your electrical goods have unbroken and tightly fitting secure plugs.
    - o If not - DON'T USE!
- Ask your landlord to install smoke alarms.
    - o Check on a regular basis that they work, especially that the batteries are regularly replaced.
- Never put metal (including tin foil and take-away foil boxes) in the microwave.
- Don't cook food when you've just come in from a night out – you will be tired. In case you are inebriated, you may be less attentive.

o   Plan ahead and leave yourself a snack if you are having a late night out.

- Never smoke in bed. Late at night is the most dangerous time, as you may fall asleep.
- Candles are romantic, but dangerous. Don't let them burn down to the end, and ALWAYS blow them out before going to bed. Beware not to put them next to a curtain or other flammable material.
- NEVER use electrical appliances in the bathroom, especially plug-in heaters.
  o   Hair drying and other personal grooming tools are best in the bedroom.
- Keep a fire blanket and fire extinguisher in the kitchen.
  o   Ask your landlord to provide this.
- If you can't put a fire out safely, get out of the building quickly and call the fire brigade. Familiarise yourself with local contact phone numbers and procedures when you move into a new building.

7. SELF-GROOMING – Looking Good!

Introduction

There was some debate as to whether this section belongs in this book. Parents and educators overwhelmingly said "Yes"! Students will probably have a "Whatever!" moment – but have a read anyway!

It may sometimes feel as though your student success is measured in terms of your academic grades, or that your future depends on you getting the highest scores. But getting the job of your choice is a combination of qualities of which this is only a part. The expression a "well-rounded individual" is all encompassing. To achieve this you may have spent years studying an extra-curricular subject; playing a musical instrument or competitive sport; participating in charitable activities and much more. All of these represent active effort you have put in to improve yourself and the impression you give to others.

However, there are other elements of ourselves that, with a little bit of care and attention, we can dramatically improve. Put another way, WITHOUT this effort, the overall impression could be spoilt. The way we present ourselves speaks loudly about who we are, and shows our care and attention to detail. Grooming is not about being vain. In fact, being well groomed takes the 'spotlight' away from you. People can pay attention to the real you: what you're saying, your thoughts and ideas, and all those parts of you that make up your true essence. It is also respectful to the people you are meeting to be clean and fresh.

Personal Hygiene

As with saying "Thank you!" - people barely notice if you do – but it stands out if you don't! - so it is with personal hygiene. If you look clean and have a neutral or pleasant smell, people will not necessarily reflect on your hygiene. Yet if you smell unpleasant and / or look dirty, scruffy or are inappropriately dressed, they may be polite enough to say nothing, but are left with a negative impression tainting their perception of you.

Good personal hygiene is not just about creating a good impression; clean means healthy; physically minimising your exposure to bacteria and dirt. Psychologically you will also feel better in washed and fresh clothes.

Good Habits:

1)   Keeping the smells at bay

Regular washing: Daily showering and bathing is preferable. In some circumstances, such as limited equipment, water, or time, or if you have a bandaged-up injury, this may not be possible – but a sponge down with bowl of warm water is essential. Areas of the body that sweat particularly need attention; underarms, groin and feet tend to sweat the most. Soap is essential, but choose anti-bacterial rather than scented, which has the added possibility of causing an allergy. Own-label brands are economical and efficient.

Deodorant / anti-perspirant: Whilst it is natural and good to sweat a little – you can control the smell, and hence increase your confidence, by using a deodorant. Remember these are NOT intended to mask an existing smell or allow you to skip a shower after oversleeping! Use product after you wash, on clean and dry skin. Again, don't choose heavily scented products, and don't rely on a product that promises 48-hour protection – that is NOT an excuse not to wash! There are recipes online for home-made deodorants. These can be cheap to make, and are free from chemicals.

Perfume (proceed with caution!): Perfume similarly is not a mask for unpleasant smells. There are many different scents on the market and we all have our own taste. Don't overdo using a scent – as it is intrusive within the airspace you are sharing with others. It can be a turnoff if someone doesn't like your choice, or worse initiate a headache or allergic reaction! In the past, top chefs have been known to ban certain scents from their restaurants –they can confuse smells from food and wine, and are also very personal. You may love a particular perfume but someone else may not. If everyone is wearing a different and strong cologne, the smell can become overwhelming. If you wear the same scent regularly, you may become immune to its power, and unwittingly use more and more. Be sparing and thoughtful about others.

> A top tip to make your perfume last longer - rub some moisturiser on your skin, before applying perfume in a short spritz burst, at least 20 centimetres from your skin.

Hair: Some people naturally have oily hair and others less so. Work out your best routine to keep your hair looking clean and shiny and smelling good. Regularly trim your hair to keep it in top condition.

Clean clothes and shoes: Try to ensure your clothes are changed at least daily, especially in the high sweat areas – clean socks, underpants and tight clothing. Avoid artificial fibres such as nylon as this makes you sweat more, choose natural fibres; cotton, wool, silk and linen. Making sure your laundry is fully dry before putting away as this will avoid another nasty smell. Keep at least two pairs of shoes and try to rotate which pair you use, as this gives each pair time to dry out thoroughly. Smelly shoes can be deodorised with a generous spoonful of bicarbonate of soda put inside and left-over night.

2) <u>Not just a pretty face</u>

Spots: As you went through puberty a few years ago, you lost your baby complexion and may have experienced an outburst of spots. Whilst your changing hormone levels cause this, there are steps that can be taken to minimise the effect. Wash your face ideally twice every day, but if you wake up with only a minute to spare – choose breakfast and make sure you clean your face after being exposed to the grime of the day! Wash your hands first, and then with an unscented, mild facial cleanser preferably containing salicylic acid – which you must rinse off thoroughly, wash with warm water. Generally, don't squeeze spots, but sometimes the pressure can cause pain on or under the skin. With clean hands, use clean tissues or a flannel / hand towel and warm water to relax and soften the skin. Then apply enough pressure to ease out the pus. Diluted lemon juice applied with cotton wool is an excellent astringent. Wash or dispose of your tools in order to avoid spreading.

Teeth cleaning: Did you know that the human tooth is only designed to last 50-60 years? Adult teeth arrive when children are approximately eight years old, which means that by the age of 60-70 our teeth may wear out. With an ever-increasing average age, and a desire to hold on to our teeth, it becomes all the more important to look after them. Brushing twice a day is essential. In the morning you need to get rid of "morning breath": The nasty odour and feeling from not drinking water all night. In the evening you need to ensure that you have cleaned away food and drink debris which can hide between teeth, harbouring bacteria and acids that attack the enamel on your teeth and rot your gums. Flossing regularly is essential. Floss before you brush, so that your toothbrush and paste better reach between your teeth.

Ears: Producing earwax is natural, and your body's way of eliminating dust and dirt. Washing outside your ears is essential, but you should not poke around deeply into the inner ear with a cotton bud. Technically ears are self-cleaning and by poking inside you could be pushing dust and infection further inside. If you feel that there is a build-up of wax, known as impaction, which may even be impairing your hearing, visit a professional to have your ears cleaned. Other symptoms could include an unpleasant smell from the affected ear, ringing (tinnitus) or other earache.

Hands and nails: Your hands should be clean at all times – which means washing hands with soap regularly, including each time after going to the toilet; before preparing and/or eating food; and in general, as regularly as possible. During normal daily activities, such as working and playing, disease-causing germs may get onto the hands and under the nails. If hands are not regularly sanitised, they can spread germs around to manifest in unwanted ways – the spread of spots, upset tummy and the general spread of airborne diseases such as a cough or cold. Dirt is particularly liable to linger under the nails – so pay attention to cleaning thoroughly.

Dress codes and standards

Whilst style and fashion may vary – clean is never out of date. Your clothes must be cleaned regularly to avoid smelling of body odour, and dried properly to avoid smelling of mildew.

Think about pictures of your parents and grandparents you may have seen when they were your age. You would possibly laugh now at the fashions and hairstyles, as they seem so dated. Visualise the clothes you wear now, and how they might be amusing in twenty years' time to your children! The clothing you choose is about establishing your identity; fitting into budgetary constraints; and your affiliation and belonging to a social group.

There is a time and place to be outrageous with your dress, and there is also a time to be conservative. Choose a basic wardrobe of classic pieces that will last and look "timeless", but of course still invest in some fun "statement" pieces!

Gentlemen

- Clean shoes communicate a meticulous and caring personality. Looking after your shoes will guarantee they look after you!
- Avoid T-shirts with offensive or meaningless messages. Your T-shirt could scream the wrong message about you before you even open your mouth or smile.
- A button-down shirt is a standard staple to look business-like or well groomed.
- Smart trousers / pants are most often a good cut in a dark colour and quality fabric. These will be a staple item in your wardrobe. Avoid high fashion with elements such as rips or low cut. Jeans are acceptable for many occasions, ripped being too fashion-led, blue being the most casual, and black being the smartest. If you are not sure, err on the side of formality rather than being too casual.
- A quality belt shows care and attention to your dressing, and looks polished.
- Ties are only for formal occasions, but make a good impression. A black tie should only be used for funerals, and avoid ties that have cartoons or inappropriate images.

Ladies

- Remember the rule to never show legs and cleavage at the same time! One can be elegant, both suggest something else!
- You may love high heels, but they are not the most practical for a day on campus. Think about comfort and protecting your feet.
- Don't overdo perfume, make-up or jewellery. Less is more. Consider a maximum of three pieces out of bracelet, earrings, watch, necklace and brooch. If any of your clothes have sequins or sparkles this also counts.
- For corporate of formal occasions, a trouser suit, skirt or dress is acceptable. Avoid colour and patterns that are too loud or bright – unless you WANT to draw attention to yourself.

Party etiquette

When invited to a party, it is important to dress appropriately so that you fit in and feel comfortable. Below are the traditional dress codes seen on invitations, but if you are in doubt, don't hesitate to call the host and ask for more information.

1. **White tie**: This is the most formal of dress codes. Men cannot deviate from the tails and white bow-tie, ladies must wear long ball gowns. These can be rented, as they are not worn often and the expense of buying is beyond most students! Ask questions if you need information, but to arrive wrongly attired is disrespectful to your host or organiser.

2. **Black tie**: This means a dinner jacket, also known as a tuxedo for men, with a dress shirt and black bow-tie. Ladies can wear party clothes, also called cocktail. The invitation may state long or short dresses. If you are not sure – ask so as to avoid embarrassment. Beware high fashion for this dress code – look back at some of the Oscar parties! Men in frilly shirt fronts in the 1980's was not a lasting look!

3. **Smart casual:** This means non-denim, and no flip flops or sports shoes. Gentlemen need not wear a tie, but can wear an open neck shirt perhaps with a jacket. For ladies this is more difficult as the range of what to wear could be so broad. If you are not sure, just ASK!

4. **Casual:** This should mean that anything goes, including denim and flip-flops. However sometimes an invite is overly casual about stating "casual"! Assess who has sent the invite and to what and where. If still unsure – ASK! Remember, it is always more comfortable to be slightly over-dressed than to be too casual.

A few final tips about looking the part:

High heels can damage wooden floors and can make a lot of noise on a hard floor (concert hall). They can also sink into grass or soft earth if outdoors. Be sure to consider in advance whether they are appropriate.

Temperature is always tricky to plan ahead for, so layers of clothes allow for adding or removing so you don't overheat or freeze.

If attending a function which includes entering a place of worship – make sure to check out the dress guidelines. For example, for some religions, bare shoulders are not appropriate, and for others a hat is essential.

Finally, white sports socks should be worn ONLY with sports shoes!

Be yourself, be comfortable, be respectful.

Chapter 6: Wellbeing - Healthy Body and Mind

by Rachael Desgouttes

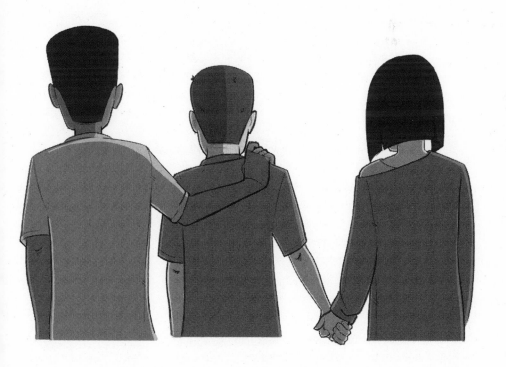

1. KEEP Yourself Emotionally Well

KEY POINTS: Keep yourself EMOTIONALLY WELL

1. Success is free and a valuable tonic! This does not just mean being top of the class, but success can mean ticking off an item on a manageable "To-do" list. When struggling, just making your bed could be your first success of the day.

2. Good sleep with respect to both quantity and quality is an essential bodily need.

3. There are controversial theories on recreational drug use – especially cannabis, used to manage mental conditions such as schizophrenia, bi-polar disorder, and depression. There is also evidence that these drugs can be a trigger for these mental illnesses. Illegal drugs are made and distributed with no control over quality of materials or the manufacturing process. The motivation for distribution is profit. It is not uncommon for drugs to be a mixture of cheap and dangerous chemicals - potentially lethal.

4. Practice immense caution with any and all drugs.

5. Remember that the buzz you may feel from alcohol, accompanied by a numbing of negative sensations, is only temporary. When the effects wear off, a hangover and tiredness are paybacks, and even worse, your problems will still be there.

THE Comfort of Home

In your final year of school, it seems that you have passed through a lengthy system, which has served its purpose. You have probably outgrown it. Final revision and taking exams at the end of your school life, whilst demanding and rigorous, are formalities – the natural stepping stones to get you to the next level: tertiary education.

You will have started planning at least one year earlier, if not more; the destination, course options, and application process will be peppered with obstacles and emotions. *Will I get in? Will I make the grades? Have I made the right choice? Can I afford it? How will I cope? Woohooo! I'm finally free!*

On Arrival

When you first arrive at university, the excitement may be tremendous. It represents a new stage in life; the beginning of a journey of self-discovery through all kinds of learning; and new experiences. Naturally everybody wants to have the best university experience possible. It should be a memorable period of your life, an enriching chapter that will shape you into the adult you are going to become. There may have been some doubts and anxieties in the lead up to leaving home, but the wave of euphoria of your peer group will likely overshadow those and convince you how fantastic everything is going to be.

Yet different students will experience different types of emotions. One overseas student, speaking about her arrival in the UK, reported that the first month was horrible; from the day she arrived, she hated everything there. In reality she might not have hated everything there, but it was so far removed from her "norm" that she felt ill at ease and lost. Plus, the constant drizzling rain literally put a damper on her mood. Other students report that they did not seem to have had a 'honeymoon' period. Some say that the first term was the hardest, and it was only in the second term that they seemed to get a bit more organised in their studies and house chores and started to make friends and socialise.

It is stereotypical to think that home has been a warm loving environment where students are nurtured through their schooling until they are prepared and independent enough to spread their wings and take on the world alone. This may be a reality for many students. For others, home may represent an environment of angst and stress, caused by issues such as financial hardship, parents arguing, or alcoholic abuse. Children accept their environment whatever it may be as the norm, because that is all they have experienced and know.

As teenagers develop heightened awareness, coping mechanisms evolve for the environments they find themselves in; at home, school, socially, and so forth. We rarely talk about our emotions. We take for granted that how we feel is how we are supposed to feel and possibly how everyone else feels. But what ARE emotions? How can we recognise them, see them coming, let them go, or even better, "manage" them?

When we analyse the emotions of students going off to university for the first time, they fall into two main opposing clichés. After all, clichés become clichés because of the realism they contain and the frequency with which they occur.

The first is the student who is delighted to break free from the confines of parental care and have a wild time in the student union bar with no curfew!

The second is the student who is devastated to fly the nest, and sits at home every evening tearfully on the phone to younger siblings and old friends.

Of course, these feelings are not static. It is important to recognise that we will all live and respond to situations differently. On arriving at university, some students may feel ecstatic then homesick, others may feel scared and nervous but then relieved to make friends. Others may just feel the same as before, no matter what!

We can learn to recognise that some emotions are internal constructs from the self – we "imagine" this moment is horrible, but it is only our perception.

2. HELPFUL Guidelines for Managing Emotions

Do	Don't
Get plenty of quality sleep, spend time in meditation, envisioning yourself further on in time, so as not to get stuck in the seemingly difficult moment. Put "now" within a wider perspective – know it will pass.	Turn to or rely on "false cures": alcohol, mad partying, or drugs.
Choose friends who give you positive energy and a sense of well-being. Avoid those who trigger negativity.	Allow yourself to believe that things are bad, without considering your perception.
Get the balance of positive social interactions but some silence too.	Allow noisy environments to take over.
Hormone changes impact moods and emotions. Recognise and accept it. Don't overreact. Breathe mindfully. Walk outdoors, even if rainy or dark.	Allow yourself to rely on social media – evidence repeatedly proves that over-use exacerbates depression.
Embrace opportunities for new experiences.	Fail to recognise you are in a rut, resorting to the same negative self-destructive patterns.
Volunteer (helping others takes us out of our narrow boundaries).	Hesitate to ask a friend, mentor or professional for help.

AN emotional roller-coaster - School to University

Don't underestimate highs and lows:

- ✓ Extra pre-departure ups and downs
- ✓ Homesickness
- ✓ Adaption
- ✓ Exam results – success, celebration, acceptance

On arrival at university, you are meeting new people from unfamiliar places, sharing stories, talking about classes and teachers, having new kinds of conversations in new venues, like bars and clubs, cafes, seminar rooms and dorm hallways and kitchen spaces. There may be physical attraction and flirting too. These new people and experiences can affect your self-esteem or conversely reduce your inhibitions. It may feel like a splendid adventure.

The "Honeymoon" Period

Whist the first semester of college typically is the 'honeymoon' phase, the function of the undergraduate period is transitioning from child to adult. Although technically an adult, there is still a lot to learn about life and emotions. You need to maintain a high level of productivity and efficiency, whilst discovering and uncovering your real self. Student life is an adjustment or transition.

Filled with mostly positive experiences it may eventually subside as new routines and patterns set in, and people become more adjusted to their new life on campus. For those who have left their country to study abroad, or moved to a new city, your feelings may begin to change as the excitement of a new place and new people becomes more familiar and routine.

Then reality hits. Your initial ability to be exuberantly happy, despite negative feelings under the surface, may have waned. The difficult moments may feel like they outnumber the positive ones.

Possible Triggers for Feeling Depressed:

You may continue to feel homesick. You still miss your parent's home-cooked meals, and the comfort and familiarity of your home environment.

Making new friends has been more difficult than you expected; you are bombarded through social media with images of everyone else's "perfect" life – you may feel some resentment, as your dear old friends are forging ahead with new relationships and no longer sharing experiences.

Partying hard may mean that you have gained weight – which doesn't feel good in our body-obsessed, body-shaming, share-everything culture. Your clothes may feel too small and uncomfortable.

If you have relocated to a different country with a new culture and language, you may feel isolated and lonely.

Cyberbullying can be relentless, weaving its' way through your phone into your private safety space.

Classes may seem difficult or begin to feel boring or uninteresting. The workload is too heavy, or you may consider that you have made a wrong choice.

Your housemates have different standards of living – including their music taste, cleanliness, lifestyle and values.

The chores may seem arduous. In fact, the whole life-balancing act seems overwhelming.

Living on a budget is more challenging than you thought it would be.

A high-school romance which you were determined to continue during college, may be under pressure when the long-distance separation becomes hard, and you may face a breakup at Thanksgiving or Christmas during the first term.

You may have rushed into a new romance in the first weeks, yet it now feels like a mistake - or your new partner may want to finish with you. You may feel embarrassed or humiliated.

You may feel you are not meeting your family's expectations: maybe letting them down, or wasting their money.

In general, a wide range of factors may start to trigger unpleasant feelings and emotions that you may have assumed you would leave behind.

Your fears may be irrational beliefs, and hence may lead to bouts of anxiety which you cannot explain or control.

DEPRESSION

> **But what is depression?**
>
> Definitions vary from expert to expert. Definitions from sufferers include:
>
> - "A suffocating feeling of dread".
> - "An all-encompassing feeling of helplessness, staring into blackness and feeling completely unable to pull yourself out of it..."
> - "A mood disorder causing a persistent feeling of sadness and loss of interest, affecting how you think, feel and behave – can lead to emotional and physical problems."
> - "Feeling unaccountably blue."

How can we Identify depression?

Mental illness affects approximately 50% of women at some time in their life, and 35% of men. Whilst at university, the change of lifestyle, the opportunity to discover yourself, and the weight of responsibility means that the opportunity to feel depressed intensifies. The obvious question is: How can we identify depression? What are the signs or clues that you are or someone else is depressed?

This is impossible to answer in absolute terms, because someone can be depressed and mask "normal" behaviour whilst suffering internal mental turmoil and anguish. Conversely someone might claim to be depressed, when really just suffering from a hangover.

Depression sufferers can seem anywhere on a scale between normal (a word that is itself difficult to define, and impossible to evaluate, especially in someone that you haven't known very long) and a departure from normal, which could be a tiny difference or an exaggerated amount.

Behavioural Changes: Could include, but are not limited to:

- ✓ Lethargy and or energy levels greatly diminished,
- ✓ Enthusiasm and lust for life subsiding,
- ✓ Changing of eating habit – either binge eating "bad items" (such as overdosing on ice-cream or chips) or not eating at all and having no interest in food,
- ✓ Experiencing a negative spectrum of emotions.

IMPORTANT: Sometimes feeling bored, or over-tired or lonely can produce the same symptoms. It is easy to throw in the term "depressed" as a catch-all when feeling blue. Remember, that it is natural for people who are well balanced and enjoy good emotional well-being to have different moods; for example, feeling happier one day compared to another. Try to develop a self-awareness to understand your normal range. You may be energised some days and sluggish on others.

"*Yesterday was a downer day for me, caused by one too many beers the night before, tiredness and fighting off man-flu. I went to the gym and that helped restore equilibrium a little. I also had a long chat with my mum. That helped too. I felt much better this morning.*"

-- Jason F., Leeds University

How Can We Self-help?

Students need to be accepting of themselves and each other. Self-awareness (that you are able to be true to yourself and hold on to your values) is important. The alternative is to be swept along on the sea of peer pressure and behave in ways which might not feel authentic.

Some students will turn to alcohol and drugs when negative feelings start to creep up, long before they would consider asking for help in dealing with a particular issue. Even if they are not enjoying the party life style and everything that comes with it, they may find other forms of escapism. These coping mechanisms include engaging in social media and entertainment for an excessive period of time instead of keeping up with course work; spending too much time indoors, not engaging in any exercise, or fruitful or productive activities.

Alcohol is a depressant. It does not cure but mask, and it plays tricks on the mind. The initial sensation is usually a "feel-good" one, and there is some debate as to what causes this initial feeling of euphoria from alcohol. Perhaps it is a release of endorphins due to the depressant qualities subduing the natural processes of inhibition that we should have running in our brain.

Before turning to alcohol, try to identify objectively what are the causes of the feelings. If you are feeling down, seek out some company or take yourself for a walk especially in a natural environment to get some fresh air. Try treating yourself to a movie with some popcorn or pamper yourself with a bubble bath. Even just having an early night with a good book might be the self-care you need. You may quickly feel better.

Talk About It!

Remember, you never have to shoulder the burden of a problem alone. "A trouble shared is a trouble halved" is a wise saying. It does have some limitations though. Be careful to whom you speak. Choose someone who is loyal, mature and supportive. Avoid anyone who might use your secret information against you in the future. Your family may typically be understanding, yet some problems are off family radar. Sometimes students feel that they have let their parents down, or for several reasons they cannot turn homeward. Friends may provide high empathy yet offer low experience. They may compare your problem to the one other person they have known with something similar – which it probably isn't!

How to Be a Support to Others

When a friend or flat mate is suffering – you want to offer your support. Peer groups identify with common circumstances – so you have a lot to offer. If you identify that someone in your midst has deviated from his or her "normal behaviour" you can't just yell, "Hey! What's up?!" You need to instil confidence and confidentiality. Get alongside them and gently ask, "Are you okay?" Let them talk, if that is what they want – or be silent with them. Silence can be cathartic too.

However, when someone has a tangible problem, causing them to feel depressed, it is important for you not to take on board the same issues. It is also not appropriate to give advice – just listen. When a circumstance sounds dire, or beyond your scope – suggest specialist services. Guide your friend to a safe place or person who can take charge. Colleges and universities often have counsellors or a student welfare department. Sometimes these are busy and don't have any available appointments for the foreseeable future. Organisations such as your university or local places of worship offer help, in addition to specific help experts such as the Samaritans who offer 24 hour pastoral care. Ironically a sufferer of depression typically does not always seek out help themselves. Be supportive in seeing what is available for them, and don't be offended if they refuse your offerings. Seeking help is scary, and it takes time to build up the courage to do so.

> **If someone reaches out for help - walk alongside them; hold their hand;**
>
> **let them know they're not alone.**

When coping with depression yourself, or supporting someone who is depressed, remember...

Friendly advice is not a substitute for medical attention. If someone has a broken leg or skin rash, the damage is visible and you know roughly what you are treating. With a mental condition, there are no obvious symptoms and without a broader understanding of someone's circumstances you may not be able to treat "feeling down" with a Band-Aid. Choose carefully who may be your best confidante. You will feel better knowing someone is supporting you. Your general practitioner may be a good start, as is the campus counsellor, or other psychotherapists. There are national and local support groups in most cities, and even online chat support, so explore what is available, convenient and comfortable for you.

Know that you're not alone. Statistics vary amongst different publications, but a 2013 survey by The American Psychology Association found that anxiety is experienced by 41% of students, depression by 36.4% and relationship problems by 35.8%. Therefore, feeling depressed is not unusual and there should be no embarrassment attached. Similarly, a British university student survey concluded that 11% of students are seeking help, which is up 8% year on year. Yet they are not providing support to all who need help, as many may be reticent to seek it out. Don't suffer in silence.

Not sure whether you, or a friend are depressed? We all feel low, nervous, anxious or overwhelmed with work from time to time. Sometimes these feelings can be "diagnosed" as not enough sleep; a hangover; or too much work – time, care, and management can nurse us back to a better place. Yet, if these feelings are the prevalent emotion, and are impacting your daily life, this is the time to seek professional help. From cognitive-behavioural therapy to medication, there are many ways to help and manage your emotions. Don't leave things until they are in crisis. On-going support could avert ever reaching this stage.

If you have a previously diagnosed mental health issue, let the university support services know as early as possible. This will not impact the way you are treated for your studies, but they will prepare support for you at the earliest time if things spiral out of control.

Counselling is the first step of an on-going process of maintenance. Sometimes a session with a counsellor may seem unproductive or too much of just a chat; but it is the first baby step of building a relationship based on trust and confidence. This paves the way for exploring topics, which may be painful or distressing. If they are deep-seated issues going back a long time – there will eventually be a feeling of release and relief. Be patient and kind.

Ensure there is pleasure and success in every day. Even though that sounds ambitious, it's all about how you frame it. One student reported that at the very deepest part of a period of depression, this simple advice was a turnaround point.

> "*I made getting out of bed my success and a coffee my pleasure. From a small acorn a mighty oak can grow. I remember the day I felt I could achieve nothing – but under guidance, making my bed every morning became a massive achievement. Now I smile each day as I make my bed and take it for granted, as I know I have left behind a very dark place.*"
>
> -- Jessie C., Stirling University

ANXIETY and Panic Attacks

Suffering from anxiety is not feeling nervous. It is a condition that manifests a range of physical and psychological symptoms. The most commonly displayed include short-term heart palpitations, or a rapidly beating heart for longer periods of time; feeling sick or dizzy or generally disorientated; or hot flashes with or without sweating. Different studies in the USA and UK concur that more than 60% of people suffer from anxiety at some time in their life.

Anxiety affects millions of people. It involves a cocktail of physical and mental ingredients; compulsive worrying, irrational fears, social anxiety and more – many of the normal pressures within the student world.

It is important to remember however, that you shouldn't try to self-diagnose, or make a guess about someone else. The Internet can be a dangerous trap, as it often portrays worst-case scenarios. There are different classifications of anxiety types including; Generalised Anxiety Disorder (GAD), Social Phobia, Panic Disorder, Agoraphobia, Post-Traumatic Stress Disorder (PTSD), Obsessive-Compulsive Disorder (OCD), and many more. It is difficult to identify the threshold between a safe level of anxiety – which keeps our adrenalin pumping and our wits sharp – and a disorder. If your anxiety is causing you problems and interfering with your daily life then you need to talk to someone.

Only a mental health professional should diagnose a disorder.

Symptoms for any stress or anxiety disorder can include a selection of the following:

- Restlessness, tiredness, lethargy, or a can't be bothered attitude
- Inability to concentrate or stick to a project
- Tension and inability to relax – especially your neck, shoulders and back
- Irritation and negative feelings – which can lead to obsession with possible worst-case scenarios
- Feeling out of control
- Antisocial behaviour – not wanting to be with friends, inability or even a phobia about meeting new people

Stress or anxiety can trigger panic attacks with the following symptoms:

- Chest or stomach pain
- Rapid heartbeat
- Dizziness
- Breathing difficulties
- Hot or cold flashes or excessive sweating
- Numbness or tingling feeling

Sometimes physical symptoms are followed a little later with mental anguish – severe anxiety about your health, or that of others, or other sorts of extreme and irrational negativity and doom. Whilst experiencing a panic attack, seek assistance for immediate recovery. Try to identify triggers, so that you can look for ways to avoid and reduce them in the future.

Anxiety can be manageable and controllable. You must first commit to understanding the anxiety, avoiding and minimising exposure, and selecting effective methods to reduce and eliminate.

SELF-HARMING

Self-harming has become prevalent amongst young people yet remains a taboo to speak about. It could be, for example, making a skin cut or burn, picking a scab to keep a wound from healing; banging a head repeatedly against a wall, or other impact bruising; ingesting toxic substances; or any other harmful physical act which can relieve a build-up of pressure or give a feeling of emotional or physical stress release. Self-harming can even give an impression of regaining control – if all other aspects of life seem uncontrollable. The feeling of relief is short lived, but negative feelings and wounds are not. Harming can become addictive, and hence self-harming becomes regular and ritualistic. Individuals who self-harm are not attention seeking. Conversely, they often have feelings of shame and embarrassment about it and may disguise what they are doing.

Self-harming challenges the ability to nurture trusting relationships, and low self-esteem or self-loathing makes it hard to ask for help. Secrets are lonely company.

Binge drinking, taking too many drugs, reckless driving and having unsafe sex are often considered the behaviour of youth, but they could be indicative of a troubled emotional state and actually a form of self-harming.

> "*I feel relieved and less anxious after I cut. The emotional pain slowly slips away into physical pain. It is a way to have control over my body, because I can't control anything else in my life.*"
>
> -- Name withheld

If you suspect someone you know is self-harming, look out for indicators such as:

✓ Evidence of scratches, wounds, bruises and scars – use original excuses to explain away
✓ Clothing changes – or cover-ups, long trousers and sleeves to hide evidence
✓ Blood stains – tissues, bed sheets, clothing, or excessive Band-Aid usage or waste
✓ Knives, blades and less obvious objects with sharp edges amongst possessions. A piece of broken glass, the metal ring-pull from a can, or even a broken plastic ruler with a sharp edge have the potential to inflict damage

Whether you need help, or wish to help someone else:

1. **Confide in someone**. It could be parents, a sibling, a friend or an adult you respect and can trust. Look in your local directory for counsellors and support groups. Confiding with someone who is non-judgmental and supportive is a huge and positive step forward. Sometimes it is easier to talk to someone you don't know well. Make sure you choose someone who will not gossip or betray your confidence. Yet, beware of burdening a vulnerable person who cannot cope with your problems in addition to their own. As difficult as it is for you to open up, it is also difficult for the person you tell — especially if it is a close friend or family member and they are not trained in pastoral care. They may react with shock, anger or fear. You could communicate by letter or by email / text dialogue. Sometimes just the process of writing or typing can also be very cathartic.

2. **Exercise:** When you are feeling low, instinct is to curl up in bed and not surface from under the covers for as long as you can go without food. However, exercise of any kind, even just a brief walk, will release endorphins. These are the body's natural pain relievers – acting to kill pain – even emotional pain. They interact with the opiate receptors in the brain – giving a similar effect to that of morphine. Best of all, there are no side effects. Some doctors even prescribe gym membership as treatment. Gym membership may be pricey – but just go for a run or walk. Go with someone for company and talk as much or as little as you choose.

3. **Laughter:** When feeling low, laughter does not come naturally. Yet, like when exercising it also triggers a release of endorphins. Spend relaxing time with friends or log on to some funny shows and let the laughter make you feel that little bit better.

4. **Triggers:** For bouts of depression or the need to self-harm, keep a mood journal. Try to identify the triggers which initiate bouts of self-harming, so that modified environment, behaviour and circumstances can stave off episodes. Identifying patterns means alternative strategies can be developed.

5. **Break overwhelming projects down into manageable chunks:** When you have a lot to do, or a big project to achieve – it seems overwhelming. Breaking it into manageable chunks makes everything seem less threatening and more manageable. Feel better as you regularly draw a line through the many small units on your "To Do" list. This will keep you on track in timely sequence. *See chapter on Time Management.*

6. **Alternatives could include:**

   - Finding a hobby – such as painting, drawing or writing. Negative emotions can find a voice in creativity.
   - Listening to music that expresses what you're feeling can offer empathy. Explore new genres.
   - Relaxing – a warm, relaxing bath with essential oils can reduce stress.
   - Stress relievers are therapeutic and calming. Repeatedly squeezing a tennis ball can have the same effect.
   - As mentioned, exercising is great to take the mind and body to a better place. Try kickboxing and punch some happier thoughts.
   - Playing an instrument – even the recorder gives a melodious feeling of well-being.

7. **Breaking a self-harming habit:** Self-harming can be addictive, but fortunately not as compelling as drugs or alcohol. Whilst breaking the habit and rehabilitating emotions and behaviour, there are alternatives to cutting and burning:

   - Rub an ice cube across the skin.
   - Make a mark with a felt tip pen.
   - Put a rubber band around wrist / knee etc. and ping the elastic to cause a sharp stinging sensation.

EATING Disorders

Anorexia nervosa, bulimia nervosa, and binge-eating seem familiar eating disorders because they are frequently mentioned in the press, often in line with a prominent celebrity sufferer. They often result from a distorted self-image. The condition may start because of obsessive portion control, but then the fixation spirals into disproportionate obsession, leading to psychological and physical consequences. Common amongst teens and young adults, eating disorders are medical illnesses, often coexisting with other psychological issues such as depression or anxiety.

Anorexia: Not taking on board enough nutrition over an extended period can obviously be life threatening. For an anorexia sufferer, rational understanding of the need to eat is less important than their self-perception of being fat and needing to lose weight. Causes could include low self-esteem and distorted body image, but in severe cases the effects include being severely underweight; paranoia over food; hair loss; bone deterioration; muscle weakening, lanugo (or the production of downy body hair); arrested menstruation in females and hence long-term fertility issues; potential damage to all vital organs; self-induced vomiting; or over frequent use of laxatives. The deeper into the black hole of an eating disorder, the harder it is to climb out.

Bulimia: For sufferers of bulimia, the main behaviour abnormality is binge eating. Because of guilt and shame, this out-of-control action is often in private. Similarly, unhappy with weight, gorging is followed by purging – often enforced vomiting. Ironically it is rare that bulimia leads to sufferers being overweight – after purging, calories do not remain. However, acid burning of the throat, oesophagus and even into the mouth and teeth can be painful, and lead to additional problems.

Binge Eating: The same is not true of Binge Eating Disorder (BED). Sufferers may be out of control with their eating, but do not purge food from their bodies or fast. Often they are unmotivated to exercise, hence are often in a negative cycle of being overweight, shame, and guilt lead to depression and hence further comfort food consumption.

SUPPORT

Our goal is to reach optimum weight level, and to ensure the uptake of a balanced diet rich in vitamins and minerals. This needs to be supplemented by appropriate and manageable levels of physical activity. Therapists offer a combination of therapies to support regulating behaviour and fixing a norm. This might be in support groups or family context, or one on one, and in severe cases may include medication – typically anti-depressants.

If you are supporting a friend with an eating disorder, ask them how you can best be of help. If relapses happen regularly, you may start to feel frustrated and resentful. It is very hard to empathise and understand why someone behaves like this when you don't experience the same thing. Eating disorders are caused by a mix of genetic, psychological, and environmental factors. Sufferers may not be aware that they have a disorder.

It is important that you don't inherit **second-hand stress** or feel that you have failed or let someone down. Reassure them that there is NO SHAME or weakness; recognise that they have an illness, they need help and support in the same way that you would care for a friend who had caught a common cold.

3. SLEEP: The Golden Chain that Ties Health & Body Together by Sheila Partrat

Sleep, the often underestimated and overlooked free essential, is as important to our wellbeing as the air we breathe, the water we drink, and the food we eat. It affects how we look, feel, and perform on a daily basis, and can have a major impact on our overall quality of life. We spend a full one third of our life "between the sheets". Far from being unproductive, the quality and quantity of our sleep has a direct impact on how successful the other two thirds are. Read on for the basics and quick tricks to improve our nights AND our days.

SLEEP and society: The trends

Less sleep: As a society, we tend to trade sleep for more productive work-related or social activities. Over time, this has led to sleeping about one to two hours less than what we used to do a few hundred years ago.

Lower quality: Add to that the relatively recent shift in the content of both work-related and social activities, most of which have us plugged in behind a screen often into the evening, which negatively impacts sleep.

It's safe to say that quality and quantity of sleep are not on an upward trend. Most of us can relate, but what is the impact and what can we do about it?

SLEEP – The basics

What happens when we sleep? Our sleep cycles follow a regular pattern, alternating between REM (rapid eye movement) and NREM (non-rapid eye movement) sleep throughout a typical night. This cycle repeats itself about every 90 minutes.

298

NREM is made up of four stages and takes up about three quarters of our night. It starts between being awake and falling asleep with a light sleep. As sleep onsets, we become disengaged from our surroundings. Breathing and heart rate are regular while our body temperature drops. Blood pressure also drops, while breathing becomes slower. Muscles relax, blood supply increases while tissue growth and repair occurs, and energy is restored. Hormones are released, such as growth hormone (which is essential for growth and development, including muscle development).

REM which is the other 25% of the night, first occurs about 90 minutes after falling asleep and recurs about every 90 minutes, getting longer later in the night. It provides energy to brain and body and supports daytime performance.

How Much Sleep Should We Be Getting?

Older adult: (65+)	7 - 8 hours
Young adult and adult (18 to 65)	7 - 9 hours
Teenager (14 to 17)	8 - 10 hours
School age: (6 to 13)	9 - 11 hours

What Happens When We Get Enough or Too Little Sleep?

Enough quality sleep	Not enough ... over time
Appetites are balanced by helping to regulate levels of the hormones ghrelin and leptin, which play a role in our feelings of hunger and fullness.	Obesity is increased by an increase in ghrelin, which is a hunger hormone. Risk for diabetes is increased because sleep deprivation increases insulin resistance.
Morning alertness. Hormone cortisol dips at bed time and increases over the night for morning alertness.	Memory loss is accelerated, with increased likelihood of problems with cognition, test scores, creativity and sexual arousal. Yup, that too!
Better psychological functioning.	Kids have a strong link to diagnosed ADHD.
We grow and repair body tissue.	Risk for diabetes is increased because sleep deprivation increases insulin resistance.
Contributes to a healthy immune system.	Weakened immune system.

TEENS And Sleep

Are you a teen and not able to fall asleep before 11pm? It's natural! Biology shifts during the teenage years towards later times for both sleeping and waking. However, it does need a little management. Teens tend to have irregular sleep patterns, often sleep deprived across the week, followed by typically staying up late and sleeping in on the weekends. Be watchful, "starve and binge" can negatively affect biological clocks and sleep quality.

"Sleep deprivation puts teenagers into a kind of perpetual cloud or haze", explains Dr. Mary Carskadon, a professor of psychiatry at Brown University and director of chronobiology and sleep research at Bradley Hospital in Rhode Island. "One of the metaphors I use is that it's like having an astigmatism. You don't realise how bad your vision is until you get glasses or in this case, good sleep." That haze, she says, can negatively affect a teenager's mood, ability to think, to react, to regulate their emotions, to learn, and to get along with others.

Looking to upgrading the quantity and quality of sleep? Check out these sleep robbers and easy fixes for a sleep upgrade.

→ Manage the lighting: Make your room as dark as possible. Why? Melatonin starts in dark and cortisol starts with the light. (Source: Lights out. T.S.Wiley)

→ Turn off the Wi-Fi and put the phone on airplane mode. We are exposed to way more electromagnetic fields in our environment today than our ancestors were. 200,000,000x in fact! This is way more than our circuits can handle. Do your bit to limit your own exposure.

→ What are the sources? Indoor cordless telephones and base units, wireless computers and their wireless routers, mice and printers, wireless security, baby monitors, microwave ovens and more. (Source: National Institute for Environmental Health Sciences).

What To Do About it

Unplug / remove wireless in bedroom when you sleep. Make sure the wireless router is not in your bedroom. Don't charge the laptop in the bedroom at night.

During the day, keep the telephones away from the head. Chord gives distance. Laptops nowhere near bed or body, use trays for laps.

300

Get more sleep enhancing nutrients: certain nutrients in foods are precursors to sleep enhancing hormones. Check out the chapter *Food Smarts for a Better Life* for advice on a well-rounded diet. If there is room for improvement, see if you can regularly add more foods with:

- ✓ **Tryptophan:** eggs, cheese, good quality whey protein or other protein powders, salmon, nuts and seeds and turkey.
- ✓ **Vitamin C:** oranges, red peppers, kale, Brussel sprouts, grapefruit, kiwi, and green peppers.

Try a screen curfew, the blue lights from smart phones, laptops and television suppress melatonin and elevate our cortisol levels. For every hour we are on our devices it suppresses our body's melatonin production by 30 minutes. Try closing the screen at least 30 minutes before you go to sleep to give your melatonin a chance to catch up. Alternately, check out Night Mode for your smart phones, which turn off the sleep depriving blue light. Check out f.lux, a free blue light-filtering app that can be downloaded on a cell phone or laptop.

Sleep in a cool environment. Most experts agree that somewhere between 17 to 20 Celsius (or 62 to 68 Fahrenheit) is an ideal sleep temperature.

Still Can't Sleep?

Try a wonderful breathing tool from yoga. Gently close off your right nostril and breathe exclusively through your left nostril deeply, slowly, evenly for three to five minutes. This slows down the constant computation of the mind and helps put distance between ourselves and our emotions.

Chapter 7: Safety

by Rachael Desgouttes

1. PUTTING Together a Medical Kit - Keep It Simple

There are many articles about first aid which recommend lists of over thirty items. These are often sponsored by manufacturers of medical equipment. It is really not necessary so long as you have core basics, keep your first aid kit up to date and know where to turn in case of more serious incidents.

You may choose to have a personal supply, especially in your first year, but you may also choose to share a group kit with your housemates. It is important to know the difference between your own personal medical supplies (such as any prescription medicine you take regularly, which is your responsibility, and will be kept somewhere for you to access easily, such as your bedside table) and a more general household first aid kit. If shared, it is something that all members of your group should contribute towards funding, and most importantly, there must be agreed upon rules: for example, should someone use something from inside, it MUST be replaced. This way, you can all be confident that in an emergency you will have what you need when the time comes.

2. IN Case of Emergency

Make sure you know the local emergency numbers as these vary from country to country. Check them out!

For any serious accident or emergency, you will be able to seek medical help through your college, local doctor, or the Accident and Emergency Department of the nearest hospital. Most universities have their own security and help phone numbers. Make sure you familiarise yourself with information and the phone numbers at the beginning of term and have the numbers readily accessible too. As well as on your phone fast dial, stick these details on the fridge door, in your diary, and on a paper at the top of your medical box.

Getting medical help if you suffer from a chronic condition:

If you have a medical history of seizures, severe asthma, diabetes, or any other condition, you must share this information with your friends and flatmates. Teach them what to do in an emergency, where your own medication is kept, plus the appropriate dosage so that in case of an episode, they will best know how to help you and not be afraid. This isn't limited to physical problems, but can also include anxiety and emotional attacks. Panic attacks can be very stressful to someone who doesn't know what's going on or what to do. Pre-warning your friends means they'll be ready to assist if the time comes.

3. FIRST Aid Box

Key Point: Some shops sell ready-made medical kits, but beware. These often cost more than buying the component parts separately. Similarly, supermarket own brands are usually more reasonable than manufactured brands.

The container for a medical kit does not need be a dramatic red box with a red cross emblazoned on the side! But it is a good idea to use an airtight plastic box to keep your supplies clean and dry. These are cheaply available. A transparent box is good, so in an emergency you can see what is inside. Label it clearly and keep it in an easy to access place.

Essential Contents of the First Aid Box

Administration

- ✓ List of emergency numbers and contacts.
- ✓ Campus Health Service phone number.
- ✓ Familiarise yourself with the local doctors and hospitals and the systems to make contact – especially for possible out of hours emergencies.
- ✓ If you have private health insurance, be aware of the Health Insurance phone number plus the process for authorisation BEFORE you are in an emergency. Living in a shared house, keep the details for each person, so you can best help someone else in an emergency.
- ✓ If you know your blood group, a note of this is a good thing to keep here. You can add to this information about chronic or reoccurring conditions.
- ✓ For medicines, you may want to list the date of expiry for each item.

Medical Supplies and Over the Counter Medications

> **Remember: the simpler it is, the easier it is to maintain.**

- **Medical disinfectant wipes:** The danger with many injuries is not the wound itself, but the risk of infection. If you cut yourself on a rusty nail or a broken glass, it is VERY important that the wound be thoroughly cleaned before dressing. Single use antiseptic wipes in sealed sachets are essential. Keeping a note of your last Tetanus injection is sensible.
    - o Whether you are cleaning your own wound or attending to someone else, remember to **wash and dry your hands** before attending any injury. Remember also to wash and dry your hands AFTER attending to an injury.

- **Antibiotic ointment:** This prevents infection in minor wounds and burns. However, it is important to keep the tube/bottle clean. Don't apply cream directly to the wound or with your finger. Use a gauze/tissue/cotton bud to avoid contaminating the rest of the ointment.

- **Simple plasters and sterile dressings**: Bandages, tape and gauze come in all shapes and sizes. You do not need to have it all. Keep several varied sizes of plaster and a general bandage kit comprising of bandage, non-stick gauze (also useful for applying cream) and medical tape. This will cover you until morning for non-urgent accidents, when a doctor or a pharmacy shop can be visited for something specific. An elasticated bandage is a good idea to give compression to a sprain. Scissors can be useful, but in many a student home, these seem to disappear! If you can choose a selection of materials without needing scissors, it is one less complication in an emergency.

- **Pain**: There are some general medications that will fix short term, mild conditions.
    - o <u>Paracetamol or Ibuprofen:</u> Great for inflammation or swelling, fever, headaches and general pain. Read the instructions and follow carefully not just the recommended dose, but also guidelines for taking before or after food, and whether they mix with alcohol or not.
    - o If an injury is severe enough that there is a risk of surgery being needed, delay taking medicine until you have sought professional medical help.
    - o <u>Ice</u> (not in the medical box!) is excellent for anti-inflammatory pain. If you have a freezer – ice is great for reducing swelling. A packet of frozen peas or anything else can be used instead. Wrap in a clean cloth before applying to skin.

- **Allergy:** If you are suffer from hay-fever or allergies regularly, then your medication might be in your own private kit. A general antihistamine is a good idea for a one-off reaction. Keeping an antihistamine cream is a great idea for a skin irritation, burn or insect bite.
  - o If you have a serious allergy, such as to nuts, insect bites or penicillin – make sure you let your friends know. Wear a bracelet if necessary, and have your anaphylactic medicine and equipment readily available.

- **Indigestion or heartburn:** Over the counter (OTC) medications are good to have on hand. Relief is almost immediate, whereas the symptoms can be miserable and stop you getting your all-important sleep. Repeated heartburn pain should be investigated by a doctor.

- **Sore throats & coughs:** Cough drops – or lozenges and syrups should be bought on an as-needed basis, but left-overs may be put in the box. Cough syrups may need to be refrigerated. Be sure not to take too many cough lozenges, as they won't actually heal; they simply numb the sore throat.
  - o Try gargling with warm water or salty water, consuming honey and lemon drinks, sucking chewable Vitamin C (read dosage), getting enough sleep, and not too much talking. No whispering either - it damages vocal chords too!

- **Thermometer**: Is it hot in here – or do you have a fever? You may not even feel you need a thermometer. There is certainly no need to invest in an expensive digital one, perhaps buy a traditional glass one in a case. Make sure you familiarise yourself with how to use it before you need it! They are not always easy at first, but practice makes perfect. Wipe the bulb of the thermometer with an alcohol swab after each use. Alternatively, you can choose a strip that you put on your forehead, which is cheap, quick and practical, but may be slightly less accurate. This also needs cleaning each time.

- **Sunscreen, after-sun cream, insect repellent**: These are the responsibility of each person. They are not medical items but for general wellbeing, and prevention of insect bites and sun burn. Depending on your location, these items will have more or less importance.

Eucalyptus / tea tree oil: As well as powerful cleaning agents, these substances are potent natural remedies. A small bottle is not expensive and makes a great gift!

- <u>For Colds or Flu:</u> Eucalyptus works as an expectorant and helps cleanse your body of toxins & microorganisms that can make you feel sick. Put several drops of the essential oil on your pillow or in a diffuser to benefit all night long. If you don't have a diffuser, make one, by adding drops of oil into a bowl of steaming water. Cover your head with a towel, lean over the bowl, breathe deeply and inhale the vapour.
- <u>Sinus, Allergies and Respiratory Problems:</u> Eucalyptus is effective in treating <u>sinusitis</u> or allergies. Gargle a solution of water with a couple of drops added, to clear the throat. Eucalyptus oil is also a highly effective treatment for respiratory problems, such as <u>asthma</u>, <u>bronchitis</u>, and pneumonia. It is proven to dilate blood vessels and allow more oxygen to the lungs. Also try mixing eucalyptus oil, <u>peppermint oil</u> and <u>coconut oil</u> with a body lotion or petroleum jelly, then rub on upper chest.
- <u>Wound Treatment:</u> Eucalyptus oil has antiseptic properties, effectively treating wounds, burns, cuts, and sores. Make into an ointment and put on bites and stings. It is a natural pain reliever, plus also keeps the area from getting infected, which speeds healing.
- <u>Hair Nourishment:</u> For a moisturising refresh, try a weekly treat of a few drops mixed with some coconut or olive oil massaged into your hair. Rinse thoroughly and see the difference.
- <u>Hand Cleaner:</u> Eucalyptus is an excellent cleanser to remove grease and grime from your hands.

It is better to buy medicine as you need it, rather than keep a massive stash of things which may expire. All oral medicines have a sell/use by date – so it is important to keep an eye on what you have. Date-label all boxes/bottles with a permanent marker, which will reduce the risk of taking old medicine. Don't throw away the box if it has the sell-by date on it!

TOP TIPS

Money tip! Supermarket own label medication is a much cheaper alternative to branded items. Compare the dosage and choose an equivalent.

Keep all medication in the original box with the instructions. The box has that all-important use by date.

Use ice for a sprain, bruise or break; use a hot water bottle for aches, pains and old injuries.

Buying branded eyewash is not necessary – cold clean water will suffice if you get something in your eye. If it is more serious than that, go to the hospital.

Have clean and dry hands for wound care. Also, keep all supplies clean and dry.

Sometimes feeling unwell can be solved with a hot drink and an early night! "Fresher's 'flu" is a common student ailment as students arrive in a new place, bringing germs from all parts of the world. They party hard, have the stress of studies, eat poorly, and are getting used to self-management. Plus, they don't have the familiar comfort of being tended to when ill at home. All these factors contribute to minor illnesses.

**Keep an eye on your flatmates – and your
flatmates will keep an eye on you!**

4. KEEPING Yourself Safe on the Street

Top Tips from Safety Expert, Mike Howard

Mike has 35 years of experience in law enforcement, principally in the investigation of international narcotics cases. He has also been the lead investigator for serious crime cases including murder, rape, armed robbery and kidnapping. For several years he spoke at international schools on the signs and dangers of drug use amongst students. He is currently working as an investigator for an international bank looking at staff misconduct and whistle-blowing allegations.

Mike has three grown children and a fourth preparing for university. His driving force is to assist young adults make the transition from home to overseas and independent living, and to ensure they are in possession of the tools they need for ensuring their own safety and security as far as is possible.

There is no better way than to introduce and explain the seriousness of potential situations, than in his own words: *"I want to give you enough information to make you safe and want to take precautions, without scaring you to death."*

It is not the intention to scare you – these statistics can do that on their own.

Check out this link: http://www.operationlookout.org

According to the U.S. Department of Justice, in 2015 over 600,000 people under the age of 21 went missing in the USA. That is over 1,600 per day. Many of these victims are now deceased, either from natural causes or due to more suspicious circumstances. Some will be runaways who have recreated a life elsewhere. One shocking fact is that at least a seventh of these will have been drugged and trafficked into prostitution. Like so many things, it is easy to feel like, "It won't happen to me." The probability is that it won't. But we should never be cavalier about safety or overlook any techniques and tips that minimise our risk and create a safer environment.

All youngsters tend to consider themselves to be "street wise". They are looking for enough self-confidence to be able to socialise. Within the context of the environment in which they have grown up, they probably know the risks. Consider your home: do you live in a small village, a small town, or an inner city with high rise blocks? Are there areas of high unemployment? Is there racial tension? Are there gangs? Are incidences of petty theft, violence, or drug arrests daily, weekly, or rare occurrences?

You may be "street wise" to the extent you need to be for your hometown. Going to a new place may present a whole different range of challenges. Of course, not all cities are crime-ridden, and not all small sleepy villages are crime free. But, as with all things – forewarned is forearmed, and you will benefit from being informed and prepared. Much of the information you need is available online and by putting it together to form a meaningful picture, you can make the best choices.

BEFORE you go to university

When you are choosing your accommodation, whether you have campus accommodation or are selecting a property yourself, you need to try to get to know the area (and importantly the surrounding areas) before you choose.

This includes:

- ✓ The areas of your lessons, which may be in more than one place
- ✓ The area in which you plan to live
- ✓ Very importantly, and often forgotten: the route through which the journey/s will take you.

You will need to research which are the local areas:

- ✓ With low – or high crime rates
- ✓ Which are culturally diverse and may have racial tension, which make the area more volatile and challenging, especially at night
- ✓ Which have an active drug scene
- ✓ which are prone to gang fighting.

Sadly, these negative factors and conditions are what push rental prices down, and hence are sometimes attractive to students because of their low prices. The more you research, the better informed you will be to make choices that will balance your safety with your budget. Talk to the university staff and students who have been in the area for some time. Don't be shy to ask questions, and search online for more information.

Consider:

- ✓ Bus routes – do they pass through undesirable areas?
- ✓ How many pubs are there en route between your transport stop and your front door – do they attract a rough crowd?
- ✓ When profiling an area, remember that the day time and evening/night time may present completely different pictures.
- ✓ What time is "chucking out" or closing time? If there are several pubs in an area – do they all close at the same time? If so, this may be a travel window for you to avoid.
- ✓ How far is the walk from the bus/train to your accommodation?
- ✓ Are there any areas you need to be wary of such as street corners or parks where teenagers gather?
- ✓ Are the ground floor windows directly on the street? If so, what security does the accommodation have?

BEFORE a night out

Plan a buddy-system strategy with your friends before you go out. Watching out for each other is a responsibility you both need to undertake. Whilst you need to remain sober and alert and watch your friend's back, you should be able to rely on your friend to do the same for you. Should your plans change during the evening (perhaps you decide to go to different places), review your plans and find a new buddy. Remember, your friends are not your parents, so never assume that you can be irresponsible simply because someone is watching your back.

> "*When you start university, you don't really know anyone and don't know what they're like on a night out. I know from experience! At the end of the day no one is responsible for you except YOU, and I know as a fresher I wouldn't put my entire safety in the hands of someone that I had met not that long ago.*"
>
> Mylena Reay.

Tips for preparing for a night out on the town:

- If you are going out alone – let your friends know your intended movements, especially an approximate time you intend to be home.
- Prepare speed dials on your phone:
  - Your parents
  - A responsible friend
  - An adult you can turn to for help – to whom you have discussed using them as a first call option
  - For moments of serious difficulty, have the police and ambulance numbers prepared too!
- If you are going to be coming home alone, perhaps someone can meet your bus/train, or even just be at the front window / door to ensure your safety as you walk down the street (if this is one of your identified danger areas).
- Money tip: Plan the things you need in your bag and wallet and don't take too much. Calculate the cash you need, plus 10%. This helps you stay within budget and minimise any loss.
- Photocopy all the things in your wallet and take a minimum number of cards and IDs. If you lose all of these documents, it can be a lengthy nightmare to replace.
- Dress for the occasion and the venue. Beware of flashing designer labels in a run-down area. They send a message of affluence and make you a target. Dress conservatively, not provocatively.
- Consider carrying one of many legal self-defence tools available on line. Pepper spray or a rape whistle are effective, and some universities even offer them to students free of charge.

DURING a night out

In a difficult situation, you need to make judgement calls constantly. If a big group of leather jacketed, bikers or loud fraternity boys pumped with testosterone enters the bar causing a rumpus, it may be time to look for somewhere else for a quiet drink *(And NO, this is not stereotyping and saying that a leather jacket equals bad behaviour! It is summing up a collection of signals that could indicate potential trouble.)*

Always try to calculate your degrees of risk.

Sit with your back to the wall. Being caught up in a jostling crowd close to the bar can be a potentially dangerous spot, should trouble erupt.

Identify key triggers that might spark trouble:

- ✓ A man flirting with another man's girlfriend.
- ✓ Excessive alcohol means a small comment can attract a lot of attention.
- ✓ Racial slurs can quickly escalate and turn aggressive.

If any of this happens between strangers – walk away. If a member of your party is a participant in a tension-stricken interaction, tactfully steer them away.

Martial arts are often promoted as the best self-defence answer in tricky circumstances. However, a fighting stance in a class or gym is only of use against an opponent who knows and plays by the same rules. In a real-life situation, during the time you take to prepare to make a blow, an assailant may have drawn a knife and stabbed you. The rules are not fair. Walk away first instead of acting all "macho". Is there a back door, emergency exit or access outside through the toilet door or window?

"I did a program where the local police offered us a self-defence workshop. The cops taught us some useful defences that any woman can use in an attack or assault. Many US universities offer self-defence classes as part of the course offerings, or through the fitness centre!"

A.C.N. Medicine

Mike's TOP TIPS:

If you see trouble coming, walk away!

If you are ever unlucky enough to be attacked, GIVE YOUR PROPERTY UP. It is not worth risking being injured, maimed or killed for your watch, wallet, car keys, or handbag.

Call the police if trouble brews – don't be a have-a-go-hero.

The very LAST option is to engage or participate in violence.

---

5. DRUGS

This book does not intend to provide a list of drugs with the associated pros and cons. There is plenty of information about the ever-evolving drug scene on the internet and your university will probably have a help department. This is a warning about a serious drug which you may have passively or unknowingly inflicted on you called GHB (Gamma Hydroxybutyrate).

GHB reduces your bodily activity and slows processes in the brain and central nervous system. Known as the "Date Rape" drug, Rophynol, "roofies", or a range of other nicknames, this common drug can come in many forms – tablet, powder, or liquid.

Whilst it was first employed to achieve a "high" at clubs and raves, now it has a reputation for being a tool to commit rape. It is similarly a tool used to manipulate theft (for instance, the perpetrator will force the victim to withdraw money from a bank cashpoint machine). Symptoms can include drowsiness, dizziness, nausea, memory haze, and visual perception. In other words, you might feel drunk. It is impossible to gauge the strength and quality of the illegal substance GHB since it is often homemade, and might be mixed with other illicit drugs or household substances. If a drink has been contaminated with GHB it is not discernible – either visually or by tasting. If ingested, it can cause disastrous consequences. Mixed with alcohol, the result can be literally deadly. There are cases of the Date Rape drug being used on men and women, by men and women. Everyone needs to remain aware.

Some common sense tips to reduce the chances of being targeted:

- ✓ NEVER leave your drink unattended and return to it later. Scarily, you only need to turn your head and someone could slip something inside. You could consider cradling your glass and keenly observing your surroundings.
- ✓ If you need the bathroom, finish your drink first, or ask ONLY your reliable buddy to hold it for you. Never trust a stranger to keep an eye on your drink.
- ✓ If you feel too intoxicated for the amount of alcohol you've consumed, feel dizzy, are slurring your words, or are struggling to walk, you may have been drugged. Tell your friends and call emergency help immediately. If in doubt, notify the manager of the establishment and insist they get medical help. Get yourself to a safe place.

6. SAVVINESS in Daily Life

Protecting your new home

Inviting your friends to your apartment is part of the growth and development of the relationship. You use your gut to decide and trust them.

Even though you may initially get on like a house on fire with your new college friends, you have little history together. When you first met, you automatically had a lot in common. You have all left school, are excited to meet new pals, and are starting a new chapter of your life away from where you grew up. However, you may never have seen your new friends drink to excess, or turn angry or depressed. You even may discover deep-rooted, fundamental differences between you – whether these differences are cultural, religious, or political.

Aside from using caution and trusting your gut with your new acquaintances, realise that your new friends may bring additional friends with them, who you have not had an opportunity to evaluate against your system of values, and whose ideas and behaviour is beyond your range of choice.

Exploring transport options

In your new destination you are going to need safe and efficient ways of getting around. Especially if you are planning on drinking alcohol, you need fool proof ways to get home. Here are some key tips mastering different transportation methods:

- ✓ **Bus, tram, or train:** Sit near a door so you can exit if trouble gets on. Know where the emergency button bell is to alert the driver in a challenging situation.
- ✓ **Car:** If you are considering a car whilst at university, think about discretion. A new sports car on campus or in a poor area of town will attract the wrong sort of attention. Don't leave valuables in your car when unattended. Even when in motion, it is not a good idea to put a wallet, purse, computer, or valuable phone on the seat where it is visible. There have even been incidents of smash and grab (a broken window, and an item stolen as quickly as when a car is stationary at a red light).
- ✓ **Bicycle:** If you have a bike, think about the area in which you live and padlock it carefully against solid, immovable items. Think about the parts that are removable and either take them with you – or lock them securely to other parts.

REMINDER: If you are ever attacked, give your property up immediately. A wallet or a handbag is a small price compared to what could potentially cost you your life. You never know if an attacker has a knife or gun, and how desperate he may be.

Never force yourself to be in a situation or environment that feels uncomfortable. If in doubt – walk away.

---

7. DIGITAL Citizenship and Safety

'Digital Citizenship' is often a misunderstood term, despite in recent years becoming frequently found on the curriculum of many schools. So, what does it really mean? And why and how does and should it concern you as you leave home to study?

This section is based on an interview with Iain Williamson, Head of Film and Media and Digital Literacy Coordinator at the South Island School in Hong Kong.

Being aware of your online persona and what impact it can have on your life is hugely important. The term 'digital citizenship' often holds a negative connotation amongst students and youngsters – it could be associated with adults in authority giving instructions and rules about what to do and what not to do with technology. Adults may not claim to "know everything" when it comes to technology, yet that does not stop them throwing around rules, "Put your phone away!" or "Get off your phone, you're being antisocial!" Then there are the punitive threats, "That's it, no phone for a week!" or "If your phone rings in school you will get a detention!" Unsurprisingly, this isn't always greatly appreciated. The probability is, you've heard it before and it can be frustrating.

On reaching adulthood, taking away the negativity from the concept of 'digital citizenship' is important. Instead, we can start to see it more as simply a part of general knowledge, or common sense. In fact, this is crucial, as careless online actions can bring current or future problems to either personal or professional situations.

In this ever-growing interconnected world, using social media has several important aspects that need to be considered; safety, legality and ethicality. Despite seeming tedious, it is a good idea to read about new popular apps, to not only gain a better insight into their perks, but also become aware of any possible associated dangers.

An important aspect of your digital footprint is the permanence of online actions. On Facebook, Twitter, Instagram or any other site, never forget that once you put something online, it is very difficult to get rid of completely. YOU may have deleted it, or blocked a teacher, your mother or an ex-friend, but people are able to make a screenshot and save information you have posted. Test this out yourself! See what your online profile looks like by Googling your name.

It is important to have awareness of your online persona as a result of what content you post. Whilst you have the freedom to garner insight about companies, potential bosses, and colleagues, they can use the same avenues to access information about you! A common cliché and scare-tactic teachers and adults use is that once you start applying for university or looking for jobs, your potential institution or company will Google you. While you shouldn't panic, all this information is so readily available that if it is sought after it can be very easily found.

"*In my first year as a teacher, I was nervous. Some of the students were only five years younger than me - the same age as my brother! The first month went quite well, and I was building up confidence. But then one of the Year 12 boys found a picture of me that my friend had innocently posted, but tagged me in, at a fancy dress party, having drunk a bit too much. It took the rest of the term to overcome the embarrassment and fully restore order.*"

-- Jane Fullerton, qualified as a teacher in 2014

Below you will find some straight-forward, common sense advice. Summarising these points, **keep your profile as 'clean' as possible**, especially if it is accessible to anyone and everyone. Picture yourself as a young professional in the workplace. Are you happy to have this post attached to your identity?

Train yourself with a mental "traffic light" check.

Something that might be funny to your close circle of friends might be offensive to a different audience. At school you were a tight group from similar backgrounds. Your university peer interaction will have a much broader range of backgrounds and social diversity.

Using the traffic light idea is a good self-imposed filter before posting. If in doubt whether to go post something that "walks the fine line" between appropriate and inappropriate, err on the side of caution. Would you show the content to your grandmother, or the headmaster of the school you attended?

The Traffic Light Test

 Just like for social chit-chat at a dinner party, avoid discussing politics, religion, and anything else which may be very controversial. Be especially leery of posts that are politically angry or aggressive.

 Nothing that is offensive, rude, bawdy, or overtly sexual. Avoid posting photos from drunken escapes, both images of yourself or anyone else who may take offence or be embarrassed. Be sensitive to others. If you wouldn't want the same picture posted of yourself, the chances are, this person doesn't want it either.

 Anything that cannot cause any offence is great! Whilst cute children and pets, happy people having a good time, views, and sunsets may seem too fluffy, they are inoffensive. Include your achievements and sporting successes. Thank other people and support their effort and success, always be polite.

Start your LinkedIn page.

LinkedIn is an important reference to have and shows you are ambitious, aware, and connected to the professional world. Analyse the way other people have presented themselves in your career to which you aspire. It may feel too early to do this, but the sooner you start your page, the easier it will be to maintain in the future. LinkedIn is a key way of business networking, and adding one activity / internship experience at a time is a lot less overwhelming than starting your page from scratch right before you need it! Also, the earlier you make your page, the more "connections" you can build, as you can connect with your teachers from high school and your old classmates before those relationships fade.

"At my university, the people who had LinkedIn from first year onwards, definitely had an advantage over those who only got it in their fourth year, right before beginning the job search."

SRM Warwick

> The definition of a digital footprint is "to engage in positive safe, legal and ethical behaviour when using technology, including social interactions online or in using network devices."

There are three important aspects to take into consideration when talking about online presence: Safety; Legality; and Ethicality.

1. Safety

The main aspect of 'safety' is using verifiable websites, and making sure that they are legitimate sources of information. Especially when moving away from home, setting up a bank account is a task typically at the top of the to do list. Use official, legitimate websites that allow you to carry out financial transactions (such as PayPal, which is a verification service). Double-check the URL of a banking site, social networking, or e-mail site before you log in. Many browsers, such as Chrome, Internet Explorer and Firefox include a colour-change on the left side of the location bar to indicate that the site has been verified as legitimate.

If you shop online, make sure that the site's address starts with "https", instead of just "http", and has a padlock icon in the URL field. This shows that the website is secure and uses encryption to stop it being intercepted by others. Beware of a website that has misspellings, bad grammar, or an inaccuracy in the logo. This could be a fake version of a legitimate website.

Talk to your bank about their security processes in order to avoid being scammed by fake calls or emails. Never assume that an email from the bank will not be a scam. If you are not expecting one, or it does not have a name you recognise, or it has an attachment – beware.

Check out this excellent website with practical tips and advice:

https://securingtomorrow.mcafee.com/consumer/consumer-threat-notices/10-tips-stay-safe-online/

An overview of good password protection: (see "Money chapter")

When making passwords to protect a bank account, they should be more complicated than for your email password. Using a variety of lowercase and uppercase letters, as well as digits and symbols should make them more complex.

Every year a list is published by an internet security firm called Splash Data. Unbelievably, people have used passwords such as; "12345678", "password", the top letter keyboard line "Qwerty", or their birth date. From banking to email accounts at university, don't choose a password that is too straightforward. "Password123" is not a good password!

In the past, seven or eight letters/digits were sufficient, but nowadays these aren't long enough. A safer password would range between around 20-25 characters, including numbers and special characters such as exclamation marks or question marks to ensure safety.

Password managers are available to help you create, store and regularly update strong passwords for all of your accounts. Ask your university or technical friends for recommendations and read reviews online.

2. Legality

It is important to understand and respect the rights and obligations of using and sharing intellectual property online. Many of us are already downloading and sharing information online, such as films, apps, photographs, music to name a few. More often than not, there is a bit of a grey area about what is considered legal and what is not.

Downloading the work of someone else and using it comes down to personal choice but has a legal implication, even if it's just borrowing. Downloading images to use in a PowerPoint presentation with citations seems pretty harmless, as it is not being used for money-making purposes. However, if the pictures are being used for promotional purposes, or for any activity which ultimately can make money, that is a different story. You are using someone else's work to potentially make a profit. You could even run the risk of being sued.

https://www.theedublogger.com/2017/01/20/copyright-fair-use-and-creative-commons/

Accessing and downloading files is fundamentally illegal if you are the person uploading content to the file sharing service. This is breaking the law. Recently, streaming and torrenting files has become increasingly popular. This is a grey area as far as legality goes.

3. Ethicality

In areas such as Hong Kong, accessing illegally uploaded files, in other words 'streaming' content, while it may be considered unethical, is technically legal. Nonetheless, uploading content is unarguably illegal.

In the UK, streaming is currently being debated in court. The best advice is simply to STAY AWARE. Many universities are, to a certain extent, able to monitor student activities on their Wi-Fi network. Often this means students caught torrenting content are essentially banned from the network and consequently need to explain themselves to the IT department and deal with the repercussions. Ask yourself, is it worth running the risk, or would it be more worthwhile to just go through legitimate sites, like Netflix or Hulu? For a small price, you are able to ensure safety, legality and quality. You are also taking the higher moral path.

> *"One of my friends ordered fake ID's during first year (the drinking age in America is 21) using the university Wifi to send money to China. It flagged up as a concern and he had to explain what he was up to to the University police! He handed over the ID's and lost $200, and luckily was let-off with a warning, but it could have been much worse!"*
>
> Name withheld

Another important aspect of being cautious online is the ability to manage personal data to maintain digital privacy and security, as well as be aware of data collection technology used to track your navigation online. That's a lot to take in, so let's break it down.

Regardless of the online activity, whether its social media signups or Google searches, the vast majority of these applications have a moderating system, such as recording IP addresses. Quite often, information from the apps we use (like Facebook and Instagram) is sold on to advertisers in terms of demographics. Have you ever mentioned a city, only to be bombarded with advertisements for hotels in that area? Essentially, there is very little that you can do online that isn't traceable, meaning there's really no such thing as complete privacy online.

Phishing is when an unauthorised party tries to obtain sensitive information, often by devious means. Under the guise of a reputable name – such as your bank, or a reputable company or brand name – these parties seek out sensitive information such as your usernames and passwords, or bank and credit card details. Sometimes an advertisement has an embedded phishing link, or an email may look authentic to lure you, but has a false URL. You are then connected to malicious sites (known as Malware) which bring all sorts of problems such as viruses.

Considerations for heading off to university:

The issue of managing personal data and stopping your data being taken hostage was first occurring with the online celebrity culture. Celebrity photos or videos from their personal cloud storage were being hacked, and private photos or videos were either virally distributed to embarrass the celebrities, or used as click bait (meaning someone was unethically and illegally making money from it).

Now data can be held hostage. This is when the owner's information is stolen, and the owner is threatened via social media. Unless a ransom is paid, the contents of their cloud will be released online. While this occurrence is luckily rare, knowing the warning signs and how to react if the situation should arise will protect you for the future.

Schools often run mandatory talks about important topics such as drugs and sex education. These topics are often neglected from a technology standpoint, a fundamentally important part of life nowadays. When it comes to sexting or sending provocative pictures, it is obviously down to the individual's choice, however it is necessary to be aware of the possible dangers of this. Recent articles show that this sort of blackmail can lead to drastic and tragic consequences. Legality can also be an issue: if you are of age but you're dating a minor (under the legal age of 18) and naked pictures are being exchanged, this qualifies as illegal activity.

In more extreme cases of data hostage, images and content are used as click bait. This sort of content tends to be targeted at boys more than girls (typically individuals around 15 - 25 years old). This is a critical age and is linked to the development of an active relationship with pornography. This can lead to the possibility of young people exposing themselves on camera, often via webcams (with the parties sometimes unaware that they are being recorded). This data can be used to blackmail people via contact through social media sites. Whilst these situations may be extreme, it is good to keep in mind that everything you do online is traceable and can be dug up, whether it is the pornographic sites (even through incognito mode) or the messages you send. Be very wary!

On-line Pornography

Recent research has looked at the effect of online pornography on the human brain. Scientists carrying out studies have found that pornography is addictive, lighting up the pleasure receptors in the brain not entirely dissimilar to those of Class A drugs. The most serious side effects of this increased exposure to pornography affects boys in that, once at university, many medical practitioners report a relatively high number of erectile dysfunction cases. This is due to the "lowered excitement" of a real relationship as compared to the portrayal of sex in pornographic films and images. They are entering a hyper-reality and as a result, the sex portrayed through porn changes reality perceptions and hence their actions within a real-life relationship. Girls feel the need to conform to the expectations of the male's sexual fantasies of pornography, which can have major implication in a relationship.

Another dangerous aspect of virtual reality is computer games which also are a form of pleasure that provide 'dopamine style hits'. If you have ever struggled with being self-disciplined using computer games at home, it is really important to consider the dangers that you may face being away from home at university. Now, there will be no teacher or parental figure keeping you in check or giving you guidance as to what is a healthy amount of gaming or computer-usage time. It can also be difficult to assess how you are actually spending your computer time. When you finally log off to fall asleep, it feels as though you have done a full day of work; but can you honestly assess what was work and what was game or other computer time? Your education can be impacted because of misappropriation of study time due to poor self-discipline or self-control, and before you know it, you might fail to hand in assignments on time. Ultimately, more severe repercussions could occur, including ultimately even being asked to leave the university.

Luckily, there is a way to balance your time between social, relaxation and work tasks. As with so many aspects of life discussed in this book, pre-planning is always a better way forward than damage control. Find a method that can support you:

- ✓ Speaking to your parents
- ✓ Using computer games as a personal reward system

Getting guidance through the university's resources (for example: a course on 'study-skills' offered at the University of Warwick).

Chapter 8: Get That Job!

by Rachael Desgouttes

Job Applications and Interview Skills

1. INTRODUCTION

The first time you look for a job, be it part-time work during your studies, a summer placement, or a full-time job after you graduate, it can be daunting getting organised and presenting yourself in your best light. There are several simple but important steps that can up your chances of job success!

2. MAKING a Job Application

When replying to a job advertisement, it is key to match your skills to the requirements, emphasising the skills they are looking for and persuade the recruiters that you are the best candidate.

TOP TIP: Follow the instructions 100% accurately. Make sure you include all the things they ask for (photo, references, sample of your work) as appropriate. If any ONE of these things is omitted it says a lot about your attention to detail! You may have fallen at the first hurdle, as this may be part of the company or organisation's first test.

Make sure you address the letter as instructed. Never make a spelling mistake with someone's name. Use the contact person's correct job title as it appears in their advert or correspondence. Never use *"to whom it may concern"* as they will have told you who is concerned with it! Use the method of communication asked for – don't send an e-mail if they ask for snail mail, and vice versa.

Apply for jobs and opportunities that will serve your resume in the future – all experience is good experience. Read a job description as the recruiter's wish list. If you fall short of a couple of minor items asked for, don't always be put off from applying. If it asks for a Mandarin speaker and you are not one, applying would be wasting your time, but if it asks for five years of experience and you have only three, you could still give it a go. If a quality is described as "preferable", then you are not out of the running – but demonstrate that you would be willing to develop this skill, or what you can offer to counterbalance not having it. Don't hide or try to disguise a skill you don't have, and directly identify where you have a shortfall and what you intend to do about it. Compensate a weakness with an excess of something else, or other talents and experiences.

A spontaneous application can also be very well received (one that is not in response to an advertisement but sent directly to an organisation that you are keen to be involved with). Even if your dream employer is not advertising, send your C.V. Explain how you think you are an ideal fit and how you could be a benefit to the company. They may be expanding and create a job for you, or keep your details for future opportunities.

3. WRITING a C.V.

C.V. stands for Curriculum Vitae – or literally – the story of your life! It can also be referred to as a resume. The things that you choose to include will tell your story.

Your C.V. is a document containing the information a recruiter needs. It should be succinct and factual. It is very rare that a C.V. needs to be longer that two sides of typed A4 paper – no matter how many qualifications you may have. The major goal of this document is to make the reader interested and curious enough to call you for an interview.

For all things you intend to include in this document, ask yourself, "Does this add to my value?" For example, if you are applying for a job that is advertised for 18-25 year olds, then you need to add your age so that you confirm you qualify. If there has been no mention of age, adding that you are 22 might work against you if the company prefers five to ten years' experience; or, adding that you are 25 will not help a company who are searching for a school leaver. The same applies to your address. Mentioning that your postal address is in Kuala Lumpur may be off-putting if the job is in the north of England. Include information about your address so that people may contact you – it is most probable that they will email or phone you, so no need for a postal address unless it has been specified.

The sections in a CV are typically:

1. Personal Information

Essential:

- ✓ **Name:** If your name is culturally unfamiliar within the recruitment area to which you are applying, think about whether you need to show your family name (perhaps in capital letters) or your given names. Many companies nowadays have "equal opportunities" clauses, meaning that candidates shouldn't be judged on name – based on your culture or gender, but on experience and abilities alone. However, you want to avoid embarrassing an employer if he does not know how to address you.

✓ **Gender:** Consider whether you want to imply gender – is it necessary and will it help? Consider aiding the interviewer to know how to address you. This can be done by simply signing off your accompanying letter Ms, Mrs or Mr.

✓ **Contact details:** Give what is asked for. No matter what, make a selection of what is necessary for the recruiters to contact you. One phone number and one email address are enough, but make sure you check these regularly!

Non-Essential

✓ **Personal data:** Be selective about including personal data such as your date of birth, nationality, and marital status. Be smart! Only include these if they are relevant and add value to your application. Beware how they can be active negatives – for instance, if your phone number has a German dialling code and you are applying to Lancashire UK, a company might fear the expense and time of needing to relocate you. Focus on positives and getting to an interview. Everything else can be discussed thereafter.

✓ **Personal overview:** This is an optional paragraph, often included at the beginning of a resume. It is a useful tool to highlight the synergy between the recruiter's needs and your background. It is often the hardest to write because it is a key moment to blow your own trumpet and summarise your achievements. It is a useful tool to be succinct and summarise a large chunk of your life (for instance, "12 years dynamic sales experience for a multinational FMCG company"). Ask people whose opinion you trust to give you an honest summary of yourself. This helps to build your positive self-image and allows you to present yourself in a dynamic light. Write in the past tense, using power words to highlight achievements.

2. Work Experience

This should include the dates of each job – the month and year of the start and finish, the name of the company, your title, if relevant the title of the person to whom you reported and a short summary of the tasks you executed within this job.

Use action words such as "achieved, managed, created, or initiated" to highlight your experience and dynamic nature. Even if a job was dull and routine, show how you took initiative to work better/smarter/more cost effectively. You may think that working behind the bar at the Student's Union has no relevance to getting a post graduate training programme with an Electrical Engineering multi-national company – but it may! Every job contributes to the overall picture of who you are. Any job shows your initiative, eagerness and enthusiasm. Depending on the nature of the work, it could suggest that you are fast, capable, good with customers, numerate, and so forth. All these qualities are worth mentioning.

Your work experience should be listed in REVERSE chronological order – in other words, your current or most recently finished job at the top, then previously finished jobs following. If you don't have any paid work experience, don't worry. As a budding professional, you can consider charitable projects in which you have demonstrated responsibility, initiative, and any other qualities that may be relevant to the recruitment officer. As your career progresses, your CV will evolve. If you are applying for a Senior Director's position, the Student Union job has very little relevance. Everything you do is a stepping stone to the next position. The most recent two or three steps are the most important. Interim steps become obvious, as you wouldn't have succeeded to the higher positions without them!

If you are not currently job hunting, don't let your CV gather dust! Your CV is a constant work in progress rather than a new piece of work you have to write every time you need it. Every time you have a "win" at work, write it down to help you remember.

3. Qualifications

These should similarly be listed in reverse chronological order. Include a course that you are currently studying for, with a projected finish date. If you have a predicted grade you could choose to include it, identifying it as being a prediction.

If you are applying for a job that requires a degree, you obviously need to detail this qualification. You can reduce the amount of information relating to the 11+ exam or the IGCSE's, the French Brevet, American SATS or a first aid certificate you took as a Girl Guide. Again, these are stepping stones. The fact that you are now studying for, or have a degree, makes it a given that you were successful in these steps.

4. Skills

This is an opportunity for you to list certified skills that may have value within your next job or career. Piano Grade 1 might not add much value, but if you speak more than one language, can drive, or have a certificate for a computer programme these could all add to the picture of your potential within this company. Space will be limited as your career grows, so be selective and choose things that directly have relevance, or can infer a skill – for example, a football player suggests you operate well in a team; Grade 8 piano suggests you are tenacious and willing to dedicate hours to reaching perfection.

You could add hobbies at the end of your CV as a tool to illustrate your strengths. Even if you feel that your strength is only being a regular, propping up the Student Union bar – correctly expressed, this can suggest to an employer that you are outgoing, sociable, and a good communicator!

A key skill is the ability to convert a negative experience into a positive – "I ran for Student Representative. Even though I wasn't elected, I am proud of myself for putting myself out there. Also, I learned that I should have been more organised, started my campaign earlier, and appealed to a more diverse faction of students." Beware not to overuse this tactic, or your CV could sound like a list of negatives and mistakes!

IN SUMMARY:

- Your CV is a living document, which will change throughout your life as your experiences and knowledge grow.

- The job of a CV is only to win you an interview.

- The most important things are always the most recent.

- Your CV should never be more than two sides of A4 paper. (In the following example it appears as three because of the paper size!) Choose a sensible break point to start the second page.

- **TIME tip!** Regularly update your CV so you can produce it at any time. It is a tool to help you remember when you left a company or passed an exam a long time ago.

- EVERYTHING you add should earn its inclusion, because it contributes towards confirming that you are the best candidate for this position.

---

(1)May Cheung
(2) **Address?**
(3) **UK Mobile: +44 (0) 7344867322 Hong Kong Mobile (852) 9897 5659**
(4) **Email MayChung@Google.com**

(5) **Personal profile:** As a multicultural child, I grew up speaking three native languages plus two additional ones, whilst living in a dynamic multi-cultural environment. Hence there was a natural draw to my degree subject; BA Communications and Modern Language. Always up to date with social media trends, I am a natural and confident communicator, able to read a situation or trend, and use initiative and common sense, often under pressure, to resolve issues and get a job done logically and efficiently.

(6) **Currently studying:** 2017 – 19 BirkBeck Uni, London. MA Linguistics & Communication

(7) **Employment History:**

June – Sept 2014, 2015, 2016	**Carlton Towers Hotel, Resort & Club.**
Job Position	Summer Internship - Communications & Marketing Department Reporting to the Vice President of Communications

(8)

- Independently managed multiple social media routes to market; Twitter, Facebook, Instagram etc, by creating original but regular posts to promote the hotel and its services to international clientele plus local club members within different sectors: Food & Beverage; Golf & Leisure; Health & Beauty and Children's Summer camps.
- Worked within the hotel and resort team gathering salient information to process a variety of information into original content, aimed at different target audiences - hence a variety of style and tone.
- Always achieved delivery on time against tight deadlines.
- Particular responsibility for delivering the Children's Summer Programme to over 1,000 members. Achieved sales target for enrolment. Followed up all activities such as competitions or days out within a newsletter.
- Coordinated all responses to social media posts; either direct response or forward to the relevant department to ensure 24 hour reply in line with corporate policy.
- Successful completion of each summer programme resulted in my being reselected for the next summer.

(9) Sept 2011- Sept 2015   **Tae Kwon Do For All Part Time**

Job position: Assistant Teacher - Tae Kwon Do

- Organized and managed classes to assist the Master.
- Demonstrated and led class for warm up and other exercises and techniques
- Managed administration and running of exam days
- Motivated and supported younger children at lower belt levels

(10) June- Sept 2015   **O'Reilly Irish Bar and Restaurant**

Job position: Hostess/Waitress

- Welcomed and tended to guests at front of house
- Answered the phone and managed telephone bookings
- Made menu recommendations and took orders
- Served food and attended to every detail of guest's enjoyment
- Prepared and presented bills for payment, processed payment.

Sept 2013- June 2014   **Foundation Local School, Hong Kong**

Job position: Volunteer Teacher - Second Language English

- Created weekly lesson plans based on key themes. Prepared relevant and creative activity material
- Helped organize classroom activities. Taught personalized material for children with learning difficulties
- Evaluated students through a series of tests to monitor language progression

(11) Other Work activities
- I have a regular clientele of private language students to whom I teach Chinese.
- To support my studies, I have proof-read and edited several PhD thesis papers and a soon to be published book.

(12) Qualifications:

2017 – 2019 (Current): MA Communication & Linguistics   Birbeck Uni, London

2013-2017 BA Communications and Modern Language   Strathclyde University. 2:1

2011– 2013 : International Baccalaureate Diploma, International Academy, Hong Kong
Total points 36

Higher Level English Literature (5)	Standard Level Mandarin B (7)
Higher French B (6)	Standard Level Mathematical Studies (5)
Higher Level Economics (6)	Standard Level Physics (5)

Bonus Points for Theory of Knowledge and Extended Essay (2)

2009 – 2011 : IGCSE's, British International School, Shanghai.

French (A*)	Mandarin First Language (A*)		Mathematics (A)
Geography (B)	History (B)	Chemistry (A)	Biology (B)
First Language English Literature (A)		First Language English (A*)	

(13) **Other Achievements:**
Tae Kwon Do – 2nd Dan Black Belt - June 2015
Jazz and Modern Dance– Hong Kong Dance Academy Show Team
Violin – Grade 8 with Merit - May 2012
Deputy Editor of the school newspaper "The Busy Bee"

Charitable Efforts:
For my CAS in the IB diploma I travelled to Cambodia to donate school supplies our class had bought with money raised through sponsored activities, including bake sales, sponsored environmental clean-ups, dog walking and baby-sitting.
Currently I am in a university dance troupe, which produces an annual, three-performance show. All proceeds go to a local children's charity.

Skills:
Languages –English (native), Mandarin (fluent), Cantonese (fluent) French (good written and spoken) Spanish (Beginner/ conversational)
(14) Fully Computer Literate
Social Media UK: Advanced Certificate in Social Networking and Search Engine Optimisation.
UK driving licence

Hobbies: I play netball and badminton regularly. Classical music and dancing are my relaxation. I love to travel, especially tasting, then recreating new cuisines. I have my own travel, food and lifestyle blog, with over 6,000 followers. I post weekly articles.

C.V. KEY

(1) Don't be over fussy with your presentation and fonts, but do make your name loud and clear. Add a gender title if your name isn't obvious.

(2) Choose whether to add your address or not – only if it helps or adds– for example, shows you are local.

(3) Only add phone numbers that have relevance. Too many may confuse.

(4) See note 4 from the application letter.

(5) The purpose of this overview is to keep the reader interested in you. Highlight most salient points.

(6) Although this will be repeated in your qualifications list – let the reader know what you are doing NOW.

(7) Note how your work history is reported in REVERSE order. The most important job is the most recent.

(8) Bullet points are easy to read and efficient. As you list your responsibilities, use POWER words: Independently managed achieved responsibility Successful

(9) Layout dates, position, company etc. in a clear and consistent way for each job.

(10) Over time, as your career develops, and your experience advances – these bullet points can be reduced to one sentence. For example, "Performed all front of house tasks to ensure all customers enjoyed a memorable dining experience."

(11) Other work may be free-lance, and concurrent with other jobs, but it is also important to include.

(12) Similarly, as you need more space for work experience, your qualifications can be summarised. "9 IGCSEs – All A8, A and B."

(13) The headings: Other Achievements, Charitable Efforts, Skills and Hobbies are non- essential, but an opportunity for you to give additional information about yourself outside the work place. Use what space you have to complete the second page, selecting a few details that best represent yourself.

(14) "Computer literate" – this should be a given! "Driving license" is only necessary in a job that may require you to drive! Chose the skills you list carefully and when space is limited only select the ones that are relevant.

4. JOB Advertisements

Job ads appear in many places and in many styles. Some are brief and give little information about a role, whilst others are detailed and specific. The principals for applying are the same. The information you present needs to be clear and helpful, prompting the recruiter to call you for an interview. Apply for several jobs at a time, but remember to keep details of what you have applied for straight, so you can track the responses you are getting. If you refocus your cover letter and CV for each application, be sure to keep a copy of the original document, followed by a labelled copy of each version you send, so you can make a new copy if asked for one.

Extract from a job advertisement:

Wanted – Social Media Executive Ref: NC092:28/2/xx

The Social Media Executive's role will be to manage the social media voice and presence for the large-scale exhibition venues of our 25 worldwide hotels via Facebook, Twitter, Instagram and Pinterest and other social media. They will need to build each brand's social voice and audience by creating unique and relevant posts across all platforms. They will manage all social media channels and pro-actively collaborate with internal team members and exhibitors to find and promote content to support marketing activities.

The Ideal Candidate: The successful Social Media Executive will be an outgoing, proactive and professional individual with a passion for marketing and content creation. They will ideally have a minimum of one-year work experience in social media marketing and have the ability to work well under pressure and to meet deadlines efficiently.

They will require excellent writing, editing, presentation and communications skills, be detail orientated and be able to work well within a team. It is essential that they have previously managed social media accounts for a brand/brands and have the ability to create compelling digital copy.

If this Social Media Executive role sounds like something you might be interested in, please apply including your C.V. and a cover letter to the Director of Communications before February 28th.

---

5. APPLICATION (or Cover) Letter

Unlike the CV which is a standard document and can remain virtually the same for each application, a cover letter can and should vary and be tailored to each job you are applying for. It can re-confirm the points asked for in the advertisement and embellish them with examples. It is also possible to change the tone according to the formality of the advertisement and the company culture. Applying for a position as an operator on a helpdesk at a music company, a primary school teacher, or an intern at a law firm will each have a different tone.

BEWARE: If you keep a template for writing application letters, MAKE SURE you always carefully review each application. Nothing will close a door in your face faster than a letter accidentally containing a detail from a previous application!

Example of an Application Letter

(1) Ms May Chung
(2) 18 Wandsworth Bridge Road
London SW6
(3) UK Mobile: +44 (0)7343466
(4) Email MayChung2001@Google.com

(5) Mr. N. Cooper
(6) Director of Communications
(7) Address as specified in the advertisement

17th February 20_ _

(8) **Application for SOCIAL MEDIA EXECUTIVE Ref: NC092-28/2/xx**

(9) Dear Mr. Cooper

I am delighted to enclose my C.V. as requested, to support my application for the post of Social Media Executive, as advertised in the Daily News Review on January 23rd, 20__. I am confident that I have all the necessary requisites to fill this position.

(10) Although I have just graduated, I meet your one year experience criteria by compounding three appropriate work placements, all executed within a a pretigious hotel, resort, spa and club. Amongst other projects, I created original and varied copy to manage the brand's varied voices in all social media arenas. (11)

Having lived my life in Asia, and finished my tertiary education in the UK, I am outgoing, understanding and open to all cultures and social trends. I am professional and efficient, always meeting deadlines. I have also supported my own blog for over two years, and gathered over 6,000 followers around the world. I can be a solo operator, yet also work well in a team; offering and accepting ideas and support. (12)
My degrees in Linguistics and Communications have deepened my love of writing. To support my studies financially, I have edited some PhD thesis papers, and also a soon to be published self-help book.

I would welcome the opportunity to meet with you and disuss this exciting opportunity further. I am available by phone or email as detailed above. I will be overseas between March 9th and 15th, but apart from this I am available for an interview at any time. (13)

I look forward to hearing from you,

Yours sincerely

May Cheung
May Cheung

APPLICATION LETTER KEY

(1) Adding your title; Ms Mr. Mrs Dr. etc, allows the recruiter to know your gender and how to address you.

(2) With all contact details, evaluate if they may help you. Give enough information to be contactable, not too much to cause confusion!

(3) You may have several phone numbers, but choose the one most useable, and with scope for a message if you may not be able to answer.

(4) If you had a fun moniker email address, now might be the time for a more sedate and professional one. PartyAnimal1@xxxx.com does not leave the best impression!

(5) Use a title, plus the name as quoted in the advestisement. Not sure of the gender? Ring the company and ask.

(6) Use the title exactly as listed in the advertisement.

(7) The address may be an email address and or a postal address – all as specified in the advertisement.

(8) Make the title stand out so it assists the recruitment department sift their mail. Make it clear what you are applying for and when and where you saw the post – they may be advertising for several similar posts.

(9) Using the first name is too familiar. Never use the Initial here.

(10) Note how this letter explains a potential deficit in the requirements, and how the candidate can overcome it.

(11) Note how the candidate's overview relates to the advertisement, reinforcing that she has the right skills, experience and qualities.

(12) Without stating the obvious, the candidate is showing her initiative and relevance.

(13) Reinforcing the contact details from the top of the page, and explaining availability for an interview makes it easy for the decision-maker, and contributes to the positive image he has of the candidate.

6. ATTENDING an Interview

If you have been invited for an interview, you should rejoice! Receiving an invitation for an interview shows that the company recognises your potential and is impressed with what you have to offer them. Think of the interview as being their verification that they need you!

Timing is important when planning your interview. Avoid the hour before lunch or the end of the day, as you and the interviewer may both have low concentration or be feeling hungry and tired. Allow yourself enough travel time, considering rush hour congestion, especially if you are unfamiliar with the area. Avoid being rushed, flustered, or stressed.

Ensure you research and verify the exact place that your interview will take place. A large company may have several offices or outlets in one town. You may be familiar with one, yet the interview be held in another.

You have applied for the job by sending your application and CV, (resume) so there shouldn't be a need to bring this along. However, it looks professional to have a hard copy with you, in case you or the interviewer should need to refer to it, or there is an additional person in the interview.

TOP TIP: Ask in advance whether they need any paperwork, such as visas, certificates, or references. Even if they don't, this paints you in a good light as someone prepared and proactive.

First impression

Body language experts claim that a decision is made within the first two minutes of you meeting the interviewer. Everything you say just reinforces that first impression and supports your CV facts. It takes a lot of hard work to overcome a negative first impression. Consider the following to support that critical first impression:

- ✓ **Appearance:** Dress the part!
    - o Whilst you won't necessarily need a corporate suit for all interviews, it is a good rule of thumb to be formal rather than too casual. Avoid sandals or flip flops, jeans, etc. If you are in doubt, you could call the company in advance and ask about their office dress code or policy.

o Avoid heavy make-up and jewellery. When it comes to jewellery, less is more! It is especially distracting if you are wearing noisy bracelets or large dangling earrings.

o Make sure your hair is clean and neat. Make sure your hands, especially your fingernails, are clean.

✓ **Handshake:** A damp, limp handshake suggests a passive, timid person. A long, tight grip like a vice is aggressive and controlling, and may force the other person's hand to be underneath – hence the expression "taking the upper hand". A firm, confident yet equal handshake is a powerful communication of competence.

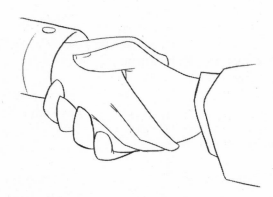

✓ **Eye contact:** Not making eye-contact suggests a shifty character or someone with something to hide! Looking directly at someone's eyes is warm and friendly, open and honest. Don't overdo it though.

✓ **Smile:** Nothing is more winning that an authentic smile (with brushed teeth of course)!

✓ **Be prepared:** Bring a few spare copies of your CV with you, as they could come in handy (for example, if there is a panel of interviewers rather than one individual). You could even bring a folder with certificates, prizes, and newspaper articles you have been featured in for reference. Make sure you have a pen and paper immediately available so you can make a note of anything you promise to do.

✓ **KEY POINT Greeting your interviewers:** Greet with a smile, direct eye contact, a firm and confident handshake, and address them by name, "Good Morning, Mr Cooper".

Questions and answers

The word "interview" comes from the French *entrevoir* or "to see between us." Remember that it is as important that YOU like what you see and hear as it is that the interviewer is impressed by you. Your adrenaline will be pumping, and your nerves will make you anxious, which will speed up your reply and make you impulsive with what you say. Slow down and breathe.

Remember, your CV has already been seen, so the decision to call you for an interview is an indication that you are already a fair fit for the job, or that you have potential. Always remain honest and open. It is absolutely fine to ask for a few seconds to think about a response, and a good habit is to take a deep breath before launching into an unthought out, speedy answer to a question.

Relax and enjoy the experience and the feedback. If you are confident and prepared, they'll be able to see that in your behaviour. Interviewers are trained to pick up on instinctive body language.

Top Questions:

From the interviewer

What the interviewer may ask:	Tips on how to answer:
Tell me about your strengths and weaknesses.	Virtually every weakness can be converted into a positive. A bossy person shows leadership; shy people are often the best listeners. Avoid rehearsed clichés such as "I am a perfectionist!"
How would your friends, colleagues, parents, or teachers describe you?	This is the same question as strengths and weaknesses, but thinly veiled so you may expose a weakness. Remember to be honest, yet convert those negatives to positives!

Where do you see yourself in 1/5/10 years' time?	This question may want to check that you are not planning to use the company as a training stepping stone before you settle down. Respond with ideas about contributing to the company alongside your personal goals.
Describe an instance when you have responded under pressure or cooperated with an unreasonable colleague.	Situational questions seek to see how you would respond under certain circumstances – typically giving you an insight into the types of pressures this job will offer. As with all questions, be honest and open. If you don't have an example of what they are asking for, be honest: *"Whilst I don't have first-hand experience of this; I anticipate that I would…"*

General advice on asking questions yourself

It's always a good idea to come prepared with questions – it shows initiative and genuine interest in the role and the company. Offer up new, relevant information that did not work its way into the conversation ("It's not a question, but there is something else I would like to tell you about that hasn't been mentioned…"). If all your prepared questions have been answered during the course of the interview, take the opportunity to repeat, in order to verify or emphasise something that has been said. Examples of this include:

- "I had been interested to know about the company's attitude on _____, but I feel really clear on that point now.
- "Might I just clarify, you mentioned earlier that…."
- "It is important for me to work within an organisation with social responsibility so I was pleased to hear you describe…."

WHAT NOT TO DO: Don't make your questions ego-centric, but based around what you can do for the company short, mid and long term. Don't ask questions of a flippant nature, but instead ask questions that show genuine interest and initiative. Never ask, "When can I expect a promotion / pay rise?"

AT THE END: A powerful way to end the question asking portion is to say, "I am really excited about the possibility of working with _____ organisation. What are the next steps that I need to take?" This is a question which underlines how interested you are. Make sure you follow through with anything they ask you to do!

Post interview follow up

When your interview finishes, thank the interviewer – you could add that you have enjoyed it, and shake hands again.

If during the interview you discussed something which you agreed to follow up on, such as forwarding a certificate or getting him the name of a book you discussed, make sure you do.

Thank you letters or emails are crucial, as you are reminding the interviewer who you are, and giving another strong impression that you are polite and efficient (qualities that he will value in a prospective employee). Remember, several candidates may have been interviewed for the same post, so this is another way of standing out from the others.

Nothing is a stronger communication then a smile!

In a first interview it is not typical to talk about salary, unless the interviewer asks you your expectations. A second interview is typically the time to enter into negotiations.

7. SALARY Negotiation Tips

When you get as close to a job as a final interview or even a job offer, it is important to know how to clinch the deal. Knowing how much salary to ask for is a delicate negotiation, which carries emotion and impacts your feeling of self-worth. Asking for too much can seem arrogant and you may sacrifice the offer. Asking for too little lacks confidence in your ability, may look desperate and even if you are successful in getting the job, could mean that you have a feeling of resentment as you toil away at your job.

Do your homework: Before you even start sending CVs or reply to ads. Research salary ranges for each position you are planning to apply for. This can be online, through a student alumni, or you can ask during job fairs at university. Don't wait until the moment you are asked for your salary expectations during a job interview.

Remember that different areas of the country or even city have different costs of living. A fair salary in a small town may be impossible to live on in a capital city. The qualifications and experience you have will affect your value as an employee. Yet this needs to be offset against the training and career progression with which the company has committed to support you.

Gauge your negotiation leeway: Many big corporations use salary grids, which reduce the potential for negotiation – for the high and the low boundaries. Try to understand how it works beforehand: For instance, if you are recruited on Jan 1st and the salary reviews are once a year in March, chances are, as a newly recruited employee, you will not get any the first year. Unless you get a proven track record of success in three months, you will have to wait 15 months before your next potential pay rise. Therefore, it would be better to negotiate a bit higher up front. Explaining this to your future employer shows that you are professional too. Back up your negotiations with preliminary research.

Leave the salary negotiation until you receive an offer. One tactic is even to avoid saying your expectations until the end. Many employers have already budgeted an amount and will have little flexibility. It is always easier to negotiate if the potential employer gives you the salary first, as well as the benefits.

Sometimes the application form asks you what salary you are looking for. Leaving this blank is an option, but you risk your application being disregarded for not having followed all instructions. Based on your research make a mid-range assessment of what you are looking for, which gives you room to manoeuvre in negotiations.

Get the whole picture: Don't just consider the salary, but the benefits, commute time, working hours, job responsibilities, career development opportunities, on-the job or accredited training etc, calculate your potential income tax with their offer: Sometimes an additional benefit may be better than a 5% higher salary. Now is the right time to re-work your budget with that offer.

Depending on your expectations, and your budget, discuss the package – that's the tough part: Assessing how far you can negotiate without annoying the potential employer or losing the offer altogether. Whatever you decide to negotiate, back it up! If you are asking for 10% more than their offer, what makes you think you are worth 10% more than other candidates? How do you prove it? Do you speak a relevant language, or have additional relevant modules in your studies etc? Having kept precise records of your accomplishments in other jobs or internships may help you.

Be honest and transparent: Don't negotiate a higher salary based on insubstantial experience hyped up, or say you have another higher offer when you don't. However it is fair to point out that the commute is expensive due to perhaps a ferry journey or road toll and see if there is any compensation or support for this.

Believe in yourself within a reasonable framework of research for your worth. Balance the experience you will receive with the package. If it seems low but you are anxious about asking for too much, it is acceptable to ask what salary progression there might be over the next few years.

Like all big decisions there will be compromise. Talk to your friends and family, read the local press to compare and decide whether this job is for you. Good Luck!

8.   ORGANISATION of Graduation!

In addition to applying for jobs, you may also be planning for your graduation ceremony and celebration! Remember the adage, "It takes a village to raise a child!" Don't forget everyone who helped you along the way. It is special if your parents, family, and friends can be part of this celebration of your achievements. It is also thoughtful to drop a note to your current and past teachers – they would love to know about and celebrate your success too!

By now you are an expert at organising! Don't allow the most memorable day of your university life to be spoilt by forgetting an important detail. Here are a few key things to remember:

- ✓ Find out what registration procedures are in place through the college for you as a graduate (especially if you are planning on not attending (graduating in absentia), or deferring your ceremony).
- ✓ Follow the guidelines for booking tickets for your guests. The early bird catches the worm, so don't be late!
- ✓ You will not be the only student graduating, so there will be heavy demand on services, including finding accommodation for your family and visitors. As early as possible, even a year (!) book accommodation and amenities needed for your family and friends.
- ✓ Ensure all your university fees and extras are paid. Check your account to ensure that graduation won't be delayed due to an outstanding charge.
- ✓ Organise your robes, gown or mortar board purchase or rental as instructed. Think carefully about what to wear for graduation events. Choose conservative clothes, shoes and hairstyle to save yourself cringing in the future!

✓ See what official photography is available through the university and book as appropriate. Alternatively, arrange your own, or make sure you appoint someone in your party to take official style pictures. It's an important day, and one you will be grateful to have official footage of!

✓ Join up with your university or college alumni clubs and associations.

Congratulations! You did it!

Further reading

Great sources for food and nutrition

- ➢ Harvard TH Chan School of Public Health. See website https://www.hsph.harvard.edu/nutritionsource/
- ➢ Pollan, Michael. In Defence of Food: An Eater's Manifesto. London: Penguin, 2009. Print.
- ➢ Robert H.Lustig, MD, MSL. Sugar Has 56 Names: A Shopper's Guide (A Penguin Special from Hudson Street Press). Sept. 2013. Print
- ➢ Schwarcz, Dr. Joe. Is That a Fact?: Frauds, Quacks, and the Real Science of Everyday Life. Toronto, Ontario: EWC, 2014. Print
- ➢ Robert H. Lustig, MD, MSL, Fat Chance: The Bitter Truth about Sugar, You Tube Video
- ➢ Holford, Patrick. Patrick Holford's The New Optimum Nutrition Bible. London: Piatkus, 2004. Print.

Sleep & breathing: Sources or dig deeper

- ➢ Park, S. Y. (2012). Sleep, Interrupted: A Physician Reveals The #1 Reason Why So Many of us are Sick and Tired. New York, NY: Jodev Press LLC.
- ➢ The Shadow Side of the Wireless Revolution. See website www.electromagneticHealth.Org

Wine

- ➢ "Bordeaux Bootcamp" by Wendy Narby is available as a paperback or eBook.